The Red Bridge Reader

THIRD EDITION

James K. Norman • Sharon J. Gerson
DeVry Institute of Technology–Kansas City

Pearson
Custom
Publishing

Cover Photo: "The Red Bridge," by James K. Norman.

10 9 8 7

Please visit our web site at www.pearsoncustom.com

ISBN 0–536–62554–9

BA 992899

 PEARSON CUSTOM PUBLISHING
75 Arlington Street, Boston, MA 02116
A Pearson Education Company

Copyright Acknowledgments

Dedicated to our children,
Reed Norman and
Stacy and Stefani Gerson

Contents

CHAPTER 1

CHAPTER 2

CHAPTER 3

CHAPTER 4

Chapter 5

Chapter 6

CHAPTER 9

Chapter 10

CHAPTER 11

Preface

In this third edition of *The Red Bridge Reader,* we have made significant changes to the overall content and design of the text. We have redesigned the content to assure reader friendly ease of access. You will notice shorter sentences and shorter paragraphs and listings which will help you to access information easily.

Moreover, we have rewritten all the introductory information so that you have more useful information to prepare you to read the essays and write your own paragraphs and essays. You will find an entirely new chapter entitled "Writing in College" that discusses the following topics:

Expressive writing

Expository writing

The writing process

Prewriting techniques

Revision techniques

Thesis statements

Introductory paragraphs

Concluding paragraphs

You will also find new introductory matter for the following chapters:

Description

Narration

Example

Process Analysis

Division/Classification

Comparison/Contrast

Cause/Effect

Definition

Argument and Persuasion

Research Paper

In addition to the all-new introductory material, you will find many new professional and student-written essays. Many of these new essays deal with topics which are up-to-date and will be easy to relate to.

At the end of each chapter introduction you will find new topic ideas and an all-new form entitled "Peer Evaluation." This form can be used by class members to evaluate student papers. Following their evaluations, the student writers can then revise and rewrite their essays prior to submitting them for grading.

We have enjoyed this revision process and hope that each of you find the third edition even more useful than the previous edition. As always, we welcome any ideas teachers or students might have to further improve our text. Remember that we wrote this book with you in mind, so please share your ideas with us for future editions. You can reach us via email at sgerson@kc.devry.edu and knorman@kc.devry.edu.

CHAPTER 1

Writing in College

In college English classes, you are taught how to write not only for your English classes but also for the other classes in your curriculum. That is why in your English classes, your teachers introduce you to several important aspects of writing:

1. Expressive writing
2. Expository writing
3. The writing process
4. Prewriting techniques
5. Revision techniques
6. Thesis statements
7. Introductory paragraphs
8. Concluding paragraphs

Once you have mastered these, you will feel more comfortable writing and be a more successful communicator.

Why Should You Learn How to Write?

Learning how to write an essay will help you to progress successfully through your college curriculum. In addition, if you attend graduate school, being able to write will help you to succeed in those classes.

College-level essay-writing courses are the foundation of much of your academic progression. Without writing skills, you will feel unprepared for many types of activities in other college classes.

Later on, after graduation, when you enter the business world, you will be expected to communicate both orally and in writing, and no boss will teach you how to do this.

Managers and supervisors don't need or want employees who can only sit in front of a computer screen. Companies hire and promote people who can interact comfortably with other people in a variety of ways. Writing is an essential skill.

Ten Objectives of the College Writer

1. Successful writing communicates to its intended audience.
2. Successful writing interests the audience.
3. Successful writing is clear and coherent.
4. Successful writing is informative.
5. Successful writing varies sentence patterns.
6. Successful writing varies words.
7. Successful writing appeals to the reader's anticipation for development.
8. Successful writing fully develops all ideas.
9. Successful writing relies on form including a thesis statement, topic sentences, body paragraphs, introductory paragraphs, and concluding paragraphs.
10. Successful writing is error free.

Overview of Expressive Writing

Expressive writing is personal writing that relies primarily on description, narration, illustrations, and examples. When you write expressively, you draw on your experiences to express your emotions, ideas, wit, memories—the basic elements of your personality. Often these types of paragraphs or essays are written in first person.

Why Write an Expressive Paragraph or Essay?

Writing an expressive paper helps you to develop a colorful and interesting style and helps develop other strong essay writing skills. Organization, coherence, tone, precise diction—these are important in expressive writing and in all types of writing. Expressive writing allows you to be subjective and encourages your imagination and creativity. Being able to effectively express yourself is an important skill for any college student.

How Do You Write Expressively?

1. Choose a subject with which you are familiar. A good subject will be one to which you respond emotionally, something that you find ironic, something you find humorous or nostalgic or moving. Drawing on personal experiences will allow you to feel confidence about the subject matter and provide you with sufficient content.

2. Don't limit yourself to only the positive side of topics. Often the conflicts inherent in the less positive side of things make for more interesting writing.

3. Write in first person so that your reader feels your involvement.

4. Use colorful adjectives and adverbs that will add interest and depth to the content, but base your writing in strong nouns and verbs.

5. Use specific, concrete diction when you describe. These words add to reader interest and also help your reader visualize what you're writing about. Don't allow your diction to leave things to the reader's imagination; let the reader see your imagination.

6. Use narration, if appropriate, to connect your ideas in a logical, coherent pattern.

7. Use dialogue, if appropriate, to add realism to descriptions of people.

8. Use specific, well-developed examples to illustrate your ideas.

9. Let your reader know why you've chosen to write what you have. Your purpose might be implicit in your writing, or you might explain your purpose explicitly in your introduction or conclusion.

10. Let the overall tone of your writing transmit your emotions to your reader. Expressive writing is personal writing. You want your reader to understand your topic, but you also want your reader to understand how you feel about the topic.

Overview of Expository Writing

To write an expository essay, you analyze a subject. When you analyze, you break a subject into its components to "expose" various aspects of the topic. A thorough discussion of these components lets the reader see your entire subject.

What Types of Essays Are Examples of Expository Writing?

Types of expository essays include process analysis, classification/division, comparison/contrast, cause/effect, definition, argument and persuasion, and research.

Why Write an Expository Essay?

Expository essays are the primary types of writing you do in your college classes. You will write expository essays in English classes, and in classes such as psychology, history, literature, business, and economics.

Many of your tests in your college classes will require that you write analytical test responses. Thus, learning to write expository essays will help you to do well in these classes.

Later on, when you write business documents either in a professional writing class or on the job, you will have to analyze subjects and write reports, memos, and letters that depend on these same writing skills. Therefore, your work in expository writing also will help prepare you to be a successful business communicator.

The Writing Process

The best way to become a good writer of either expository writing or business documents is to use the writing process.

The writing process puts as much emphasis on the process as on the product, that is, the finished essay or business document. This process consists of three parts:

- *Prewriting*
- *Writing*
- *Rewriting*

Prewriting—The first part of the writing process is prewriting. This should take about 25 percent of the time you spend on a written document.

You prewrite for several reasons:

1. Sometimes it's difficult to write "cold."
2. Prewriting can help you to generate ideas and jog your memory.
3. You can think about your topic before you actually have to write.
4. It helps to dispel nervousness and the "blank page syndrome," which often act as blocks to writing.
5. Prewriting helps you plan by allowing you to focus on audience and objectives.

Several types of prewriting techniques that will help you get started include the following:

1. Answering the reporter's questions—By applying the questions *who, what, where, when, why,* and *how* to your topic, you can generate ideas to include in your essay.
2. Mind mapping—Envision a wheel with your topic in the center. Radiating from this center, like spokes of a wheel, are different ideas about your topic.
3. Brainstorming/listing—You randomly think of ideas about your topic and then list them. This can be done individually or in a group.

4. Branching—Your main topic is like the trunk of a tree. Each component of the topic represents a separate branch.

5. Outlining—This traditional method of gathering and organizing information allows you to break up your topic into major and minor components.

6. Journals—Keeping a journal can be an excellent way for you to collect ideas that might prove useful in an essay.

Writing—After you formulate your ideas, then write the essay, preferably on a word processor so that you can begin editing simultaneously. The actual rough draft stage should take about 25 percent of the time you spend on an essay. Unfortunately, too many writers stop with this rough draft stage and never follow through with a thorough revision.

When you compose your rough draft, simply set down all your paragraphs so that your ideas are in front of you. At this stage, concentrate on your content and overall organization. Don't spend too much time worrying about spelling, grammar, diction, or other items that you will address in your revision. Once you have completed your draft, walk away from it. This is the "cooling off" period, a time for you to achieve some distance and perspective of your subject.

Rewriting and Proofreading—The last stage of the writing process gets 50 percent of the time you spend on a writing project. Spend 45 percent revising and 5 percent proofreading.

When you revise, consider these seven revision techniques:

1. Add—Do you need material to fully develop your topic or major points?

2. Delete—Have you included unnecessary information that you now see needs to be deleted?

3. Simplify complex words and ideas—Did you use any terminology that your audience will not understand? Are any of your examples, definitions, or illustrations too complex to easily understand?

4. Move—Would your essay be more effective if some material was rearranged?

5. Reformat—Are any of your paragraphs too long, too short, or just plain weak in terms of sentence length or number?

6. Enhance—Have you used words or phrases that are boring or repetitive or immature? Review your word choices and sentence constructions to be sure you have variety and a mature style that will appeal to the level of your audience.

7. Correct—Carefully study your essay, and look for all grammar, punctuation, and spelling errors that your computer failed to catch (and *always* take advantage of whatever software is available). Spell check will not catch words spelled correctly but

incorrectly used in context. You can't depend on software programs to catch all your human errors.

Once you complete revision, then proofread. Even though only 5 percent of your time is devoted to proofreading, failure to proofread can result in a less than perfect essay.

The Usefulness of the Writing Process

Following the writing process . . .

1. Helps you to avoid the blank page syndrome.
2. Lets you generate ideas.
3. Speeds up the writing task.
4. Encourages creativity.
5. Helps you to avoid the discomfort many people feel about writing.
6. Provides you with training in effective writing techniques.
7. Applies to all writing situations whether they are in the classroom or on the job.
8. Keeps you from developing a dependency on the teacher and lets you develop your own skill set.
9. Fosters your ability to think clearly and quickly.
10. Provides a framework for analytical thinking and develops your critical thinking skills.

Thesis Statements

A thesis statement is a sentence that declares the main point or controlling idea of your entire essay.

Where Do You Place Your Thesis Statement?

The thesis statement can be placed at the beginning or the end of the introductory paragraph. For the beginning essay writer, the best place for your thesis statement is the last sentence in the introductory paragraph. Placed last in this first paragraph, the thesis statement serves as a bridge to the first body paragraph. More than that, the thesis statement will also serve as a contract with you so you know what to write about and a contract with your readers so they know what to expect in the essay.

How Do You Phrase the Thesis Statement?

To write a thesis statement, you need to state the topic plus your attitude plus a focus.

For example, if you are writing about a movie such as *Die Hard*, you could compose a thesis statement that says it's a good movie because of several reasons. You might write the following statement: "*Die Hard*, starring Bruce Willis, is a good movie because of the special effects, the colorful scenes, and the dramatic story line."

This thesis statement then leads into body paragraphs that discuss the special effects, the colorful scenes, and the dramatic story line. You have, therefore, mapped out the overall organization of your essay for your reader.

Do Different Types of Essays Require Different Types of Thesis Statements?

A thesis statement will be phrased differently for each type of essay, including comparison/contrast, definition, classification/division, causal analysis, argument/persuasion, and process analysis.

To illustrate how to write different thesis statements for these essays, take the topic "dating."

Comparison/Contrast

I enjoyed my date with Steve because of where he took me, everything we did, and how much attention he gave me, and I didn't enjoy my date with Jim for the very same reasons.

Definition

A date is a particular social event involving just two persons with a mutual attraction, and it is characterized by location, activities, and interaction.

Classification/Division

Dates can be categorized into three types: "nerdy" dates, the "macho male" date, and the "football jock" date.

Argument/Persuasion

Dating is the most over-rated, expensive, and complicated thing to ever occur to the young American male college student.

Process Analysis

To prepare for a date, I follow six basic steps.

Causal Analysis

Because I had nine bad dates in a row, I decided that before I accept another date, I will know the man better, lower my expectations, and refuse any blind dates.

Errors to Avoid in Your Thesis Statements

1. Don't say "In this essay . . ." or "The subject of my paper is . . . " or "I think . . . " or "I believe . . . " or "I will write about . . . " or "In my opinion . . . "

2. Don't have unreasonable expectations of your readers, such as expecting them to know more about a topic than they are likely to.

3. Don't merely state well-known facts such as "War is terrible . . . " or "Child abuse is wrong . . . " or "TV is a waste of time . . . "

4. Don't phrase the thesis as a question ending in a question mark.

5. Don't be rude, sarcastic, or unkind in your thesis.

6. Don't present ideas in your thesis statement that you fail to cover in your essay.

Criteria to Follow in Writing a Good Thesis Statement

1. State your main opinion about a subject.

2. Choose a limited number of criteria to state in the thesis. You can't write about everything.

3. Limit the length of your thesis to one sentence.

4. Use specific words to state your thesis.

5. Place your thesis last in the introductory paragraph.

Introductory Paragraphs

In an essay, an effective introductory paragraph will achieve the following:

1. *Catch your reader's attention.* Studies show that you have only a few seconds, three to four sentences, in which to capture and hold your reader's attention. Failing to do so will prevent you from fully engaging your reader's interest in your essay.

2. *Provide the focus for the entire essay.* Without an interesting, informative introductory paragraph, you might have an essay which wanders and fails to direct your reader.

3. *State clearly the main points to be developed.* Use a thesis statement to map out the topic and the divisions of the essay after you have captured reader interest in the opening sentences.

4. *Lead into your body paragraphs.* By placing your thesis statement last in the introductory paragraph, you will create a "bridge" to the topic sentence in the first body paragraph.

How Can You Introduce Your Essay?

You have a variety of ways to write your introductory paragraph. You could begin with an anecdote, a quotation, a startling fact, figures, a question, a description, brief dialogue, or a refutation of an established theory or idea.

Use no more than five to seven sentences to introduce your essay and lead into the thesis statement.

Errors to Avoid in Introductory Paragraphs

When you write an introductory paragraph, avoid the following:

1. Don't begin with subject matter which fails to relate directly to the topic in the essay.

2. Don't write an introduction which is too long. Use only five to seven sentences averaging approximately fifteen words each to begin your essay.

3. Avoid apologizing or complaining. You shouldn't say "I don't know much about . . . ," or "This argument is boring . . . ," or "I really hate writing."

4. Don't assume your audience already knows all there is to know about your topic. By relying on personal experience and sufficient details, you will create a fresh appeal in any topic.

This is an example of a boring, weak introductory paragraph:

There are many types of magazines, and for each type of magazine there is a good and a bad. In fishing magazines, this comparison seems to be between *Bassmaster's Magazine,* which calls itself America's most popular fishing publication, and the *In-Fisherman,* another popular angling periodical. *Bassmaster's* types of articles, knowledge behind the articles and photographic illustrations can, in no way, compare to the *In-Fisherman.*

This is an example of an attention-getting, interesting introductory paragraph:

Early in the morning, as the sun rises over the broad bay, the bat boat prowls silently across the mirror-like surface. As if in perfect unison, the caped crusaders cast their bat-lures in search of unsuspecting prey. Feeling a tug on his bat-pole, the Boy Wonder sets the hook. After a grueling battle, Robin lands his catch. "Holy catfish, Batman." "No, Robin, actually it's a channellus catius. If you had read your latest issue of the *In-Fisherman,* you would have known that." It's precisely that kind of knowledge that fishermen across the country are looking for. Batman finds this knowledge in the *In-Fisherman,* a popular angling periodical. Robin, on the other hand, has been beached in the shallows of *Bassmaster's Magazine.* The types of articles found in *Bassmaster,* the knowledge behind the articles and the photographic illustrations can, in no way, compare to the *In-Fisherman.*

Concluding Paragraphs

All essays need to be concluded. After you write your last body paragraph, you should indent and begin a conclusion. Some writers, however, find that a concluding paragraph is one of the most difficult to write, and they may be right: good conclusions are not easy to write. They require thought, precision, and plenty of revision to be effective.

In the conclusion, you can bring together all the disparate ideas you wrote about in the essay and effectively refocus your reader. The conclusion doesn't have to be long; in fact, only a few sentences will be your best choice of length for a conclusion.

What Should You Include in a Concluding Paragraph?

Gather your ideas so that your reader feels the essay is ending. You might consider summarizing the main points, restating the thesis, or calling your reader to action, especially in a persuasive essay. If you've arranged your essay from least to most important, the conclusion might be where you reveal why you think your last major point was the most important. If you've presented complicated information or written a particularly long essay, you may need to recap the major points for the reader. In a narrative essay, you need to establish a resolution or a sense of where the major complication of the essay now stands. Other essays might require that you use the conclusion to reflect on the events or opinions you've just delivered in the body paragraphs. The main point is to avoid leaving your reader hanging, to give your reader a sense of closure or "finished-ness." The best conclusions do this in a natural manner, not appearing tacked on or written as mere formality. Be prepared to try several different approaches before considering your conclusion complete.

CHAPTER 2

Description

To describe effectively, a writer creates precise pictures in words about objects, people, scenes, events, or situations.

Why Write a Descriptive Essay?

These pictures help develop your writing by bringing to life these people or scenes. Without descriptions, writing would seem dull and colorless. You will find that effective description increases the strength of your writing, helping you to drive home your points with force and vividness. What you see or hear or touch creates an image in your own mind. To communicate that very same image to your reader is a difficult task, but without at least attempting to use specific, concrete, vivid details of description, you're asking your reader to merely guess at what that picture may be. The challenge of writing effective description is to transmit to your reader that precise image you have inside your own head and allow your reader to perceive it the same way you do.

How to Describe

We describe by appealing to sensory impressions (our senses of seeing, feeling, hearing, smelling, touching, tasting). Precise sensory impressions are the heartbeat of descriptive writing. Most well-written description blends several sense impressions, rather than relying on just one.

A writer should also create a dominant impression (or one clear focus) which emerges from the description as a whole.

When to Describe

Although a writer can write either a descriptive paragraph or a descriptive essay, often we employ description in other types of essays including comparison/contrast, classification/division, argument/persuasion, etc.

In addition, in the business world you will rely on description in generating many different types of documents. For example, you might rely on description to create a sales letter or a sales brochure, describing the service or the product you are selling. Or you might use descriptive writing in a proposal for the modification of existing hardware.

Learning how to describe effectively will help you to be both a successful essay writer and also a successful writer of business and technical documents.

Key Aspects of Descriptive Writing

1. Rely on sensory impressions. Precise sensory impressions are the basis of strong descriptive writing. If you can physically examine or reexamine the subject you are describing as you are writing the description, do so. If not, concentrate on your memory of it; then capture its features with appropriate words. Most successful descriptive writing blends several sense impressions, rather than focusing on just one.

2. Have a specific focus in mind when you write descriptively. Do you want to emphasize the feelings and emotions the subject matter evokes? Do you want your reader to have a strong sense of the physical aspects of the subject? Your focus should communicate to your reader the central idea that brings you to this subject, the reason you have chosen this particular subject over any other.

3. Create a dominant impression. A good writer selects and expresses sensory perceptions with an eye toward creating a dominant impression, one that will emerge from the description as a whole. Your paragraph or essay may be a collection of details, but the details should all combine to create one unified effect.

4. Choose a point of view either as a moving or fixed observer. A moving observer views things from a number of positions, signaling changes in location with phrases such as "moving down the street" or "as I walked around the corner." A fixed observer remains in one place and reports only what can be perceived from that one unique perspective.

5. Carefully select details. Effective description stems as much from exclusion as from inclusion. Never try to be a camera and cover every single thing. Instead, select details deliberately to help you build the impression you intend to create.

6. Details need to be consciously arranged. The arrangement might be spatial, or from most to least important, or chronological, or some other pattern. Whichever you choose is up to you, but a good reader will notice your organization and gain insight from how you structure your details as well as from the details themselves.

7. Create a specific framework. Begin with a topic sentence naming the object to be described. Then in the paragraph following,

describe the object. In an essay, begin with a thesis statement naming the object, usually the first or last sentence of your first paragraph, if the essay is relatively short. The body paragraphs in the essay then fully describe this object.

8. Avoid using worn out expressions or stale words. Avoid difficult or confusing words, as well. Don't force your reader to go to the dictionary to understand your writing

Topic Ideas

Last minute holiday shopping

The best or worst rock concert you've ever been to

An exercise class

A graduation audience

A shopping center

A busy city intersection

A bad job interview

A fast food restaurant

The worst party you've ever attended

Your wedding

College registration

A loading dock

Waiting in line

A car wreck you were in

A teacher or professor who greatly influenced you in some way, perhaps an influence that you did not notice until months or years later

A memorable first day or night on a new job (not necessarily as negative as the one described in "A Guard's First Night on the Job," but sometimes negative experiences do give you more material to work with)

Peer Evaluation for Descriptive Papers (Paragraph or Essay)

1. Does the paragraph begin with a topic sentence (for a paragraph) or a thesis statement (for an essay)?

2. What topic is being described? Can you encapsulate it in a few words?

3. What pattern of organization is followed? Would another pattern be more effective?

4. What dominant impression is being created?

5. Which senses are appealed to as methods of development?

6. From what vantage point has the writer written?

7. Are the word choices clear, precise, descriptive, colorful, emotional? Do any of the words need to be changed?

8. Does the paragraph have unity and coherence? If not, how might they be added?

9. Does the writer conclude the paragraph or essay effectively? Does the ending seem natural? Does it give a sense of closure?

10. Has the writer avoided using repetitive words?

11. Does the writer avoid grammar and punctuation errors?

A Guard's First Night
on the Job

William Recktenwald

When I arrived for my first shift, 3 to 11 P.M., I had not had a minute of training except for a one-hour orientation lecture the previous day. I was a "fish," a rookie guard, and very much out of my depth.

A veteran officer welcomed the "fish" and told us: "Remember, these guys don't have anything to do all day, 24 hours a day, but think of ways to make you mad. No matter what happens, don't lose your cool. Don't lose your cool!"

I had been assigned to the segregation unit, containing 215 inmates who are the most trouble. It was an assignment nobody wanted.

To get there, I passed through seven sets of bars. My uniform was my only ticket through each of them. Even on my first day, I was not asked for any identification, searched, or sent through a metal detector. I could have been carrying weapons, drugs, or any other contraband. I couldn't believe this was what's meant by a maximum-security institution. In the week I worked at Pontiac, I was subjected to only one check, and that one was cursory.

The segregation unit consists of five tiers, or galleries. Each is about 300 feet long and has 44 cells. The walkways are about 3 1/2 feet wide, with the cells on one side and a rail and cyclone fencing on the other. As I walked along one gallery, I noticed that my elbows could touch cell bars and fencing at the same time. That made me easy pickings for anybody reaching out of a cell.

The first thing they told me was that a guard must never go out on a gallery by himself. You've got no weapons with which to defend yourself, not even a radio to summon help. All you've got is the man with whom you're working.

My partner that first night was Bill Hill, a soft-spoken six-year veteran who immediately told me to take the cigarettes out of my shirt pocket because the inmates would steal them. Same for my pen, he said—or "They'll grab it and stab you."

We were told to serve dinner on the third tier, and Hill quickly tried to fill me in on the facts of prison life. That's when I learned about cookies and the importance they have to the inmates.

"They're going to try and grab them, they're going to try and steal them any way they can," he said. "Remember, you only have enough cookies for the gallery, and if you let them get away, you'll have to explain to the guys at the end why there weren't any for them."

Hill then checked out the meal, groaning when he saw the drippy ravioli and stewed tomatoes. "We're going to be wearing this," he remarked, before deciding to simply discard the tomatoes. We served nothing to drink. In my first six days at Pontiac, I never saw an inmate served a beverage.

Hill instructed me to put on plastic gloves before we served the meal. In view of the trash and waste through which we'd be wheeling the food cart, I thought he was joking. He wasn't.

"Some inmates don't like white hands touching their food," he explained.

Everything went routinely as we served the first 20 cells, and I wasn't surprised when every inmate asked for extra cookies.

Suddenly, a huge arm shot through the bars of one cell and began swinging a metal rod at Hill. As he ducked away, the inmate snared the cookie box.

From the other side of the cart, I lunged to grab the cookies and was grabbed in turn. A powerful hand from the cell behind me was pulling my arm. As I jerked away, objects began crashing about, and a metal can struck me in the back.

Until that moment I had been apprehensive. Now I was scared. The food cart virtually trapped me, blocking my retreat.

Whirling around, I noticed that mirrors were being held out of every cell so the inmates could watch the ruckus. I didn't realize the mirrors were plastic and became terrified that the inmates would start smashing them to cut me up.

The ordinary din of the cell house had turned into a deafening roar. For the length of the tier, arms stretched into the walkway, making grabbing motions. Some of the inmates swung brooms about.

"Let's get out of here—now!" Hill barked. Wheeling the food cart between us, we made a hasty retreat.

Downstairs, we reported what had happened. My heart was thumping; my legs felt weak. Inside the plastic gloves, my hands were soaked with sweat. Yet the attack on us wasn't considered unusual by the other guards, especially in segregation. That was strictly routine, and we didn't even file a report.

What was more shocking was to be sent immediately back to the same tier to pass out medication. But as I passed the cells from which we'd been attacked, the men in them simply requested their medicine. It was as if what had happened minutes before was already ancient history. From another cell, however, an inmate began raging at us. "Get my medication," he said. "Get it now, or I'm going to kill you." I was learning that whatever you're handing out, everybody wants it, and those who don't get it frequently respond by threatening to kill or maim you. Another fact of prison life.

Passing cell no. 632, I saw that a prisoner I had helped take to the hospital before dinner was back in his cell. When we took him out, he had been disabled by mace and was very wobbly. Hill and I had been extremely gentle, handcuffing him carefully, then practically carrying him down the stairs. As we went by his cell this time, he tossed a cup of liquid on us.

Back downstairs, I learned I would be going back to that tier for a third time, to finish serving dinner. This time, we planned to slip in the other side of the tier so we wouldn't have to pass the trouble cells. The plates were already prepared.

"Just get in there and give them their food and get out," Hill said. I could see he was nervous, which made me even more so. "Don't stop for anything. If you get hit, just back off, 'cause if they snare you or hook you some way and get you against the bars, they'll hurt you real bad."

Everything went smoothly. Inmates in the three most troublesome cells were not getting dinner, so they hurled some garbage at us. But that's something else I had learned; getting no worse than garbage thrown at you is the prison equivalent of everything going smoothly.

Take This Fish and Look at It

Sam Scudder

It was more than fifteen years ago that I entered the laboratory of Professor Agassiz, and told him I had enrolled my name in the Scientific School as a student of natural history. He asked me a few questions about my object in coming, my antecedents generally, the mode in which I afterwards proposed to use the knowledge I might acquire, and, finally, whether I wished to study any special branch. To the latter I replied that, while I wished to be well grounded in all departments of zoology, I proposed to devote myself specially to insects.

"When do you wish to begin?" he asked.

"Now," I replied.

This seemed to please him, and with an energetic "Very well!" he reached from a shelf a huge jar of specimens in yellow alcohol. "Take this fish," he said, "and look at it; we call it a haemulon; by and by I will ask what you have seen."

With that he left me, but in a moment returned with explicit instructions as to the care of the object entrusted to me.

"No man is fit to be a naturalist," said he, "who does not know how to take care of specimens."

I was to keep the fish before me in a tin tray, and occasionally moisten the surface with alcohol from the jar, always taking care to replace the stopper tightly. Those were not the days of ground-glass stoppers and elegantly shaped exhibition jars; all the old students will recall the huge necklace glass bottles with their leaky, wax-besmeared corks, half eaten by insects, and begrimed with cellar dust. Entomology was a cleaner science than ichthyology, but the example of the Professor, who had unhesitatingly plunged to the bottom of the jar to produce the fish, was infectious; and though this alcohol had a "very ancient and fishlike smell," I really dared not show any aversion within these sacred precincts, and treated the alcohol as though it were pure water. Still I was conscious of a passing feeling of disappointment, for gazing at a fish did not commend itself to an ardent entomologist. My friends at home, too, were annoyed when they discovered that no amount of eau-de-Cologne would drown the perfume which haunted me like a shadow.

In ten minutes I had seen all that could be seen in that fish, and started in search of the Professor—who had, however, left the Museum; and when I returned, after lingering over some of the odd animals stored in the upper apartment, my specimen was dry all over. I dashed the fluid over the fish as if to resuscitate the beast from a fainting fit, and looked with anxiety for a return of the normal sloppy appearance. This little excitement over, nothing was to be done but to return to a steadfast gaze at my mute companion. Half an hour passed—an hour—another hour; the fish began to look loathsome. I turned it over and around; looked it in the face—ghastly; from behind, beneath, above, sideways, at three-quarters' view— just as ghastly. I was in despair; at an early hour I concluded that lunch was necessary; so, with infinite relief, the fish was carefully replaced in the jar, and for an hour I was free.

On my return, I learned that Professor Agassiz had been at the Museum, but had gone, and would not return for several hours. My fellow-students were too busy to be disturbed by continued conversation. Slowly I drew forth that hideous fish, and with a feeling of desperation again looked at it. I might not use a magnifying-glass; instruments of all kinds were interdicted. My two hands, my two eyes, and the fish: it seemed a most limited field. I pushed my finger down its throat to feel how sharp the teeth were. I began to count the scales in the different rows, until I was convinced that was nonsense. At last a happy thought struck me—I would draw the fish; and now with surprise I began to discover new features in the creature. Just then the Professor returned.

"That is right," said he; "a pencil is one of the best of eyes. I am glad to notice, too, that you keep your specimen wet, and your bottle corked."

With these encouraging words, he added: "Well, what is it like?"

He listened attentively to my brief rehearsal of the structure of parts whose names were still unknown to me: the fringed gill-arches and movable operculum; the pores of the head, fleshy lips and lidless eyes; the lateral line, the spinous fins and forked tail; the compressed and arched body. When I finished, he waited as if expecting more, and then with an air of disappointment: "You have not looked very carefully; why," he continued more earnestly, "you haven't even seen one of the most conspicuous features of the animal, which is plainly before your eyes as the fish itself; look again, look again!" and he left me to my misery.

I was piqued; I was mortified. Still more of that wretched fish! But now I set myself to my task with a will, and discovered one new thing after another, until I saw how just the Professor's criticism had been. The afternoon passed quickly; and when, towards its close, the Professor inquired: "Do you see it yet?"

"No," I replied, "I am certain I do not, but I see how little I saw before."

"That is next best," said he, earnestly, "but I won't hear you now; put away your fish and go home; perhaps you will be ready with a better answer in the morning. I will examine you before you look at the fish."

This was disconcerting. Not only must I think of my fish all night, studying, without the object before me, what this unknown but most visible feature might be; but also, without reviewing my discoveries, I must give an exact account of them the next day. I had a bad memory; so I walked home by Charles River in a distracted state, with my two perplexities.

The cordial greeting from the Professor the next morning was reassuring; here was a man who seemed to be quite as anxious as I that I should see for myself what he saw.

"Do you perhaps mean," I asked, "that the fish has symmetrical sides with paired organs?"

His thoroughly pleased "Of course! of course!" repaid the wakeful hours of the previous night. After he had discoursed most happily and enthusiastically—as he always did—upon the importance of this point, I ventured to ask what I should do next.

"Oh, look at your fish!" he said, and left me again to my own devices. In a little more than an hour he returned, and heard my new catalogue.

"That is good, that is good!" he repeated; "but that is not all; go on"; and so for three long days he placed that fish before my eyes, forbidding me to look at anything else, or to use any artificial aid. "Look, look, look," was his repeated injunction.

This was the best entomological lesson I ever had—a lesson whose influence has extended to the details of every subsequent study; a legacy the Professor had left to me, as he has left it to so many others, of inestimable value, which we could not buy, with which we cannot part.

A year afterward, some of us were amusing ourselves with chalking outlandish beasts on the Museum blackboard. We drew prancing starfishes; frogs in mortal combat; hydra-headed worms; stately crawfishes, standing on their tails, bearing aloft umbrellas; and grotesque fishes with gaping mouths and staring eyes. The Professor came in shortly after, and was as amused as any at our experiments. He looked at the fishes.

"Haermulons, every one of them," he said; Mr.—drew them."

True; and to this day, if I attempt a fish, I can draw nothing but haemulons.

The fourth day, a second fish of the same group was placed beside the first, and I was bidden to point out the resemblances and differences between the two; another and another followed, until the entire family lay before me, and a whole legion of jars covered the table and surrounding shelves; the odor had become a pleasant perfume; and even now, the sight of an old, six-inch worm-eaten cork brings fragrant memories.

The whole group of haemulons was thus brought in review; and, whether engaged upon the dissection of the internal organs, the preparation and examination of the bony framework, or the description of the various parts, Agassiz's training in the method of observing facts and their orderly arrangement was ever accompanied by the urgent exhortation not to be content with them.

"Facts are stupid things," he would say, "until brought into connection with some general law."

At the end of eight months, it was almost with reluctance that I left these friends and turned to insects; but what I had gained by this outside experience has been of greater value than years of later investigation in my favorite groups.

Graduation

Maya Angelou

The children in Stamps trembled visibly with anticipation. Some adults were excited too, but to be certain the whole young population had come down with graduation epidemic. Large classes were graduating from both the grammar school and the high school. Even those who were years removed from their own day of glorious release were anxious to help with preparations as a kind of dry run. The junior students who were moving into the vacating classes' chairs were tradition-bound to show their talents for leadership and management. They strutted through the school and around the campus exerting pressure on the lower grades. Their authority was so new that occasionally if they pressed a little too hard it had to be overlooked. After all, next term was coming, and it never hurt a sixth grader to have a play sister in the eighth grade, or a tenth-year student to be able to call a twelfth grader Bubba. So all was endured in a spirit of shared understanding. But the graduating classes themselves were the nobility. Like travelers with exotic destinations on their minds, the graduates were remarkably forgetful. They came to school without their books, or tablets or even pencils. Volunteers fell over themselves to secure replacements for the missing equipment. When accepted, the willing workers might or might not be thanked, and it was of no importance to the pregraduation rites. Even teachers were respectful of the now quiet and aging seniors, and tended to speak to them, if not as equals, as beings only slightly lower than themselves. After tests were returned and grades given, the student body, which acted like an extended family, knew who did well, who excelled, and what piteous ones had failed.

Unlike the white high school, Lafayette County Training School distinguished itself by having neither lawn, nor hedges, nor tennis court, nor climbing ivy. Its two buildings (main classrooms, the grade school and home economics) were set on a dirt hill with no fence to limit either its boundaries or those of bordering farms. There was a large expanse to the left of the school which was used alternately as a baseball diamond or basketball court. Rusty hoops on swaying poles represented the permanent recreational equipment, although bats and balls could be borrowed from the P.E. teacher if the borrower was qualified and if the diamond wasn't occupied.

Over this rocky area relieved by a few shady tall persimmon trees the graduating class walked. The girls often held hands and no longer bothered to speak to the lower students. There was a sadness about them, as if this old world was not their home and they were bound for higher ground. The boys, on the other hand, had become more friendly, more outgoing. A decided change from the closed attitude they projected while studying for finals. Now they seemed not ready to give up the old school, the familiar paths and classrooms. Only a small percentage would be continuing on to college—one of the South's A & M (agricultural and mechanical) schools, which trained Negro youths to be carpenters, farmers, handymen, masons, maids, cooks and baby nurses. Their future rode heavily on their shoulders, and blinded them to the collective joy that had pervaded the lives of the boys and girls in the grammar school graduating class.

Parents who could afford it had ordered new shoes and ready-made clothes for themselves from Sears and Roebuck or Montgomery Ward. They also engaged the best seamstresses to make the floating graduating dresses and to cut down second-hand pants which would be pressed to a military slickness for the important event.

Oh, it was important, all right. Whitefolks would attend the ceremony, and two or three would speak of God and home, and the Southern way of life, and Mrs. Parsons, the principal's wife, would play the graduation march while the lower-grade graduates paraded down the aisles and took their seats below the platform. The high school seniors would wait in empty classrooms to make their dramatic entrance.

In the Store I was the person of the moment. The birthday girl. The center. Bailey had graduated the year before, although to do so he had had to forfeit all pleasures to make up for his time lost in Baton Rouge.

My class was wearing butter-yellow piqué dresses, and Momma launched out on mine. She smocked the yoke into tiny crisscrossing puckers, then shirred the rest of the bodice. Her dark fingers ducked in and out of the lemony cloth as she embroidered raised daisies around the hem. Before she considered herself finished she had added a crocheted cuff on the puff sleeves, and a pointy crocheted collar.

I was going to be lovely. A walking model of all the various styles of fine hand sewing and it didn't worry me that I was only twelve years old and merely graduating from the eighth grade. Besides, many teachers in Arkansas Negro schools had only that diploma and were licensed to impart wisdom.

The days had become longer and more noticeable. The faded beige of former times had been replaced with strong and sure colors. I began to see my classmates' clothes, their skin tones, and the dust that waved off pussy willows. Clouds that lazed across the sky were objects of great concern to me. Their shiftier shapes might have held a message that in my new happiness and with a little bit of time I'd soon decipher. During that period I looked at the arch of heaven so religiously my neck kept a steady ache. I had taken to smiling more often, and my jaws hurt from the unaccustomed activity. Between the two physical sore spots, I suppose I could have been uncomfortable, but that was not the case. As a member of the winning team (the graduating class of 1940) I had outdistanced unpleasant sensations by miles. I was headed for the freedom of open fields.

Youth and social approval allied themselves with me and we trammeled memories of slights and insults. The wind of our swift passage remodeled my features. Lost tears were pounded to mud and then to dust. Years of withdrawal were brushed aside and left behind, as hanging ropes of parasitic moss.

My work alone had awarded me a top place and I was going to be one of the first called in the graduating ceremonies. On the classroom blackboard, as well as on the bulletin board in the auditorium, there were blue stars and white stars and red stars. No absences, no tardiness, and my academic work was among the best of the year. I could say the preamble to the Constitution even faster than Bailey. We timed ourselves often: "We the people of the United States in order to form a more perfect union. . . ." I had memorized the Presidents of the United States from Washington to Roosevelt in chronological as well as alphabetical order.

My hair pleased me too. Gradually the black mass had lengthened and thickened, so that it kept at last to its braided pattern, and I didn't have to yank my scalp off when I tried to comb it.

Louise and I had rehearsed the exercises until we tired out ourselves. Henry Reed was class valedictorian. He was a small, very black boy with hooded eyes, a long, broad nose and an oddly shaped head. I had admired him for years because each term he and I vied for the best grades in our class. Most often he bested me, but instead of being disappointed I was pleased that we shared top places between us. Like many Southern Black children, he lived with his grandmother, who was as strict as Momma and as kind as she knew how to be. He was courteous, respectful and soft-spoken to elders, but on the playground he chose to play the roughest games. I admired him. Anyone, I reckoned, sufficiently afraid or sufficiently dull could be polite. But to be able to operate at a top level with both adults and children was admirable.

His valedictory speech was entitled "To Be or Not to Be." The rigid tenth-grade teacher had helped him write it. He'd been working on the dramatic stresses for months.

The weeks until graduation were filled with heady activities. A group of small children were to be presented in a play about buttercups and daisies and bunny rabbits. They could be heard throughout the building practicing their hops and their little songs that sounded like silver bells. The older girls (nongraduates, of course) were assigned the task of making refreshments for the night's festivities. A tangy scent of ginger, cinnamon, nutmeg and chocolate wafted around the home economics building as the budding cooks made samples for themselves and their teachers.

In every corner of the workshop, axes and saws split fresh timber as the wood-shop boys made sets and stage scenery. Only the graduates were left out of the general bustle. We were free to sit in the library at the back of the building or look in quite detachedly, naturally, on the measures being taken for our event.

Even the minister preached on graduation the Sunday before. His subject was, "Let your light so shine that men will see your good works and praise your Father, who is in Heaven." Although the sermon was purported to be addressed to us, he used the occasion to speak to backsliders, gamblers, and general ne'er-do-wells. But since he had called our names at the beginning of the service we were mollified.

Among Negroes the tradition was to give presents to children going only from one grade to another. How much more important this was when the person was graduating at the top of the class. Uncle Willie and Momma had sent away for a

Mickey Mouse watch like Bailey's. Louise gave me four embroidered handkerchiefs. (I gave her crocheted doilies.) Mrs. Sneed, the minister's wife, made me an undershirt to wear for graduation, and nearly every customer gave me a nickel or maybe even a dime with the instruction "Keep on moving to higher ground," or some such encouragement.

Amazingly the great day finally dawned and I was out of bed before I knew it. I threw open the back door to see it more clearly, but Momma said, "Sister, come away from that door and put your robe on."

I hoped the memory of that morning would never leave me. Sunlight was itself young, and the day had none of the insistence maturity would bring it in a few hours. In my robe and barefoot in the backyard, under cover of going to see about my new beans, I gave myself up to the gentle warmth and thanked God that no matter what evil I had done in my life He had allowed me to live to see this day. Somewhere in my fatalism I had expected to die, accidentally, and never have the chance to walk up the stairs in the auditorium and gracefully receive my hard-earned diploma. Out of God's merciful bosom I had won reprieve.

Bailey came out in his robe and gave me a box wrapped in Christmas paper. He said he had saved his money for months to pay for it. It felt like a box of chocolates, but I knew Bailey wouldn't save money to buy candy when we had all we could want under our noses.

He was as proud of the gift as I. It was a soft-leather-bound copy of a collection of poems by Edgar Allan Poe, or, as Bailey and I called him, "Eap." I turned to "Annabel Lee" and we walked up and down the garden rows, the cool dirt between our toes, reciting the beautifully sad lines.

Momma made a Sunday breakfast although it was only Friday. After we finished the blessing, I opened my eyes to find the watch on my plate. It was a dream of a day. Everything went smoothly and to my credit, I didn't have to be reminded or scolded for anything. Near evening I was too jittery to attend to chores, so Bailey volunteered to do all before his bath.

Days before, we had made a sign for the Store, and as we turned out the lights Momma hung the cardboard over the doorknob. It read clearly: CLOSED, GRADUATION.

My dress fitted perfectly and everyone said that I looked like a sunbeam in it. On the hill, going toward the school, Bailey walked behind with Uncle Willie, who muttered, "Go on, Ju." He wanted him to walk ahead with us because it embarrassed him to have to walk so slowly. Bailey said he'd let the ladies walk together, and the men would bring up the rear. We all laughed, nicely.

Little children dashed by out of the dark like fireflies. Their crepe-paper dresses and butterfly wings were not made for running and we heard more than one rip, dryly, and the regretful "uh uh" that followed.

The school blazed without gaiety. The windows seemed cold and unfriendly from the lower hill. A sense of ill-fated timing crept over me, and if Momma hadn't reached for my hand I would have drifted back to Bailey and Uncle Willie, and possibly beyond. She made a few slow jokes about my feet getting cold, and tugged me along to the now-strange building.

Around the front steps, assurance came back. There were my fellow "greats," the graduating class. Hair brushed back, legs oiled, new dresses and pressed pleats, fresh pocket handkerchiefs and little handbags, all homesewn. Oh, we were up to snuff, all right. I joined my comrades and didn't even see my family go in to find seats in the crowded auditorium.

The school band struck up a march and all classes filed in as had been rehearsed. We stood in front of our seats, as assigned, and on a signal from the choir director, we sat. No sooner had this been accomplished than the band started to play the national anthem. We rose again and sang the song, after which we recited the pledge of allegiance. We remained standing for a brief minute before the choir director and the principal signaled to us, rather desperately I thought, to take our seats. The command was so unusual that our carefully rehearsed and smooth-running machine was thrown off. For a full minute we fumbled for our chairs and bumped into each other awkwardly. Habits change or solidify under pressure, so in our state of nervous tension we had been ready to follow our usual assembly pattern: the American national anthem, then the pledge of allegiance, then the song every Black person I knew called the Negro National Anthem. All done in the same key, with the same passion and most often standing on the same foot.

Finding my seat at last, I was overcome with a presentiment of worse things to come. Something unrehearsed, unplanned, was going to happen, and we were going to be made to look bad. I distinctly remember being explicit in the choice of pronoun. It was "we," the graduating class, the unit, that concerned me then.

The principal welcomed "parents and friends" and asked the Baptist minister to lead us in prayer. His invocation was brief and punchy, and for a second I thought we were getting on the high road to right action. When the principal came back to the dais, however, his voice had changed. Sounds always affected me profoundly and the principal's voice was one of my favorites. During assembly it melted and lowed weakly into the audience. It had not been in my plan to listen to him, but my curiosity was piqued and I straightened up to give him my attention.

He was talking about Booker T. Washington, our "late great leader," who said we can be as close as the fingers on the hand, etc. . . . Then he said a few vague things about friendship and the friendship of kindly people to those less fortunate than themselves. With that his voice nearly faded, thin, away. Like a river diminishing to a stream and then to a trickle. But he cleared his throat and said, "Our speaker tonight, who is also our friend, came from Texarkana to deliver the commencement address, but due to the irregularity of the train schedule, he's going to, as they say, 'speak and run.'" He said that we understood and wanted the man to know that we were most grateful for the time he was able to give us and then something about how we were willing always to adjust to another's program, and without more ado—"I give you Mr. Edward Donleavy."

Not one but two white men came through the door offstage. The shorter one walked to the speaker's platform, and the tall one moved to the center seat and sat down. But that was our principal's seat, and already occupied. The dislodged gentleman bounced around for a long breath or two before the Baptist minister gave him his chair, then with more dignity than the situation deserved, the minister walked off the stage.

Donleavy looked at the audience once (on reflection, I'm sure that he wanted only to reassure himself that we were really there), adjusted his glasses and began to read from a sheaf of papers.

He was glad "to be here and to see the work going on just as it was in the other schools."

At the first "Amen" from the audience I willed the offender to immediate death by choking on the word. But Amens and Yes, sir's began to fall around the room like rain through a ragged umbrella.

He told us of the wonderful changes we children in Stamps had in store. The Central School (naturally, the white school was Central) had already been granted improvements that would be in use in the fall. A well-known artist was coming from Little Rock to teach art to them. They were going to have the newest microscopes and chemistry equipment for their laboratory. Mr. Donleavy didn't leave us long in the dark over who made these improvements available to Central High. Nor were we to be ignored in the general betterment scheme he had in mind.

He said that he had pointed out to people at a very high level that one of the first-line football tackles at Arkansas Agricultural and Mechanical College had graduated from good old Lafayette County Training School. Here fewer Amen's were heard. Those few that did break through lay dully in the air with the heaviness of habit.

He went on to praise us. He went on to say how he had bragged that "one of the best basketball players at Fisk sank his first ball right here at Lafayette County Training School."

The white kids were going to have a chance to become Galileos and Madame Curies and Edisons and Gauguins, and our boys (the girls weren't even in on it) would try to be Jesse Owenses and Joe Louises.

Owens and the Brown Bomber were great heroes in our world, but what school official in the white-goddom of Little Rock had the right to decide that those two men must be our only heroes? Who decided that for Henry Reed to become a scientist he had to work like George Washington Carver, as a bootblack, to buy a lousy microscope? Bailey was obviously always going to be too small to be an athlete, so which concrete angel glued to what country seat had decided that if my brother wanted to become a lawyer he had to first pay penance for his skin by picking cotton and hoeing corn and studying correspondence books at night for twenty years?

The man's dead words fell like bricks around the auditorium and too many settled in my belly. Constrained by hard-learned manners I couldn't look behind me, but to my left and right the proud graduating class of 1940 had dropped their heads. Every girl in my row had found something new to do with her handkerchief. Some folded the tiny squares into love knots, some into triangles, but most were wadding them, then pressing them flat on their yellow laps.

On the dais, the ancient tragedy was being replayed. Professor Parsons sat, a sculptor's reject, rigid. His large, heavy body seemed devoid of will or willingness, and his eyes said he was no longer with us. The other teachers examined the flag (which was draped stage right) or their notes, or the windows which opened on our now-famous playing diamond.

Graduation, the hush-hush magic time of frills and gifts and congratulations and diplomas, was finished for me before my name was called. The accomplishment was nothing. The meticulous maps, drawn in three colors of ink, learning and spelling decasyllabic words, memorizing the whole of *The Rape of Lucrece*—it was for nothing. Donleavy had exposed us.

We were maids and farmers, handymen and washerwomen, and anything higher that we aspired to was farcical and presumptuous.

Then I wished that Gabriel Proser and Nat Turner had killed all whitefolks in their beds and that Abraham Lincoln had been assassinated before the signing of the Emancipation Proclamation, and that Harriet Tubman had been killed by that blow on her head and Christopher Columbus had drowned in the *Santa Maria*.

It was awful to be a Negro and have no control over my life. It was brutal to be young and already trained to sit quietly and listen to charges brought against my color with no chance of defense. We should all be dead. I thought I should like to see us all dead, one on top of the other. A pyramid of flesh with the whitefolks on the bottom, as the broad base, then the Indians with their silly tomahawks and teepees and wigwams and treaties, the Negroes with their mops and recipes and cotton sacks and spirituals sticking out of their mouths. The Dutch children should all stumble in their wooden shoes and break their necks. The French should choke to death on the Louisiana Purchase (1803) while silkworms ate all the Chinese with their stupid pigtails. As a species, we were an abomination. All of us.

Donleavy was running for election, and assured our parents that if he won we could count on having the only colored paved playing field in that part of Arkansas. Also—he never looked up to acknowledge the grunts of acceptance—also, we were bound to get some new equipment for the home economics building and the workshop.

He finished, and since there was no need to give any more than the most perfunctory thank-you's, he nodded to the men on the stage, and the tall white man who was never introduced joined him at the door. They left with the attitude that now they were off to something really important. (The graduation ceremonies at Lafayette County Training School had been a mere preliminary.)

The ugliness they left was palpable. An uninvited guest who wouldn't leave. The choir was summoned and sang a modern arrangement of "Onward, Christian Soldiers," with new words pertaining to graduates seeking their place in the world. But it didn't work. Elouise, the daughter of the Baptist minister, recited "Invictus," and I could have cried at the impertinence of "I am the master of my fate, I am the captain of my soul."

My name had lost its ring of familiarity and I had to be nudged to go and receive my diploma. All my preparations had fled. I neither marched up to the stage like a conquering Amazon, nor did I look in the audience for Bailey's nod of approval. Marguerite Johnson, I heard the name again, my honors were read, there were noises in the audience of appreciation, and I took my place on the stage as rehearsed.

I thought about colors I hated: ecru, puce, lavender, beige and black.

There was shuffling and rushing around me, then Henry Reed was giving his valedictory address, "To Be or Not to Be." Hadn't he heard the whitefolks? We couldn't be, so the question was a waste of time. Henry's voice came out clear and strong. I feared to look at him. Hadn't he got the message? There was no "nobler in the mind" for Negroes because the world didn't think we had minds, and they let us know it. "Outrageous fortune"? Now, that was a joke. When the ceremony was over I had to tell Henry Reed some things. That is, if I still cared. Not "rub," Henry, "erase." "Ah, there's the erase." Us.

Henry had been a good student in elocution. His voice rose on tides of promise and fell on waves of warnings. The English teacher had helped him to create a sermon winging through Hamlet's soliloquy. To be a man, a doer, a builder, a leader, or to be a tool, an unfunny joke, a crusher of funky toad-stools. I marveled that Henry could go through with the speech as if we had a choice.

I had been listening and silently rebutting each sentence with my eyes closed; then there was a hush, which in an audience warns that something unplanned is happening. I looked up and saw Henry Reed, the conservative, the proper, the A student, turn his back to the audience and turn to us (the proud graduating class of 1940) and sing, nearly speaking,

> *"Lift ev'ry voice and sing*
> *Till earth and heaven ring*
> *Ring with the harmonies of Liberty . . ."*

It was the poem written by James Weldon Johnson. It was the music composed by J. Rosamond Johnson. It was the Negro national anthem. Out of habit we were singing it.

Our mothers and fathers stood in the dark hall and joined the hymn of encouragement. A kindergarten teacher led the small children onto the stage and the buttercups and daisies and bunny rabbits marked time and tried to follow:

> *"Stony the road we trod*
> *Bitter the chastening rod*
> *Felt in the days when hope, unborn, had died.*
> *Yet with a steady beat*
> *Have not our weary feet*
> *Come to the place for which our fathers sighed?"*

Each child I knew had learned that song with his ABC's and along with "Jesus Loves Me This I Know." But I personally had never heard it before. Never heard the words, despite the thousands of times I had sung them. Never thought they had anything to do with me.

On the other hand, the words of Patrick Henry had made such an impression on me that I had been able to stretch myself tall and trembling and say, "I know not what course others may take, but as for me, give me liberty or give me death."

And now I heard, really for the first time:

> *"We have come over a way that with tears*
> *has been watered,*
> *We have come, treading our path through*
> *the blood of the slaughtered."*

While echoes of the song shivered in the air, Henry Reed bowed his head, said "Thank you," and returned to his place in the line. The tears that slipped down many faces were not wiped away in shame.

We were on top again. As always, again. We survived. The depths had been icy and dark, but now a bright sun spoke to our souls. I was no longer simply a member of the proud graduating class of 1940; I was a proud member of the wonderful, beautiful Negro race.

Oh, Black known and unknown poets, how often have your auctioned pains sustained us? Who will compute the lonely nights made less lonely by your songs, or the empty pots made less tragic by your tales?

If we were a people much given to revealing secrets, we might raise monuments and sacrifice to the memories of our poets, but slavery cured us of that weakness. It may be enough, however, to have it said that we survive in exact relationship to the dedication of our poets (including preachers, musicians and blues singers).

Summer Rituals

Ray Bradbury

Yes, summer was rituals, each with its natural time and place. The ritual of lemonade or ice-tea making, the ritual of wine, shoes, or no shoes, and at last, swiftly following the others, with quiet dignity, the ritual of the front-porch swing.

On the third day of summer in the late afternoon Grandfather reappeared from the front door to gaze serenely at the two empty eye rings in the ceiling of the porch. Moving to the geranium-pot-lined rail like Ahab surveying the mild day and the mild-looking sky, he wet his finger to test the wind, and shucked his coat to see how shirt sleeves felt in the westering hours. He acknowledged the salutes of other captains on yet other flowered porches, out themselves to discern the gentle ground swell of weather, oblivious to their wives chirping or snapping like fuzzball hand dogs hidden behind black porch screens.

"All right, Douglas, let's let it up."

In the garage they found, dusted, and carried forth the howdah, as it were, for the quiet summer-night festivals, the swing chair which Grandpa chained to the porch-ceiling eyelets.

Douglas, being lighter, was first to sit in the swing. Then, after a moment, Grandfather gingerly settled his pontifical weight beside the boy. Thus they sat, smiling at each other, nodding, as they swung silently back and forth, back and forth.

Ten minutes later Grandma appeared with water buckets and brooms to wash down and sweep off the porch. Other chairs, rockers and straight-backs, were summoned from the house.

"Always like to start sitting early in the season," said Grandpa, "before the mosquitoes thicken."

About seven o'clock you could hear the chairs scraping back from the tables, someone experimenting with a yellow-toothed piano, if you stood outside the dining-room window and listened. Matches being struck, the first dishes bubbling in the suds and tinkling on the wall racks, somewhere, faintly, a phonograph playing.

And then as the evening changed the hour, at house after house on the twilight streets, under the immense oaks and elms, on shady porches, people would begin to appear, like those figures who tell good or bad weather in rain-or-shine clocks.

Uncle Bert, perhaps Grandfather, then Father, and some of the cousins; the men all coming out first into the syrupy evening, blowing smoke, leaving the women's voices behind in the cooling-warm kitchen to set their universe alight. Then the first male voices under the porch brim, the feet up, the boys fringed on the worn steps or wooden rails where sometime during the evening something, a boy or a geranium pot, would fall off.

At last, like ghosts hovering momentarily behind the door screen, Grandma, Great-grandma, and Mother would appear, and the men would shift, move, and offer seats. The women carried varieties of fans with them, folded newspapers, bamboo whisks, or perfumed kerchiefs, to start the air moving about their faces as they talked.

What they talked of all evening long, no one remembered next day. It wasn't important to anyone what the adults talked about; it was only important that the sounds came and went over the delicate ferns that bordered the porch on three sides; it was only important that the darkness filled the town like black water being poured over the houses, and that the cigars glowed and that the conversations went on, and on. The female gossip moved out, disturbing the first mosquitoes so they danced in frenzies on the air. The male voices invaded the old house timbers; if you closed your eyes and put your head down against the floor boards you could hear the men's voices rumbling like a distant, political earthquake, constant, unceasing, rising or falling a pitch.

Douglas sprawled back on the dry porch planks, completely contented and reassured by these voices, which would speak on through eternity, flow in a stream of murmurings over his body, over his closed eyelids, into his drowsy ears, for all time. The rocking chairs sounded like crickets, the crickets sounded like rocking chairs, and the moss-covered rain barrel by the dining-room window produced another generation of mosquitoes to provide a topic of conversation through endless summers ahead.

Sitting on the summer-night porch was so good, so easy and so reassuring that it could never be done away with. These were rituals that were right and lasting; the lighting of pipes, the pale hands that moved knitting needles in the dimness, the eating of foil-wrapped, chill Eskimo Pies, the coming and going of all the people. For at some time or other during the evening, everyone visited here; the neighbors down the way, the people across the street; Miss Fern and Miss Roberta humming by in their electric runabout, giving Tom or Douglas a ride around the block and then coming up to sit down and fan away the fever in their cheeks; or Mr. Jonas, the junkman, having left his horse and wagon hidden in the alley, and ripe to bursting with words, would come up the steps looking as fresh as if his talk had never been said before, and somehow it never had. And last of all, the children, who had been off squinting their way through a last hide-and-seek or kick-the-can, panting, glowing, would sickle quietly back like boomerangs along the soundless lawn, to sink beneath the talking of the porch voices which would weigh and gentle them down.

Oh, the luxury of lying in the fern night and the grass night and the night of susurrant, slumbrous voices weaving the dark together. The grownups had forgotten he was there, so still, so quiet Douglas lay, noting the plans they were making for his and their own futures. And the voices chanted, drifted, in moonlit clouds of cigarette smoke while the moths, like late appleblossoms come alive, tapped faintly about the far street lights, and the voices moved on into the coming years. . . .

The New
American Man

Robert Bly

We talk a great deal about "the American man," as if there were some quality that remained stable over decades, or even within a single decade. . . .

Even in our own era the agreed-on model has changed dramatically. During the fifties, for example, an American character appeared with some consistency that became a model of manhood adopted by many men: the Fifties male.

He got to work early, labored responsibly, supported his wife and children, and admired discipline. . . . This sort of man didn't see women's souls well, but he appreciated their bodies; and his view of culture and America's part in it was boyish and optimistic. Many of his qualities were strong and positive, but underneath the charm and bluff there was, and there remains, much isolation, deprivation, and passivity. Unless he has an enemy, he isn't sure that he is alive.

The Fifties man was supposed to like football, be aggressive, stick up for the United States, never cry, and always provide. But receptive space or intimate space was missing in this image of a man. The personality lacked some sense of flow. . . .

The Fifties male had a clear vision of what a man was, and what male responsibilities were, but the isolation and one-sidedness of his vision were dangerous.

During the sixties, another sort of man appeared. The waste and violence of the Vietnam war made men question whether they knew what an adult male really was. If manhood meant Vietnam, did they want any part of it? Meanwhile, the feminist movement encouraged men to actually look at women, forcing them to become conscious of concerns and sufferings that the Fifties male labored to avoid. As men began to examine women's history and women's sensibility, some men began to notice what is called their *feminine* side and pay attention to it. This process continues this day and I would say that most contemporary men are involved in it some way.

There's something wonderful about this development—I mean the practice of men welcoming their own "feminine" consciousness and nurturing it—this is important—and yet I have the sense that there is something wrong. The male in the past twenty years has become more thoughtful, more gentle. But by this process he has not become more free. He's a nice boy who pleases not only his mother but also the young woman he is living with.

In the seventies I began to see all over the country a phenomenon that we might call the "soft male." Sometimes even today when I look out at an audience, perhaps half the young males are what I'd call soft. They're lovely, valuable people— I like them—they're not interested in harming the earth or starting wars. There's a gentle attitude toward life in their whole being and style of living.

But many of these men are not happy. You quickly notice the lack of energy in them. They are life-preserving but not exactly life-giving. Ironically you often see these men with strong women who positively radiate energy.

Here we have a finely tuned young man, ecologically superior to his father, sympathetic to the whole harmony of the universe, yet he himself has little vitality to offer.

The strong or life-giving women who graduated from the sixties, so to speak, or who have inherited an older spirit, played an important part in producing this life-preserving, but not life-giving, man.

I remember a bumper sticker during the sixties that read "WOMEN SAY YES TO MEN WHO SAY NO." We recognize that it took a lot of courage to resist the draft, go to jail, or move to Canada, just as it took courage to accept the draft and go to Vietnam. But the women of twenty years ago were definitely saying that they preferred the softer receptive male.

So the development of men was affected a little in this preference. Nonreceptive maleness was equated with violence, and receptive maleness was rewarded.

Some energetic women, at that time and now in the nineties, chose and still choose soft men to be their lovers and, in a way, perhaps, to be their sons. The new distribution of "yang" energy among couples didn't happen by accident. Young men for various reasons wanted their women harder, and women began to desire softer men. It seemed like a nice arrangement for a while, but we've lived with it long enough now to see that it isn't working out.

I first learned about the anguish of "soft" men when they told their stories in early men's gatherings. In 1980, the Lama Community in New Mexico asked me to teach a conference for men only, their first, in which about forty men participated. Each day we concentrated on one Greek god and one old story, and then late in the afternoons we gathered to talk. When the younger men spoke it was not uncommon for them to be weeping within five minutes. The amount of grief and anguish in these younger men was astounding to me.

Part of their grief rose out of remoteness from their fathers, which they felt keenly, but partly, too, grief flowed from trouble in their marriages or relationships. They had learned to be receptive, but receptivity wasn't enough to carry their marriages through troubled times. In every relationship something *fierce* is needed once in a while: both the man and the woman need to have it. But at the point when it was needed, often the young man came up short. He was nurturing, but something else was required—for his relationship, and for his life.

The "soft" male was able to say, "I can feel your pain, and I consider your life as important as mine, and I will take care of you and comfort you." But he could not say what he wanted, and stick by it. *Resolve* of that kind was a different matter.

In *The Odyssey*, Hermes instructs Odysseus that when he approaches Circe, who stands for a certain kind of matriarchal energy, he is to lift or show his sword. In these early sessions it was difficult for many of the younger men to distinguish between showing the sword and hurting someone. One man, a kind of incarnation of certain spiritual attitudes of the sixties, a man who had actually lived in a tree for a year outside Santa Cruz, found himself unable to extend his arm when it held a sword. He had learned so well not to hurt anyone that he couldn't lift the steel, even to catch the light of the sun on it. But showing a sword doesn't necessarily mean fighting. It can also suggest a joyful decisiveness.

The journey many American men have taken into softness, or receptivity, or "development of the feminine side," has been an immensely valuable journey but more travel lies ahead. No stage is the final stop.

A Fable for Tomorrow

Rachel Carson

There was once a town in the heart of America where all life seemed to live in harmony with its surroundings. The town lay in the midst of a checkerboard of prosperous farms, with fields of grain and hillsides of orchards where, in spring, white clouds of bloom drifted above the green fields. In autumn, oak and maple and birch set up a blaze of color that flamed and flickered across a backdrop of pines. Then foxes barked in the hills and deer silently crossed the fields, half hidden in the mists of the fall mornings.

Along the roads, laurel, viburnum and alder, great ferns and wildflowers delighted the traveler's eye through much of the year. Even in winter the roadsides were places of beauty, where countless birds came to feed on the berries and on the seed heads of the dried weeds rising above the snow. The countryside was, in fact, famous for the abundance and variety of its bird life, and when the flood of migrants was pouring through in spring and fall people traveled from great distances to observe them. Others came to fish the streams, which flowed clear and cold out of the hills and contained shady pools where trout lay. So it had been from the days many years ago when the first settlers raised their houses, sank their wells, and built their barns.

Then a strange blight crept over the area and everything began to change. Some evil spell had settled on the community: mysterious maladies swept the flocks of chickens; the cattle and sheep sickened and died. Everywhere was a shadow of death. The farmers spoke of much illness among their families. In the town the doctors had become more and more puzzled by new kinds of sickness appearing among their patients. There had been several sudden and unexplained deaths, not only among adults but even among children, who would be stricken suddenly while at play and die within a few hours.

There was a strange stillness. The birds, for example—where had they gone? Many people spoke of them, puzzled and disturbed. The feeding stations in the backyards were deserted. The few birds seen anywhere were moribund; they trembled violently and could not fly. It was a spring without voices. On the mornings that had once throbbed with the dawn chorus of robins, catbirds, doves, jays, wrens, and scores of other bird voices there was now no sound; only silence lay over the fields and woods and marsh.

On the farms the hens brooded, but no chicks hatched. The farmers complained that they were unable to raise any pigs—the litters were small and the young survived only a few days. The apple trees were coming into bloom but no bees droned among the blossoms, so there was no pollination and there would be no fruit.

The roadsides, once so attractive, were now lined with browned and withered vegetation as though swept by fire. These, too, were silent, deserted by all living things. Even the streams were now lifeless. Anglers no longer visited them, for all the fish had died.

In the gutters under the eaves and between the shingles of the roofs, a white granular powder still showed a few patches; some weeks before it had fallen like snow upon the roofs and the lawns, the fields and streams.

No witchcraft, no enemy action had silenced the rebirth of new life in this stricken world. The people had done it themselves.

This town does not actually exist, but it might easily have a thousand counterparts in America or elsewhere in the world. I know of no community that has experienced all the misfortunes I describe. Yet every one of these disasters has actually happened somewhere, and many real communities have already suffered a substantial number of them. A grim specter has crept upon us almost unnoticed, and this imagined tragedy may easily become a stark reality we all shall know.

What Do Women Want?

Sara Davidson

Danielle Laurent was about to be married, at the age of thirty-three. "Is this your first marriage?" people asked, as she drove around Jerusalem on her motor scooter, ordering flowers and cakes.

"Yes."

"*Mazel tov!*"

Danielle was a French Jew, raised in Paris, but for seven years she had been living in Jerusalem, teaching literature at the Hebrew University. Her fiancé was a professor of physics, thirty-six, also new to marriage. A week before the wedding, Danielle invited friends to come to the home of her aunt, Simone, to spend the evening sewing the wedding dress.

I happened to be visiting Jerusalem and was invited. "Please, make an effort," Danielle had said. "I need you."

Simone's small house in Abu Tor, overlooking King David's Tower, was filled with women, professional women, ranging from twenty-six to thirty-five. Four were American, one was Spanish, one was Romanian, two were French and three were native Israelis. None was legally married at the time, except Simone.

At seventy, Simone is still a beauty, tall and erect, wearing her gray hair in a chignon. Simone has had two lengthy marriages, raised four children and enjoyed a career as a concert violinist. She lived in a villa outside Paris until her first husband died, at forty-two. Her children were away at school by then, so Simone, long a Zionist, immigrated to Israel, where she fell in love with her current husband, Moshe.

"I am someone who has lived by love, in love, all my life," she told me as she sat on the couch, her feet propped on pillows. "I have to be an example to the girls."

It had been Simone's idea to have the young women sew Danielle's dress by hand, from fabric Simone had bought in India: white silk, with delicate gold embroidery. As we came in, she made us wash our hands and cover our laps with sheets, so the fabric would not be soiled.

It was peaceful, sewing together, keeping a watchful circle around Danielle. But there was also a feeling of irony and self-mocking: we were not girls of sixteen, believing in the dress as a passport to the golden land.

Simone asked that we go around the circle and take turns telling stories and legends. Danielle, who was first, shook her head no. Her long dark hair covered her eyes as she bent over her sewing. For years, Danielle had been telling herself that what she wanted more than anything was to have a partner, a "permanent ally," and a house full of children. All through her twenties, she had given priority to her work, and assumed she would never have the patience to care for infants. But around the time she turned thirty, it became painful to walk past a children's store. She began to long, to ache for someone to share life with. For thirteen years she had been a waif, fending for herself and traveling across three continents; now that was to change. But could she adjust? Would the love she felt abide?

"Sara, you must provide us with a story," Simone said. For a moment, I could think of nothing that seemed appropriate; then I remembered an Arthurian legend I had heard from a friend, Winifred Rosen, who was adapting the tale for a children's book.

I began to relate the story, as best I could, from memory. "In the time of King Arthur and the Round Table, the King was out riding in the forest when he was surprised by a strange knight in full battle dress. The knight drew his sword, but the King said, 'Wait. I'm not armed, you can't do this, it would violate our honor code.' So the knight, whose name was Sir Gromer Somer Joure, had to relent. He made the King promise that he would return to the same spot, alone and unarmed, one year later. The King's life would be spared only if he brought back the answer to this riddle: What do women want, more than anything?"

Danielle interrupted the story. "That's what Freud is supposed to have asked. 'What do women want, dear God?'" Simone laughed. "The question did not originate with Freud. It recurs through the ages." She turned to me. "What did King Arthur do?"

"He rode back to the palace and met his nephew, Sir Gawain, who was, you know, the most beautiful and perfect knight in all the kingdom. He told Sir Gawain his plight, and Sir Gawain said, 'Don't worry, I'll ride in one direction, you'll ride in the other, and we'll ask every man and woman we meet, what do women want?'

"So the two of them rode off, and for a year, they asked every person, high and low, wise and simple, what do women want? They were given hundreds of answers."

I stopped to ask the women in Simone's sitting room, "How would you answer if you had to, 'What do women want more than anything?'"

They paused in their stitching.

"Love."

"A child."

"Respect."

"To be worshiped."

The Romanian lady said, "I think women want to be men."

Simone smiled, as if she knew none of the above would have saved the King.

I continued: "At the end of the year, Sir Gawain and the King each had a book full of answers. But King Arthur knew he did not have the right answer and he was prepared to meet his fate, when he saw a woman approaching. This woman was the ugliest hag in creation. She was fat and wrinkled; she had a big nose with snot dripping and hairs sprouting from her face. She gave off a terrible odor. Her teeth were like tusks. She had warts and pus oozing from her eyes. Her name was Dame Ragnell. She rode straight up to the King and said, 'Sir, I alone have the answer that will save you. I'll tell you on one condition: that you give me Sir Gawain as my husband.'

"The King was horrified. 'I can't give you Sir Gawain.' He would rather have died than commit his nephew to such a fate. But Sir Gawain insisted he would marry the hag, gladly, if it would save the King's life.

"So King Arthur accepted the terms. 'Now, tell me, what do women want more than anything?'

"Dame Ragnell said, 'Sovereignty.'"

I paused in my story. We looked at each other, silently, covered with yards of white silk. Everyone seemed to sense instantly how satisfying the answer was.

"When King Arthur returned to meet Sir Gromer Somer Joure, he told him the answer, and his life *was* spared. Overjoyed, he rode back to the palace, but he found Dame Ragnell waiting to be married. And she wanted a grand wedding, with all the royal court. After the ceremony, Dame Ragnell gave a little tug at Sir Gawain's sleeve and croaked, 'My lord, I'm your wife now, you have certain duties . . .'"

There were groans in the room.

"Sir Gawain could barely bring himself to look at her hairy snout, but he was bound by honor. He screwed up his courage, shut his eyes and turned to kiss her, and as he did, she was transformed into the most beautiful, delicate, sensuous creature he had ever dreamed of seeing. They spent the night making love, and as the sun was rising, Dame Ragnell said, 'My beauty will not hold all the time, so you must make a choice. Either have me beautiful by day, when the world can see, and ugly at night; or ugly by day and beautiful in your bed.'"

I said to the women, "Which would you choose, if you were Gawain?"

The Spanish woman said, "Beautiful by day." But she was quickly outvoted. Danielle said, "If he was a wise man, he would have her beautiful for him alone." Simone abstained, and asked me to continue.

"What Sir Gawain said was this: 'My lady, I leave it up to you.' And at that, she became beautiful all the time."

Cheers broke out; cakes were passed around. Danielle clapped her hands. "He was a very wise man." Simone, quieting the group, said, "You know, sovereignty is not a problem when you rule alone in your kingdom, but when two sovereign people want to merge their domains . . ." She looked pointedly at her niece. "Ah, that is the riddle you have yet to answer."

An Athlete's Locker Room

Student

One of the most distinctive, and perhaps most easily recognizable, atmospheres is that of an athlete's locker room. As you enter, the unmistakable odor of perspiring bodies, damp leather, and dirty clothes hits your nostrils; it is a familiar one for the athlete, but sometimes unbearable for others. The room is usually large, and dim, and long enough to be lined with rows of army-green lockers. The dryers hum in the background while the steam from the showers settles and penetrates every nook and cranny, making the floor and walls seem damp and wet. We bring our emotions into this sanctuary, away from prying eyes and ears, to release our jubilation, disappointments and discouragements, and sometimes our tears. The language would make an English professor cringe, yet nothing could ever change it. It may sound offensive in many respects, but to an athlete it is part of his life that he cherishes and never forgets when those days are set aside for a different kind of life.

My Grandma

Student

Monday through Friday my Grandma was a hard working woman with little time for fun. However, staying at Grandma's house on a Saturday night was something my cousins and I looked forward to; with no other adults around, Grandma's personality sparkled and she would cast aside her inhibitions in the desire to show us a good time. At times, we would laugh as she would dance around the room with a fringed tablecloth thrown dramatically around her shoulders, a flower clenched in her teeth, henna colored hair tossing to and fro. Other nights she would drag out her beat-up banjo and teach us the bluegrass and gospel music she learned as a girl in the hills of Arkansas. Grandma's twangy voice fit right in with the rhythm of toe tappin' and banjo pickin', and every part of her being would be caught up in her music. She would always encourage us to join in, but we could only be a pale imitation of her vibrancy. When arthritis bent her fingers and it became too painful to play the banjo, she got a player piano and had us do the pumping, leaving her free to demonstrate a Charleston or jitterbug. Arthritis finally took its toll and she could no longer play an instrument or dance around a room. Some of the magic went out of her life then; I know a very special part of my childhood was taken from me. I will never forget the laughter, song, and fun of spending Saturday night at Grandma's house.

An Urban Legend

Student

Many cities around the country have their own versions of a similar story, that is not true, but assumed true. This is called an urban legend. More than likely we have all heard them; sometimes you believe them. The one urban legend that sticks out in my mind is the buried treasure. It was told to me about fifteen years ago. This story was about an old man who lived in my neighborhood, who had just lost his wife in a car accident. The man was a wealthy real estate agent, and owned thirty acres of woods that was behind his house. There were always scary stories about the wooded lot, so I had never explored them much. The old man slowly lost his sanity and could no longer trust anyone, so he never left his house anymore. Now he was the subject of rumors, and it made the man all the more interesting to talk about. The next door neighbor claims to have seen the old man walk into the woods with a cigar box and a shovel, coming out empty handed. She said he repeated this ritual at least twice a week. One year later the man passed on, but his family could not find the money he had saved up in his savings account, leaving the whereabouts of the money a mystery. This story was told to me and my friends by older kids who said they thought the money was in the woods. They had decided enough was enough, and became tired of looking. My friends and I were bored anyway, so we started the search. This search would last four years before we had any clues! There were holes dug all over the woods where we tried to find the cigar boxes. One of my friends found an empty cigar box near an old pond in the woods. My friends and I dug fiercely around the old pond, but to our dismay we came up empty handed. That was when we decided to quit, and pass on the legend to my friend's little brother. Years have passed now and the legend is still out there, and so are the holes that we dug in the earth embedding our memories into the mysterious wooded lot.

Learning Experience

Student

It was eight years ago, and I can still remember how my friends coerced me into joining the National Guard. I was sitting around at a party with some of my older friends when they started talking about the fun things they did when they were at guard camp. I was 17 years old and about 5 years younger than the youngest of them. All the maneuvers and such sounded like a lot of fun, the way they explained it. There was just one catch. I would have to go to boot camp for 13 weeks. So the summer in between my junior and senior year came, and I was on a plane to Fort Benning, Georgia. Here I was, 17 years old, spending my summer under the supervision of Drill Sergeant Remmington while all of my friends were back home partying away.

I'll never forget the first morning when the Drill Sergeant walked in at 4:45 with a tin trash can in one hand and his night stick in the other hand. It made for a really unpleasant alarm clock, but it was very effective. I was 5 feet 9 inches tall, and I weighed about 120 pounds soaking wet. The only thing that I ever heard out of the Drill Sergeant's mouth was screaming and yelling. My underwear had to be folded a certain way, my socks had to be folded just right and my tee shirts had to look like my battle buddies. For the first week I threw up at least once a day, so the doctor put me on some nerve pills. The whole time I would think back to my friends that told me how fun guard camp was, and wonder how I could be so gullible.

That was eight years ago, and to this day I still reflect a lot of my present accomplishments to the training that I received that summer. It has definitely made me a better husband and father. Today, I can control my temper much better than when I was a young teenager. Whenever someone starts to get on my nerves or something, I know that the best thing to do is to walk away or ignore them. This, I learned from ignoring the Drill Sergeant as he was yelling at me. Sometimes my wife gets upset with me because I try to keep things too squared away, but in the end she forgives me because she knows what I have been through. Over all, the experience that I endured while at Fort Benning, Georgia, was one that will continue to help me for years to come.

CHAPTER 3

Narration

When you narrate, you tell a story. Storytelling is a powerful tool for the writer because it gives you a way to dramatize your ideas so that your reader can relate to them. By using well-chosen words, you can bring the story to life on the written page.

Why Write a Narrative Essay?

Everyone enjoys a good story, so if you use narration in an essay, you can effectively capture your reader's attention. You can rely on your personal experiences as the basis for the narrative. By relying on a personal experience, you are assured of having the details of the experience in your memory, and you will have plenty of material. For example, if you had to write an essay about why you are attending this college, you could do so in narrative format, and simply retell the story of what brought you here.

Narration is an effective method of expressing meaningful events in your life.

How to Write a Narrative

You will find that a good narrative relies heavily on the power of description. Recounting events involving people and places without also describing them is difficult. You will also find that dialogue is frequently employed in narrative writing to add interest and variation.

To narrate effectively, you need to remember that any good story has a main point or a purpose. In addition, to get to this main point, you will take your reader through a series of actions and events which have a chronology, a time sequence.

To write a narrative, you need a beginning, a middle, and an end (just like any story). You introduce the story, tell the story by emphasizing the major events and skimming over minor events, and conclude the story by making some final point.

The beginning of your essay, the first one or two paragraphs, is exposition. Here you expose the situation for the reader: the setting, the people involved, etc. Once this is established, the action of the narrative begins to rise.

An interesting narrative must have an element of conflict within it. You may remember the standard conflicts that your English teachers have talked about: man against man, man against nature, etc. Conflicts create complications in your story, causing rising action as the complications move toward a climax. At this point, the conflict has become the central focus of your narrative. From the climax, the action now begins to fall, ultimately toward a resolution, at which point the complications have been resolved.

Several points to consider: First, conflicts and complications don't have to be negative. Complications are usually based on un-met expectations. You expect something good to happen, but something bad happens instead. But this can just as easily be a case of expecting something bad to happen and then being pleasantly surprised when something good happens. Think of any movie or situation comedy you've ever seen, any short story or novel you've ever read—they always have an element of conflict or dissonance or irony at their hearts. Second, don't feel that you must explicitly describe a resolution for your narrative. Often times in real life, as we all know, resolutions are only hinted at or don't occur at all.

Criteria for Writing a Narrative Essay

1. Prewrite to be sure you jog your memory. You need to recapture the sequence of events so that you can recount them.

2. Reflect on the reporter's questions of who, what, when, where, why, and how to help you to gather your ideas and reconnect to the event.

3. Determine the focus and the purpose of the story. Why did you pick this particular event to narrate? What is important about it that you want to share with your audience?

4. Establish a conflict or a point of dissonance or an exciting high point to encourage reader interest.

5. Decide what your audience can learn from reading your narrative. The reader should finish the narrative and either learn from it or be entertained by it and perceive it as some model for future action.

6. Pick out the details to include in the narrative. Your purpose and audience should guide you. By reflecting on purpose and audience, you can determine which details should be developed elaborately and which should be handled quickly and briefly.

7. Decide whether or not to use dialogue. You need to think about

the difference between showing and telling. If the reader will learn more from being transported to the event, then use dialogue so that the event unfolds. If a word for word recounting of the event is unnecessary, then tell the reader what happened.

8. Develop your narrative in a variety of ways including use of description, explanation, and dialogue.

9. Choose your point of view. This refers to the person, the vantage point, and the narrator's attitude. The person tells the story: an uninvolved observer, a character in the narrative, or an omniscient (all-knowing, all-seeing) narrator. Choosing a type of narrator helps you to decide on which attitude to use. Consistently follow this attitude, or you will destroy the focus and coherence of the narrative.

10. Write a thesis statement that begins the narrative and establishes the purpose and focus of your paper if this not clearly implied in your first paragraph.

11. Arrange the sequence of events so that you create a beginning, a middle, and an end.

12. Rely on chronology to create overall coherence.

13. Use transitions that promote the passage of time such as *next, suddenly, at this point, first, then, afterwards,* etc. Begin new paragraphs when changes in setting occur, when new characters enter or leave the scene, and when changing speakers in dialogue.

14. Experiment with the order of events. Sometimes telling the end of the story first and then going back to the beginning can be an effective technique. Unfortunately, this can also be very confusing for your reader if you don't handle it well.

Topic Ideas for Narration

The worst date you ever had

A car wreck

A surprise party you attended

The birth of your child

Your worst day on the job

A time you got away with something that you should have been punished for

A time you were punished for something you didn't do

The first time you were ever treated as an adult

Your most embarrassing moment

Peer Evaluation for Narration

1. Does the writer begin in an interesting way?
2. Does the writer establish a focus for the narrative?
3. Did the writer use a thesis statement or clearly imply the thesis?
4. Is the narrative organized chronologically?
5. Is there a beginning, a middle, and an end?
6. Is there an element of conflict or dissonance or excitement in the narrative?
7. Did the writer use transitional words and phrases to signal passage of time?
8. Are the points in the narrative arranged logically?
9. Did the writer fully develop the ideas in the narrative?
10. Did the writer vary methods of development?
11. Did the writer rely on an appeal to the reader's senses to develop ideas?
12. If dialogue is used, did the writer use it effectively?
13. Did the writer reach a logical resolution or conclusion to the narrative?
14. Did the writer check for grammar, punctuation and spelling errors?
15. Has the writer used varied sentences and vocabulary?

Mind Your Tongue, Young Man

Sandra Flahive Maurer

It was one of those days filled with the little vexations of life. In the morning, insult was added to injury when I got a speeding ticket after having a root canal. At work, the computer fouled me up by going down. By noon, the banana I'd brought for lunch had turned black and squishy, and finally, as I sped for home at the end of the day, the needle on the car's fuel indicator shook convulsively in its demand for a thirst–quenching gulp of gas.

Although I don't remember that I uttered any profanities upon encountering the day's irritations, in all likelihood I did. Like most people, I've never been known to have a lily-white mouth.

On that particular evening, I was eager to get home because I was giving a dinner party. However, my main concern was that I couldn't make it without first obliging the car's needs. I whipped off the freeway and headed for the nearest convenience store, only to find all eight pumps taken.

"Damn," I remember exclaiming as I impatiently waited my turn. But I soon found myself using another expletive when a cheeky woman in a Volvo tried to nudge ahead of me and cheat me of my already established territorial rights.

Eventually I was able to sidle up to a pump and fill the tank. Then I darted inside to pay—only to have to wait in line for the privilege of forking over money. As I stood, swearing under my breath about another delay in my life, I was only vaguely aware of a young man in front of me. He had plunked a Pepsi on the counter and was reaching into his pockets for money.

"Ninety-four cents, please," declared the middle-aged clerk. "Oh, and I'll take this pack of cigarettes, too," the young man stated matter-of-factly, as he pitched his selection on the counter.

"ID," countered the clerk, in a tone that suggested he had made this request many times before. The casual command caused me to focus on the person ahead of me. He was extremely slight with delicate features and a face as smooth as a baby's heel. I silently agreed with the clerk's decision to question his age. He could have been 21—or he could have been 15. It was impossible to tell.

"ID," said the clerk a second time, after the customer failed to respond with anything but a surly look.

Apparently the question about his age was more than he could stand, and upon being asked twice, the young man burst forth with a string of verbal garbage. "Goddam it! I don't have any f—ing identification with me. I don't haul the f—ing thing everywhere I go!" To which the clerk calmly remarked, "Then, it will be 94 cents for the Pepsi. No ID, no cigarettes."

With that rejection, the angry young man spewed a stream of obscenities that have become part of today's vocabulary. "I just ain't got my f—ing ID with me today. I told you."

I'd been observing the exchange more out of a sense of indifference than anything. All I wanted was to pay for my gas and get on my way. But my indifference vanished when the clerk, reacting to the profanity, suddenly reached across the counter with both arms, grabbed the fellow by the collar and literally plucked him off the floor. With fire in his eyes and passion in his voice, he growled, "That is enough! You watch what you say in here, do you understand? There's a lady present!" Then he shoved the guy away with obvious contempt.

The foulmouthed offender was stunned. So was I! Instinctively, I looked around to see where the "lady" was. I glanced up and down the nearby aisles and peered high into the corners where mirrors reveal all activity in the store. I had an image of some little old woman in a housedress, shuffling along in sturdy orthopedic shoes, her white hair done up in a bun, her purse dangling from her arm. I didn't see her anywhere.

All I saw in the mirror was the reflection of the two combatants—and my own. The obvious hit me hard. *I* was the "lady." I was flabbergasted by the clerk's stern admonition on my behalf. No one had tried to protect me from offensive language before.

With considerable speed the astonished young man paid for his drink and scurried from the store. I did likewise, still so startled by the clerk's actions that I didn't respond to his gallantry.

It was only after I began driving from the convenience store that I realized the significance of the episode. Profanity seems to be one of those problems about which almost everyone agrees something should be done. Yet few of us ever do anything about it. On the contrary, most of us contribute, if not to its proliferation, at least to its continuation, by swearing ourselves or making no attempt to curb it in others.

I recalled with guilt all the less-than-delicate language that had rolled off my tongue through the years—when I was mad, when I was glad, when I was trying to be dramatic and, yes, even when I had to wait in line for a few seconds. But nothing as crass as what I'd just heard.

And now, in an act of omission myself, I had failed to respond. Why hadn't *I* told the culprit to knock it off when his first raunchy words foamed out of his mouth? Why hadn't I given so much as a second's thought to rebuking him about his language? It's so familiar that it passes unnoticed, just runs off our backs. At the very least, why hadn't I thanked the clerk for taking a stand against offensive language in his store?

Recently I read a newspaper article that stated although Americans do have a concern about all the unbridled profanity around us every day, the reality is that we are swearing more, hearing it less.

Unfortunately, there must be some truth to the story—as shown by my experience in the convenience store. Granted it seems only natural that someone might be in shock after being subjected to a string of raw expressions while waiting to pay for gas. What surprises me is how much more astonished I was by the store clerk's gallant intervention and stand against vulgarity in his establishment than by the cussing of an angry young punk denied a pack of cigarettes.

A Total Eclipse

Annie Dillard

It began with no ado. It was odd that such a well-advertised public event should have no starting gun, no overture, no introductory speaker. I should have known right then that I was out of my depth. Without pause or preamble, silent as orbits, a piece of the sun went away. We looked at it through welders' goggles. A piece of the sun was missing; in its place we saw empty sky.

I had seen a partial eclipse in 1970. A partial eclipse is very interesting. It bears almost no relation to a total eclipse. Seeing a partial eclipse bears the same relation to seeing a total eclipse as kissing a man does to marrying him, or as flying in an airplane does to falling out of an airplane. Although the one experience precedes the other, it in no way prepares you for it. During a partial eclipse the sky does not darken—not even when 94 percent of the sun is hidden. Nor does the sun, seen colorless through protective devices, seem terribly strange. We have all seen a sliver of light in the sky; we have all seen the crescent moon by day. However, during a partial eclipse the air does indeed get cold, precisely as if someone were standing between you and the fire. And blackbirds do fly back to their roosts. I had seen a partial eclipse before, and here was another.

What you see in an eclipse is entirely different from what you know. It is especially different for those of us whose grasp of astronomy is so frail that, given a flashlight, a grapefruit, two oranges, and fifteen years, we still could not figure out which way to set the clocks for Daylight Saving Time. Usually it is a bit of a trick to keep your knowledge from blinding you. But during an eclipse it is easy. What you see is much more convincing than any wild-eyed theory you may know.

You may read that the moon has something to do with eclipses. I have never seen the moon yet. You do not see the moon. So near the sun, it is as completely invisible as the stars are by day. What you see before your eyes is the sun going through phases. It gets narrower and narrower, as the waning moon does, and, like the ordinary moon, it travels alone in the simple sky. The sky is of course background. It does not appear to eat the sun; it is far behind the sun, The sun simply shaves away; gradually, you see less sun and more sky.

The sky's blue was deepening, but there was no darkness. The sun was a wide crescent, like a segment of tangerine. The wind freshened and blew steadily over the hill. The eastern hill across the highway grew dusky and sharp. The towns and orchards in the valley to the south were dissolving into the blue light. Only the thin river held a trickle of sun.

Now the sky to the west deepened to indigo, a color never seen. A dark sky usually loses color. This was a saturated, deep indigo, up in the air. Stuck up into that unworldly sky was the cone of Mount Adams, and the alpenglow was upon it. The alpenglow is that red light of sunset which holds out on snowy mountaintops long after the valleys and tablelands are dimmed. "Look at Mount Adams," I said, and that was the last sane moment I remember.

I turned back to the sun. It was going. The sun was going, and the world was wrong. The grasses were wrong: they were platinum. Their every detail of stem, head, and blade shone lightless and artificially distinct as an art photographer's platinum print. This color has never been seen on earth. The hues were metallic: their finish was matte. The hillside was a nineteenth-century tinted photograph from which the tints had faded. All the people you see in the photograph, distinct and detailed as their faces look, are now dead. The sky was navy blue. My hands were silver. All the distant hills' grasses were fine-spun metal which the wind laid down. I was watching a faded color print of a movie filmed in the Middle Ages; I was standing in it, by some mistake. I was standing in a movie of hillside grasses filmed in the Middle Ages. I missed my own century, the people I knew, and the real light of day.

I looked at Gary [her husband]. He was in the film. Everything was lost. He was a platinum print, a dead artist's version of life. I saw on his skull the darkness of night mixed with the colors of day. My mind was going out, my eyes were receding the way galaxies recede to the rim of space. Gary was light-years away, gesturing inside a circle of darkness, down the wrong end of a telescope. He smiled as if he saw me; the stringy crinkles around his eyes moved. The sight of him, familiar and wrong, was something I was remembering from centuries hence, from the other side of death: yes, *that* is the way he used to look, when we were living. When it was our generation's turn to be alive. I could not hear him: the wind was too loud. Behind him the sun was going. We had all started down a chute of time. At first it was pleasant: now there was no stopping it. Gary was chuting away across space, moving and talking and catching my eye, chuting down the long corridor of separation. The skin on his face moved like thin bronze plating that would peel.

The grass at our feet was wild barley. It was the wild einkorn wheat which grew on the hilly flanks of the Zagros Mountains, above the Euphrates valley, above the valley of the river we called *River*. We harvested the grass with stone sickles. I remember. We found the grasses on the hillsides; we built our shelter beside them and cut them down. That is how he used to look then, that one, moving and living and catching my eye, with the sky so dark behind him, and the wind blowing. God save our life.

From all the hills came screams. A piece of sky beside the crescent sun was detaching. It was a loosened circle of evening sky, suddenly lighted from the back.

It was an abrupt black body out of nowhere; it was a flat disk; it was almost over the sun. That is when there were screams. At once this disk of sky slid over the sun like a lid. The sky snapped over the sun like a lens cover. The hatch in the brain slammed. Abruptly it was dark night, on the land and in the sky. In the night sky was a tiny ring of light. The hole where the sun belongs is very small. A thin ring of light marked its place. There was no sound. The eyes dried, the arteries drained, the lungs hushed. There was no world. We were the world's dead people rotating and orbiting around and around, embedded in the planet's crust, while the earth rolled down. Our minds were light-years distant, forgetful of almost everything. Only an extraordinary act of will could recall to us our former, living selves and our contexts in matter and time. We had, it seems, loved the planet and loved our lives. But could no longer remember the way of them. We got the light wrong. In the sky was something that should not be there. In the black sky was a ring of light. It was a thin ring, an old, thin silver wedding band, an old, worn ring. It was an old wedding band in the sky, or a morsel of bone. There were stars. It was all over.

Passport to Knowledge

Mark Mathabane

When my mother began dropping hints that I would soon be going to school, I vowed never to go because school was a waste of time. She laughed and said, "We'll see. You don't know what you're talking about." My philosophy on school was that of a gang of ten-, eleven- and twelve-year-olds whom I so revered that their every word seemed that of an oracle.

These boys had long left their homes and were now living in various neighborhood junkyards, making it on their own. They slept in abandoned cars, smoked glue and benzene, ate pilchards and brown bread, sneaked into the white world to caddy and, if unsuccessful, came back to the township to steal beer and soda bottles from shebeens, or goods from the Indian traders on First Avenue. Their lifestyle was exciting, adventurous and full of surprises; and I was attracted to it. My mother told me that they were no-gooders, that they would amount to nothing, that I should not associate with them, but I paid no heed. What does she know? I used to tell myself. One thing she did not know was that the gang's way of life had captivated me wholly, particularly their philosophy on school: they hated it and considered an education a waste of time.

They, like myself, had grown up in an environment where the value of an education was never emphasized, where the first thing a child learned was not how to read and write and spell, but how to fight and steal and rebel; where the money to send children to school was grossly lacking, for survival was first priority. I kept my membership in the gang, knowing that for as long as I was under its influence, I would never go to school.

One day my mother woke me up at four in the morning.

"Are they here? I didn't hear any noises," I asked in the usual way.

"No," my mother said. "I want you to get into that washtub over there."

"What," I balked, upon hearing the word *washtub*. I feared taking baths like one feared the plague. Throughout seven years of hectic living the number of baths

55

I had taken could be counted on one hand with several fingers missing. I simply had no natural inclination for water; cleanliness was a trait I still had to acquire. Besides, we had only one bathtub in the house, and it constantly sprung a leak.

"I said get into that tub!" My mother shook a finger in my face.

Reluctantly, I obeyed, yet wondered why all of a sudden I had to take a bath. My mother, armed with a scrub brush and a piece of Lifebuoy soap, purged me of years and years of grime till I ached and bled. As I howled, feeling pain shoot through my limbs as the thistles of the brush encountered stubborn callouses, there was a loud knock at the door.

Instantly my mother leaped away from the tub and headed, on tiptoe, toward the bedroom. Fear seized me as I, too, thought of the police. I sat frozen in the bathtub, not knowing what to do.

"Open up, Mujaji [my mother's maiden name]," Granny's voice came shrilling through the door. "It's me."

My mother heaved a sigh of relief, her tense limbs relaxed. She turned and headed to the kitchen door, unlatched it and in came Granny and Aunt Bushy.

"You scared me half to death," my mother said to Granny. "I had forgotten all about your coming."

"Are you ready?" Granny asked my mother.

"Yes—just about," my mother said, beckoning me to get out of the washtub.

She handed me a piece of cloth to dry myself. As I dried myself, questions raced through my mind: What's going on? What's Granny doing at our house this ungodly hour of the morning? And why did she ask my mother, "Are you ready?" While I stood debating, my mother went into the bedroom and came out with a stained white shirt and a pair of faded black shorts.

"Here," she said, handing me the togs, "put these on."

"Why?" I asked.

"Put them on I said!"

I put the shirt on; it was grossly loose-fitting. It reached all the way down to my ankles. Then I saw the reason why: it was my father's shirt!

"But this is Papa's shirt," I complained. "It don't fit me."

"Put it on," my mother insisted. "I'll make it fit."

"The pants don't fit me either," I said. "Whose are they anyway?"

"Put them on," my mother said. "I'll make them fit."

Moments later I had the garments on; I looked ridiculous. My mother started working on the pants and shirt to make them fit. She folded the shirt in so many intricate ways and stashed it inside the pants, they too having been folded several times at the waist. She then choked the pants at the waist with a piece of sisal rope to hold them up. She then lavishly smeared my face, arms and legs with a mixture of pig's fat and vaseline. "This will insulate you from the cold," she said. My skin gleamed like the morning star and I felt as hot as the center of the sun and I smelled God knows like what. After embalming me, she headed to the bedroom.

"Where are we going, Gran'ma?" I said, hoping that she would tell me what my mother refused to tell me. I still had no idea I was about to be taken to school.

"Didn't your mother tell you?" Granny said with a smile. "You're going to start school."

"What!" I gasped, leaping from the chair where I was sitting as if it were made of hot lead. "I am not going to school!" I blurted out and raced toward the kitchen door.

My mother had just reappeared from the bedroom and guessing what I was up to, she yelled, "Someone get the door!"

Aunt Bushy immediately barred the door. I turned and headed for the window. As I leaped for the windowsill, my mother lunged at me and brought me down. I tussled, "Let go of me! I don't want to go to school! Let me go!" but my mother held fast onto me.

"It's no use now," she said, grinning triumphantly as she pinned me down. Turning her head in Granny's direction, she shouted, "Granny! Get a rope quickly!"

Granny grabbed a piece of rope nearby and came to my mother's aid. I bit and clawed every hand that grabbed me, and howled protestations against going to school; however, I was no match for the two determined matriarchs. In a jiffy they had me bound, hands and feet.

"What's the matter with him?" Granny, bewildered, asked my mother. "Why did he suddenly turn into an imp when I told him you're taking him to school?"

"You shouldn't have told him that he's being taken to school," my mother said. "He doesn't want to go there. That's why I requested you come today, to help me take him there. Those boys in the streets have been a bad influence on him."

As the two matriarchs hauled me through the door, they told Aunt Bushy not to go to school but stay behind and mind the house and the children.

The sun was beginning to rise from beyond the veld when Granny and my mother dragged me to school. The streets were beginning to fill with their everyday traffic: old men and women, wizened, bent and ragged, were beginning their rambling; workless men and women were beginning to assemble in their usual coteries and head for shebeens in the backyards where they discussed how they escaped the morning pass raids and contemplated the conditions of life amidst intense beer drinking and vacant, uneasy laughter, young boys and girls, some as young as myself, were beginning their aimless wanderings along the narrow, dusty streets in search of food, carrying bawling infants piggyback.

As we went along some of the streets, boys and girls who shared the same fears about school as I were making their feelings known in a variety of ways. They were howling their protests and trying to escape. A few managed to break loose and make a mad dash for freedom, only to be recaptured in no time, admonished or whipped, or both, and ordered to march again.

As we made a turn into Sixteenth Avenue, the street leading to the tribal school I was being taken to, a short, chubby black woman came along from the opposite direction. She had a scuttle overflowing with coal on her *doek*-covered (cloth-covered) head. An infant, bawling deafeningly, was loosely swathed with a piece of sheepskin onto her back. Following closely behind the woman, and picking up pieces of coal as they fell from the scuttle and placing them in a small plastic bag, was a half naked, potbellied and thumb-sucking boy of about four. The woman stopped abreast. For some reason we stopped too.

"I wish I had done the same to my oldest son," the strange woman said in a regretful voice, gazing at me. I was confounded by her stopping and offering her unsolicited opinion.

"I wish I had done that to my oldest son," she repeated, and suddenly burst into tears; amidst sobs, she continued, "before . . . the street claimed him . . . and . . . turned him into a *tsotsi*."

Granny and my mother offered consolatory remarks to the strange woman.

"But it's too late now," the strange woman continued, tears now streaming freely down her puffy cheeks. She made no attempt to dry them. "It's too late now," she said for the second time, "he's beyond any help. I can't help him even if I wanted to. *Uswile* [He is dead]."

"How did he die?" my mother asked in a sympathetic voice.

"He shunned school and, instead, grew up to live by the knife. And the same knife he lived by ended his life. That's why whenever I see a boy-child refuse to go to school, I stop and tell the story of my dear little *mbitsini* [heartbreak]."

Having said that, the strange woman left as mysteriously as she had arrived.

"Did you hear what that woman said!" my mother screamed into my ears. "Do you want the same to happen to you?"

I dropped my eyes. I was confused.

"Poor woman," Granny said ruefully. "She must have truly loved her son."

Finally, we reached the school and I was ushered into the principal's office, a tiny cubicle facing a row of privies and a patch of yellowed grass.

"So this is the rascal we'd been talking about," the principal, a tall, wiry man, foppishly dressed in a black pin-striped suit, said to my mother as we entered. His austere, shiny face, inscrutable and imposing, reminded me of my father. He was sitting behind a brown table upon which stood piles of dust and cobweb-covered books and papers. In one upper pocket of his jacket was arrayed a variety of pens and pencils; in the other nestled a lily-white handkerchief whose presence was more decorative than utilitarian. Alongside him stood a disproportionately portly black woman, fashionably dressed in a black skirt and a white blouse. She had but one pen, and this she held in her hand. The room was hot and stuffy and buzzing with flies.

"Yes, Principal," my mother answered, "this is he."

"I see he's living up to his notoriety," remarked the principal, noticing that I had been bound. "Did he give you too much trouble?"

"Trouble, Principal," my mother sighed. "He was like an imp."

"He's just like the rest of them, Principal," Granny sighed. "Once they get out into the streets, they become wild. They take to the many vices of the streets like an infant takes to its mother's milk. They begin to think that there's no other life but the one shown them by the *tsotsis*. They come to hate school and forget about the future."

"Well," the principal said. "We'll soon remedy all that. Untie him."

"He'll run away," my mother cried.

"I don't think he's that foolish to attempt that with all of us here."

"He *is* that foolish, Principal," my mother said as she and Granny began untying me. "He's tried it before. Getting him here was an ordeal in itself."

The principal rose from his seat, took two steps to the door and closed it. As the door swung closed, I spotted a row of canes of different lengths and thicknesses hanging behind it. The principal, seeing me staring at the canes, grinned and said, in a manner suggesting that he had wanted me to see them, "As long as you behave, I won't have to use any of those on you."

Use those canes on me? I gasped. I stared at my mother—she smiled, at Granny—she smiled too. That made me abandon any inkling of escaping.

"So they finally gave you the birth certificate and the papers," the principal addressed my mother as he returned to his chair.

"Yes, Principal," my mother said, "they finally did. But what a battle it was. It took me nearly a year to get all them papers together." She took out of her handbag a neatly wrapped package and handed it to the principal. "They've been running us around for so long that there were times when I thought he would never attend school, Principal," she said.

"That's pretty much standard procedure, Mrs. Mathabane," the principal said, unwrapping the package. "But you now have the papers and that's what's important.

"As long as we have the papers," he continued, minutely perusing the contents of the package, "we won't be breaking the law in admitting your son to this school, for we'll be in full compliance with the requirements set by the authorities in Pretoria."

"Sometimes I don't understand the laws from Pitori," Granny said. "They did the same to me with my Piet and Bushy. Why, Principal, should our children not be allowed to learn because of some piece of paper?"

"The piece of paper you're referring to, Mrs. Mabaso [Granny's maiden name]," the principal said to Granny, "is as important to our children as a pass is to us adults. We all hate passes; therefore, it's only natural we should hate the regulations our children are subjected to. But as we have to live with passes, so our children have to live with the regulations, Mrs. Mabaso. I hope you understand, that is the law of the country. We would have admitted your grandson a long time ago, as you well know, had it not been for the papers. I hope you understand."

"I understand, Principal," Granny said, "but I don't understand," she added paradoxically.

One of the papers caught the principal's eye and he turned to my mother and asked, "Is your husband a Shangaan, Mathabane?"

"No, he's not, Principal," my mother said. "Is there anything wrong? He's Venda and I'm Shangaan."

The principal reflected for a moment or so and then said, concernedly, "No, there's nothing seriously wrong. Nothing that we can't take care of. You see, Mrs. Mathabane, technically, the fact that your child's father is a Venda makes him ineligible to attend this tribal school because it is only for children whose parents are of the Shangaan tribe. May I ask what language the children speak at home?"

"Both languages," my mother said worriedly, "Venda and Shangaan. Is there anything wrong?"

The principal coughed, clearing his throat, then said, "I mean which language do they speak more?"

"It depends, Principal," my mother said, swallowing hard. "When their father is around, he wants them to speak only Venda. And when he's not, they speak Shangaan. And when they are out at play, they speak Zulu and Sisotho."

"Well," the principal said, heaving a sigh of relief. "In that case, I think an exception can be made. The reason for such an exception is that there's currently no school for Vendas in Alexandra. And should the authorities come asking why we took in your son, we can tell them that. Anyway, your child is half-half."

Everyone broke into a nervous laugh, except me. I was bewildered by the whole thing. I looked at my mother, and she seemed greatly relieved as she watched the principal register me; a broad smile broke across her face. It was as if some enormously heavy burden had finally been lifted from her shoulders and her conscience.

"Bring him back two weeks from today," the principal said as he saw us to the door. "There're so many children registering today that classes won't begin until two weeks hence. Also, the school needs repair and cleaning up after the holidays. If he refuses to come, simply notify us, and we'll send a couple of big boys to come fetch him, and he'll be very sorry if it ever comes to that."

As we left the principal's office and headed home, my mind was still against going to school. I was thinking of running away from home and joining my friends in the junkyard.

I didn't want to go to school for three reasons: I was reluctant to surrender my freedom and independence over to what I heard every school-going child call "tyrannous discipline." I had heard many bad things about life in tribal school— from daily beatings by teachers and mistresses who worked you like a mule to long school hours—and the sight of those canes in the principal's office gave ample credence to rumors that school was nothing but a torture chamber. And there was my allegiance to the gang.

But the thought of the strange woman's lamentations over her dead son presented a somewhat strong case for going to school: I didn't want to end up dead in the streets. A more compelling argument for going to school, however, was the vivid recollection of all that humiliation and pain my mother had gone through to get me the papers and the birth certificate so I could enroll in school, What should I do? I was torn between two worlds.

But later that evening something happened to force me to go to school.

I was returning home from playing soccer when a neighbor accosted me by the gate and told me that there had been a bloody fight at my home.

"Your mother and father have been at it again," the neighbor, a woman, said. "And your mother left."

I was stunned.

"Was she hurt badly?"

"A little bit," the woman said. "But she'll be all right. We took her to your grandma's place."

I became hot with anger.

"Is anyone in the house?" I stammered, trying to control my rage.

"Yes, your father is. But I don't think you should go near the house. He's raving mad. He's armed with a meat cleaver. He's chased out your brother and sisters, also. And some of the neighbors who tried to intervene he's threatened to carve them to pieces. I have never seen him this mad before."

I brushed aside the woman's warnings and went. Shattered windows convinced me that there had indeed been a skirmish of some sort. Several pieces of broken bricks, evidently broken after being thrown at the door, were lying about the door. I tried opening the door; it was locked from the inside. I knocked. No one answered. I knocked again. Still no one answered, until, as I turned to leave:

"Who's out there?" my father's voice came growling from inside.

"It's me, Johannes," I said.

"Go away, you bastard!" he bellowed. "I don't want you or that whore mother of yours setting foot in this house. Go away before I come out there and kill you!"

"Let me in!" I cried. "Dammit, let me in! I want my things!"

"What things? Go away, you black swine!"

I went to the broken window and screamed obscenities at my father, daring him to come out, hoping that if he as much as ever stuck his black face out, I would pelt him with the half-a-loaf brick in my hand. He didn't come out. He continued launching a tirade of obscenities at my mother and her mother, calling them whores and bitches and so on. He was drunk, but I wondered where he had gotten the money to buy beer because it was still the middle of the week and he was dead broke. He had lost his entire wage for the past week in dice and had had to borrow bus fare.

"I'll kill you someday for all you're doing to my mother," I threatened him, overwhelmed with rage. Several nosey neighbors were beginning to congregate by open windows and doors. Not wanting to make a spectacle of myself, which was something many of our neighbors seemed to always expect from our family, I backtracked away from the door and vanished into the dark street. I ran, without stopping, all the way to the other end of the township where Granny lived. There I found my mother, her face swollen and bruised and her eyes puffed up to the point where she could scarcely see.

"What happened, Mama?" I asked, fighting to hold back the tears at the sight of her disfigured face.

"Nothing, child, nothing," she mumbled, almost apologetically, between swollen lips. "Your papa simply lost his temper, that's all."

"But why did he beat you up like this, Mama?" Tears came down my face. "He's never beaten you like this before."

My mother appeared reluctant to answer me. She looked searchingly at Granny, who was pounding millet with pestle and mortar and mixing it with sorghum and nuts for an African delicacy. Granny said, "Tell him, child, tell him. He's got a right to know. Anyway, he's the cause of it all."

"Your father and I fought because I took you to school this morning," my mother began. "He had told me not to, and when I told him that I had, he became very upset. He was drunk. We started arguing, and one thing led to another."

"Why doesn't he want me to go to school?"

"He says he doesn't have money to waste paying for you to get what he calls a useless white man's education," my mother replied. "But I told him that if he won't pay for your schooling, I would try and look for a job and pay, but he didn't want to hear that, also. 'There are better things for you to work for,' he said. 'Besides, I don't want you to work. How would I look to other men if you, a woman I owned, were to start working?' When I asked him why shouldn't I take you to school, seeing that you were now of age, he replied that he doesn't believe in schools. I told him that school would keep you off the streets and out of trouble, but still he was belligerent."

"Is that why he beat you up?"

"Yes, he said I disobeyed his orders."

"He's right, child," Granny interjected. "He paid *lobola* [bride price] for you. And your father ate it all up before he left me."

To which my mother replied, "But I desperately want to leave this beast of a man. But with his *lobola* gone I can't do it. That worthless thing you call your husband shouldn't have sold Jackson's scrawny cattle and left you penniless."

"Don't talk like that about your father, child," Granny said. "Despite all, he's still your father, you know. Anyway, he asked for *lobola* only because he had to get back what he spent raising you. And you know it would have been taboo for him to let you or any of your sisters go without asking for *lobola*."

"You and Papa seemed to forget that my sisters and I have minds of our own," my mother said. "We didn't need you to tell us whom to marry, and why, and how. If it hadn't been for your interference, I could have married that schoolteacher."

Granny did not reply; she knew well not to. When it came to the act of "selling" women as marriage partners, my mother was vehemently opposed to it. Not only was she opposed to this one aspect of tribal culture, but to others as well, particularly those involving relations between men and women and the upbringing of children. But my mother's sharply differing opinion was an exception rather than the rule among tribal women. Most times, many tribal women questioned her sanity in daring to question well-established mores. But my mother did not seem to care; she would always scoff at her opponents and call them fools in letting their husbands enslave them completely.

Though I disliked school, largely because I knew nothing about what actually went on there, and the little I knew had painted a dreadful picture, the fact that a father would not want his son to go to school, especially a father who didn't go to school, seemed hard to understand.

"Why do you want me to go to school, Mama?" I asked, hoping that she might, somehow, clear up some of the confusion that was building in my mind.

"I want you to have a future, child," my mother said. "And, contrary to what your father says, school is the only means to a future. I don't want you growing up to be like your father."

The latter statement hit me like a bolt of lightning. It just about shattered every defense mechanism and every pretext I had against going to school.

"Your father didn't go to school," she continued, dabbing her puffed eyes to reduce the swelling with a piece of cloth dipped in warm water, "that's why he's doing some of the bad things he's doing. Things like drinking, gambling and neglecting his family. He didn't learn how to read and write; therefore, he can't find a decent job. Lack of any education has narrowly focused his life. He sees nothing beyond himself. He still thinks in the old, tribal way, and still believes that things should be as they were back in the old days when he was growing up as a tribal boy in Louis Trichardt. Though he's my husband, and your father, he doesn't see any of that."

"Why didn't he go to school, Mama?"

"He refused to go to school because his father led him to believe that an education was a tool through which white people were going to take things away from him, like they did black people in the old days. And that a white man's education was worthless insofar as black people were concerned because it prepared them for jobs they can't have. But I know it isn't totally so, child, because times have changed somewhat. Though our lot isn't any better today, an education will get you a decent job. If you can read or write you'll be better off than those of us who can't. Take my situation: I can't find a job because I don't have papers, and I can't get papers because white people mainly want to register people who can read and write. But I want things to be different for you, child. For you and your brother and sisters. I want you to go to school, because I believe that an education is the key you need to open up a new world and a new life for yourself, a world and life different from that of either your father's or mine. It is the only key that can do that, and only those who seek it earnestly and perseveringly will get anywhere in the white man's world. Education will open doors where none seem to exist. It'll make people talk to you, listen to you and help you; people who otherwise wouldn't bother. It will make you soar, like a bird lifting up into the endless blue sky, and leave poverty, hunger and suffering behind. It'll teach you to learn to embrace what's good and shun what's bad and evil. Above all, it'll make you a somebody in this world. It'll make you grow up to be a good and proud person. That's why I want you to go to school, child, so that education can do all that, and more, or you."

A long, awkward silence followed, during which I reflected upon the significance of my mother's lengthy speech. I looked at my mother; she looked at me.

Finally, I asked, "How come you know so much about school, Mama? You didn't go to school, did you?"

"No, child," my mother replied. "Just like your father, I never went to school." For the second time that evening, a mere statement of fact had a thunderous impact on me. All the confusion I had about school seemed to leave my mind, like darkness giving way to light. And what had previously been a dark, yawning void in my mind was suddenly transformed into a beacon of light that began to grow larger and larger, until it had swallowed up, blotted out, all the blackness. That beacon of light seemed to reveal things and facts, which, though they must have always existed in me, I hadn't been aware of up until now.

"But unlike your father," my mother went on, "I've always wanted to go to school, but couldn't because my father, under the sway of tribal traditions, thought it unnecessary to educate females. That's why I so much want you to go, child, for if you do, I know that someday I too would come to go, old as I would be then. Promise me, therefore, that no matter what, you'll go back to school. And I, in turn, promise that I'll do everything in my power to keep you there."

With tears streaming down my cheeks and falling upon my mother's bosom, I promised her that I would go to school "forever." That night, at seven and a half years of my life, the battlelines in the family were drawn. My mother on the one side, illiterate but determined to have me drink, for better or for worse, from the well of knowledge. On the other side, my father, he too illiterate, yet determined to have me drink from the well of ignorance. Scarcely aware of the magnitude of the decision I was making or, rather, the decision which was being emotionally thrusted upon me, I chose to fight on my mother's side, and thus my destiny was forever altered.

The Perfect Picture

James Alexander Thom

It was early in the spring about 15 years ago—a day of pale sunlight and trees just beginning to bud. I was a young police reporter, driving to a scene I didn't want to see. A man, the police-dispatcher's broadcast said, had accidentally backed his pickup truck over his baby granddaughter in the driveway of the family home. It was a fatality.

As I parked among police cars and TV-news cruisers, I saw a stocky white-haired man in cotton work clothes standing near a pickup. Cameras were trained on him, and reporters were sticking microphones in his face. Looking totally bewildered, he was trying to answer their questions. Mostly he was only moving his lips, blinking and choking up.

After a while the reporters gave up on him and followed the police into the small white house. I can still see in my mind's eye that devastated old man looking down at the place in the driveway where the child had been. Beside the house was a freshly spaded flower bed, and nearby a pile of dark, rich earth.

"I was just backing up there to spread that good dirt," he said to me, though I had not asked him anything. "I didn't even know she was outdoors." He stretched his hand toward the flower bed, then let it flop to his side. He lapsed back into his thoughts, and I, like a good reporter, went into the house to find someone who could provide a recent photo of the toddler.

A few minutes later, with all the details in my notebook and a three-by-five studio portrait of the cherubic child tucked in my jacket pocket, I went toward the kitchen where the police had said the body was.

I had brought a camera in with me—the big, bulky Speed Graphic which used to be the newspaper reporter's trademark. Everybody had drifted back out of the house together—family, police, reporters and photographers. Entering the kitchen, I came upon this scene:

On a Formica-topped table, backlighted by a frilly curtained window, lay the tiny body, wrapped in a clean white sheet. Somehow the grandfather had managed to stay away from the crowd. He was sitting on a chair beside the table, in profile to me and unaware of my presence, looking uncomprehendingly at the swaddled corpse.

The house was very quiet. A clock ticked. As I watched, the grandfather slowly leaned forward, curved his arms like parentheses around the head and feet of the little form, then pressed his face to the shroud and remained motionless.

In that hushed moment I recognized the makings of a prize-winning news photograph. I appraised the light, adjusted the lens setting and distance, locked a bulb in the flashgun, raised the camera and composed the scene in the view finder.

Every element of the picture was perfect: the grandfather in his plain work clothes, his white hair backlighted by sunshine, the child's form wrapped in the sheet, the atmosphere of the simple home suggested by black iron trivets and World's Fair souvenir plates on the walls flanking the window. Outside, the police could be seen inspecting the fatal rear wheel of the pickup while the child's mother and father leaned in each other's arms.

I don't know how many seconds I stood there, unable to snap that shutter. I was keenly aware of the powerful story-telling value that photo could have, and my professional conscience told me to take it. Yet I couldn't make my hand fire that flashbulb and intrude on the poor man's island of grief.

At length I lowered the camera and crept away, shaken with doubt about my suitability for the journalistic profession. Of course I never told the city editor or any fellow reporters about that missed opportunity for a perfect news picture.

Everyday on the newscasts and in the papers, we see pictures of people in extreme conditions of grief and despair. Human suffering has become a spectator sport. And sometimes, as I'm watching news film, I remember that day.

I still feel right about what I did.

My Experience with Hunting

Student

When I was seven, my father and a few of his friends took me on my first hunting trip. I excitedly thought of stalking wild prey through the forest, like Daniel Boone facing the untold dangers of the wild. But for me, the sport of hunting did not give the satisfaction I had expected. In most sports, we tend to think of the thrill of victory and the agony of defeat. For me, however, hunting involved the thrill of defeat and the agony of victory. The thrill of defeat is the feeling that I experienced when my father missed a shot at a deer and the deer ran off unharmed. The agony of victory is the guilt feelings experienced when one has taken a life.

During the beginning of the trip I could not wait to get out into the forest. While we unpacked the truck and set up camp, all I did was brag about the giant buck I was going to bag. Once out in the field I wanted to be the first to bag a deer and show my father and his friends that I was no longer a child. I walked ahead of them, stalking through the forest with my rifle in hand, imagining myself as the seasoned combat veteran searching the jungles for enemy patrols. I didn't spot any enemy patrols; I didn't spot any deer either.

My father's friend Jim was the first to see any deer. He called us over to use his binoculars: we saw a small herd of maybe ten deer. As we stalked closer to the herd, we stumbled upon a large doe. Everyone decided since this was my first trip, I should be the one to take the first shot. I suddenly felt nervous and I wanted someone else to take the shot, but I couldn't let my father or any of his friends know this. As I drew down and brought the deer into focus, I could see her big brown eye's staring at me. This caused me to hesitate, feeling the conflict of not wanting to take the animal's life and not wanting to let my father down in front of his friends. I forced myself to squeeze the trigger and the shot rang out. The deer ran about thirty feet and fell. My father and friends all cheered and congratulated me on my first kill.

To me, being congratulated for killing the animal did not seem quite appropriate, especially at the sight of the shivering fawn I spotted only twenty feet from its now dead mother. I never imagined the amount of intense guilt that could be felt by one person. I felt as if I was in a state of limbo and extremely disappointed with myself. I never thought I would take a life because I was afraid to disappoint someone. The deer that I killed was an innocent creature that did not deserve to die in the name of sport. To me, the premeditated killing of defenseless animals is not a sport.

It might sound strange, but I still enjoy hunting. I love being outdoors in the country, the fresh air, the trees, streams, animals and birds. The excitement felt when out in the wilderness stalking a wild animal is one of the most intense feelings I have ever felt. But now when I hunt and get an animal in my sights, I squeeze a shutter release instead of a trigger. This still gives me all the excitement of the hunt, without having to take a life. I still get to bring home a trophy of my prey, but I leave the animal alive and unharmed in its home. This is my idea of a successful hunt.

An Eventful Flight

Student

It is two A.M., and our mission briefing has been completed as I walk toward the flight line. The flood lights glow dimly on the aircraft, as the sweet smell of the sea breeze gently awakens the senses. I go through the ritual of preparing myself for the flight. I have no thoughts, except for those which guide me through my routine. I don the smooth Nomex flight suit, my leather boots and finally my issue flight vest. I check for my ID tags, that my collar is up and that my helmet is on and visor is down. "Clear on the 'P'?" shouts the pilot. "Clear," I respond. The sound of ignitors ticking fills the air as the small starting engine surges and comes to life.

The pilots go through their pre-flight check list as I walk around the helicopter one last time to insure that everything is in proper order, or at least appears that way. With the radio checks finished, flight control checks complete, and navigation settings entered, we begin to fire up the aircraft. "Clear on '1' and '2'?" bursts through my helmet. "'1' and '2' are clear sir," I garble back. The low painful moaning of the two turbo-shaft engines is felt throughout my body. Slowly and begrudgingly, the engines respond with obvious protest. Rotor blades begin to turn and the bitter sweet smell of jet fuel fills the air. In less than two minutes, we will be skating along the wave tops at 175 miles per hour, with a full load to bring across the pond to the waiting personnel in need of our goods. The rotors are now turning at full flight speed, and the helicopter is begging to fly. I take one last look around and satisfied I climb in and we become airborne.

This is my thirty-second trip across. With a fifty-five minute flight time, the opportunity for one's mind to wander is great. Our destination, once known as "The Paris of the Middle East," now resembles a scene from "Escape from New York." The oil refinery to the south still smolders from a Syrian rocket launched more than a week ago. I think of previous missions and our importance here. I recall all the events which brought me to this alien place. I wonder about my family and loved ones, and how I wish I could tell them exactly where I am. Yet always in the back of my mind the question remains, "Will I be back at the block at the end of this day or end up fish-bait?"

My introspection is suddenly interrupted by the announcement that we're ten minutes out. I pass out our Kevlar vests and sit on the extra one. The pilots arm the chaff dispenser and warm up the radar jamming equipment. The moon's reflection casts an eerie green hue through my PVS-6 night vision goggles. I notice the color of the water has changed from crystal blue to the brown-green produced by the pollution of the city and the trash carelessly discarded into the sea. The lights of the city seem to be inching ever closer and I can see the revolving light from the forbidden international airport eight kilometers to the south.

Standard procedure for this mission call for only one ship at the target landing zone at a time. With this in mind, we make a standard break, and continue heading for the shoreline. Ninety seconds later, we make the radio call "Feet Dry," indicating we have made landfall. Once splendid destination resorts lay in ruins below us, along with relics of exotic playgrounds. Every time I see this version of hell, I am amazed at the destructive power of the human race. We execute a hard cyclic climb, which is followed by a one hundred and eighty degree pedal turn. Then finally we drop the collective and plant the Lz.

Cargo and personnel are rapidly removed from the aircraft. The one hundred and twenty seconds we spend at the landing zone, always seems like one hundred and twenty hours. The missile lock indicator glows a devilish red, and we occasionally receive stray small arms fire. With the new cargo for the return trip loaded, I inform the pilots we are ready for take off. After a jerk of power and a rush of gravity we become airborne once again. Thirty seconds later, we are "Feet Wet" and heading for the holding point.

Our sister ship passes us on her way inbound in complete darkness. I try to relax. Though we had been in and out the threat was still present and we were by no means out of danger. Waiting for the other helicopter is always the worst part of this mission. Finally we got the call "Feet Wet." With this, we leave our holding pattern and turn away from the coast, heading for home. Relief slowly starts to overcome me and the adrenaline rush begins to subside. Ten minutes out, the Kevlar is removed and stowed and the chaff dispenser is returned to the safe position. With the hard part of the mission accomplished, I settle back for the trip home and start to consider what I will have for breakfast.

Suddenly, the pitch of the engine increases dramatically, followed by a sharp cracking sound. I glance toward the cockpit and see the starboard side engine fire light illuminated. Before the pilots can ask, I lean out the window as far as my harness will allow. Heavy black smoke is now pouring out the exhaust duct. I confirm the engine fire and emergency shut down procedures are initiated. Before the engine can be shut down, it decides to go south. This leaves us in a very precarious position. With only one engine left operating and a full load of cargo that cannot be dumped overboard due to its sensitive nature, our choices are limited. I begin to recall the weekend of water egress training I received before being accepted for this mission. I try to step through in my mind all the things I need to remember, find a reference point, secure all loose items, and most importantly, remain calm. The pilots are also in a very difficult position. Either we try to make it home on one engine over eighty miles of open water, return to the landing zone or ditch the aircraft and swim. None of the aforementioned options appeals to me all that much.

Thoughts of my family and friends rush through my head. I consider the very real possibility I will never see them again. An eternity seems to pass until the pilots make the decision to return to the landing zone. The original Lz has already been vacated and the evidence of our arrival removed. With only one engine, now severely over torqued, we need a runway to land on. With this in mind, we have only one choice. An old highway turned runway is located ten kilometers to the north; this will be our destination.

We make the radio calls to our sister ship, flight following service and ground control radio, to inform them of our condition and our intentions. Now the fun begins.

As we turn to the north and begin preparations for landing, we are notified that another aircraft has been scrambled to fly cover for us. Unfortunately, it will not be on station for an hour and by that time we will be down and en route to the embassy complex. We turn to heading zero-nine-zero and begin our base leg to the "runway," call "Feet Dry" and prepare for what will be the most important landing of our lives. The second helicopter of our flight is no longer holding off shore. She is now approximately sixty feet above and to our starboard side flying cover. Turning to heading one-eight-zero, we begin our final approach with the air thick with anticipation. The runway comes into sight and we begin to decrease the air speed. The customary ease to the ground is now replaced with a sharp drop and increased anxieties. Now over the threshold of the runway, the power is decreased even more and we land with an abrupt jolt to everything in the aircraft. The helicopter rolls to a stop and we shut it down. Our flying cover informs us they must continue back to base, due to an ever decreasing fuel level.

In this city of bedlam, it is virtually impossible to distinguish the friendlies from the non-friendlies. This is officially a humanitarian mission, so we carry absolutely no weapons. As the rotor blades coast to a stop a pair of jeeps, a cargo truck and an armored personnel carrier rush toward the aircraft. We have no idea as to who is driving these vehicles. To our relief, this is our guard unit and they inform us we have thirty minutes to prepare to leave.

Thirty minutes is not nearly enough time for us to accomplish all the tasks needed to abandon the aircraft. I concentrate on the secure radios, avionics, and sensitive electronics, while the pilots remove the contents we loaded at the original landing zone. I work with abandon, while the minutes fly by like never before in my life. All the equipment is loaded into the cargo truck. Then, in turn, we climb into the APC and head for the embassy. As we drive away, I turn to peek through the rifle slot to get one last look at my helicopter. I wonder if I will ever see her again.

The seven kilometer trip to the embassy complex is thankfully uneventful. We arrive to a flurry of activity and are immediately herded into a briefing room. We are informed that a fifteen man guard squad has been sent to secure the airfield and protect the aircraft. Through a window, I can see the sun beginning its ascent above the distant horizon. The adrenaline flow from the previous hour's events is starting to subside. I then realize how truly lucky we had been.

Several of the embassy staff enter the room, with coffee and some danishes. Even though we have been up for ten hours already, it is breakfast time. I am thankful for the chance to try to smooth out the knots in my stomach. Half way through my coffee, the Chief Liaison Officer enters the room and quickly begins briefing us on the situation and the plan for our removal from this place. We are informed that all non-essential equipment will be removed from the helicopter and we will be flying it back to the base. The plan calls for us to join up with a Lebanese Army gunship at nine o'clock. The gunship will escort us to a rendezvous point. Once there, we will join a flight of a helicopters from our base and two marine super cobra attack helicopters. The only other option is to destroy the aircraft in its place. There is no possible way to replace or repair the broken engine on this side of the pond.

Two hours later we are back inside the APC and heading for the air strip. When we arrive, we notice a large crowd gathered outside the airfield fence. If I didn't know better, I would think the circus was in town. The mood of the crowd is one of excitement and curiosity. We perform our standard preflight checks, except we do not need to check the starboard engine. The pilots climb in. I remain outside to observe the starting procedures. The engine is started and the rotor blades begin to turn. I am filled with doubt concerning our return trip.

With the rotors turning at full flight speed, we wait for the radio call from our Lebanese companion. Finally, it comes and we begin to roll forward. We travel down the rough runway and once at eighty knots the helicopter lifts off. The rest of the trip goes exactly as planned. We meet our next escort and follow them home. The events of this day have made me very aware of the uncertainties in life. Before this event, I thought I would be ready for anything that might arise. However, now I merely hope that when put in another position like this one, my luck will remain as it was that eventful day in September.

CHAPTER 4

Example

An example is an illustration used to help a writer make a point. When you write an essay, you use your experiences, your observations and your background as sources for examples. With an example, you can show your reader something rather than simply telling what you mean or believe.

You can use an example to support abstract ideas or to provide specifics to explain a generalization. Your examples will provide definite references to clarify otherwise vague statements. You will probably rely on both description and narration to supply the details you'll use to develop your examples.

Why Write an Example Essay?

Your examples will make your writing more lively, interesting and colorful. A careful choice of an example can influence your reader's response to a topic.

Types of Examples

You will either use brief examples or extended examples. Usually a combination of these lends variety to the essay.

Criteria for Writing an Example Essay

1. Prewrite to come up with strong examples which relate to your topic.
2. Determine the purpose of the essay and your intended audience. Making these determinations will affect your choice of examples to illustrate the topic.
3. Use an interesting introductory paragraph which lets the reader know the direction you plan to take in the essay.

4. Control the essay with a clearly stated thesis statement that will organize your essay.

5. Choose relevant examples. If you're showing the positive side of your college experience, for example, don't write about how drunk you got last night at a party.

6. Use both brief and extended examples with which your audience can identify.

7. Establish a clear pattern of organization. You could use examples in the order of least to most important. On the other hand, you might use a spatial pattern of organization of examples in another essay. Yet another essay might be organized chronologically. Your topic and purpose will determine the organization.

8. Help to create coherence and unity through connecting expressions of transition such as *for example, to illustrate, for instance.*

9. Develop your examples through description, narration, details and explanations so that the example seems vivid and interesting to your readers.

Topic Ideas for Example Essays

The contents of your grandmother's attic or basement

Miscommunication among friends

Quarrels between a boyfriend and a girlfriend

Obstacles between you and college graduation

Movie action heroes

Clothing styles through the decades

Music through the decades

Unfamiliar customs

Ways to celebrate New Year's Eve

Beliefs you have outgrown

Cultural stereotypes

Peer Evaluation for Example Essays

1. Has the writer chosen an interesting topic?
2. Does the writer have an introduction which captures your attention?
3. Does the writer use a thesis statement to give focus to the essay?
4. Which pattern of organization does the writer use?
5. Is the essay well organized?

—— *Example* ——————————————————————— 75

6. Which transitional words or phrases are used? Are they sufficient to establish coherence?
7. Has the writer used both brief and extended examples?
8. Does the writer sufficiently develop the examples?
9. Are the examples well-chosen and relevant?

Civil Rites

Caroline Miller

I was taking my kids to school not long ago when I had one of those experiences particular to parents—a moment that nobody else notices, but that we replay over and over because in it we see something new about our children.

On this morning the bus was standing-room-only as we squeezed on at our regular stop. Several blocks later my son, Nick, found a free seat halfway back on one side of the bus and his little sister, Elizabeth, and I took seats on the other.

I was listening to Lizzie chatter on about something when I was surprised to see Nick get up. I watched as he said something quietly to an older, not quite grandmotherly woman who didn't look familiar to me. Suddenly I understood: He was offering her his seat.

A little thing, but still I was flooded with gratitude. For all the times we have talked about what to do and what not to do on the bus—say "Excuse me," cover your mouth when you cough, don't point, don't stare at people who are unusual looking—this wasn't something I had trained him to do. It was a small act of gallantry, and it was entirely his idea.

For all we try to show our kids and tell them how we believe people should act, how we hope *they* will act, it still comes as a shock and a pleasure—a relief, frankly—when they do something that suggests they understand. All the more so because in the world in which Nick is growing up, the rules that govern social interaction are so much more ambiguous than they were when we were his age. Kids are exposed to a free-for-all of competing signals about what's acceptable, let alone what's admirable. It's a world, after all, in which *in your face* is the style of the moment. Civility has become a more or less elusive proposition.

I was reminded of this incident on the train the other day, on another crowded morning, as I watched a young man in an expensive suit slip into an open seat without so much as losing his place in *The New York Times,* smoothly beating out a silver-haired gentleman and a gaggle of young women in spike heels.

—— *Example* —————————————————————————————— 77

My first thought was that his mother would be ashamed of him. And then I thought, with some amusement, that I am hopelessly behind the times. For all I know, the older man would've been insulted to be offered a seat by someone two or three decades his junior. And the women, I suppose, might consider chivalry a sexist custom. Besides, our young executive or investment banker probably had to compete with women for the job that's keeping him in Italian loafers; why would he want to offer a potential competitor a seat?

Of course, this sort of confusion is about much more than etiquette on public transportation. It's about what we should do for each other, and expect of each other, now that our roles are no longer closely dictated by whether we are male or female, young or old.

Not for a minute do I mourn the demise of the social contract that gave men most of the power and opportunity, and women most of the seats on the bus. But operating without a contract can be uncomfortable, too. It's as if nobody quite knows how to behave anymore; the lack of predictability on all fronts has left all our nerve endings exposed. And the confusion extends to everything from deciding who goes through the door first to who initiates sex.

Under the circumstances, civility requires a good deal more imagination than it once did, if only because it's so much harder to know what the person sitting across from you—whether stranger or spouse—expects, needs, wants from you. When you don't have an official rulebook, you have to listen harder, be more sensitive, be ready to improvise.

But of course improvising is just what Americans do best. And unlike the European model, our particular form of civility here in the former colonies aims to be democratic, to bridge our diverse histories with empathy and respect. At a moment when so many people are clamoring for attention, and so many others are nursing their wounds, the need for empathy and respect is rather acute.

And so, as we encourage our children to define themselves actively, to express themselves with confidence, we hope they will also learn to be generous—with those they don't know, as well as with those they love. And we hope they will care enough, and be observant enough, to be able to tell when someone else needs a seat more than they do.

What the Nose Knows

James Gorman

Society is losing its odor integrity. Some enterprising souls are actually marketing aerosol cans filled with the aromas of pizza, new cars, anything that might entice people to buy something they would otherwise not. From the inexhaustible engine of commerce have come Aroma Discs, which when warmed in a special container (only $22.50) emit such scents as Passion, Fireplace and After Dinner Mints. And, in what may be the odor crime of the century, a company in Ohio is selling a cherry-scented garden hose.

I may seem like a weird curmudgeon looking for something new to complain about, but it's only the fake smells I don't like, the ones that are meant to fool you. This is a dangerous business because the human nose is emotional and not very bright. Inside the brain, smell seems snuggled right up to the centers for cooking, sex and memory.

I recently discovered a substance whose odor stimulates my memory of childhood like nothing else: Crayola crayons.

I don't expect you to experience the effect of this odor memory just by thinking about crayons, since most people can't recall smells the way they can recall pictures or sounds. But once you get a good whiff of waxy crayon odor, the bells of childhood will ring. Go out and buy a box. Get your nose right down on the crayons and inhale deeply. Pull that crayon smell right up into the old reptile brain. You'll be flooded with a new crayon, untouched-coloring-book feeling—you're young, the world is new, the next thing you know your parents may bring home a puppy.

The smell is part of our culture, in the same class as the Howdy Doody song. Long after my daughters have stopped drawing with crayons, they will have in their brains, as I do now, the subconscious knowledge that if you smell stearic acid—the major component in the smell of Crayola crayons—you're about to have a good time.

—— *Example* ————————————————— 79

Crayons have odor integrity. The Crayola people didn't stick stearic acid into their product to make you buy it. Nobody in his right mind would buy something because it smelled like a fatty acid. If there were a national odor museum, I would give crayons pride of place in it. And I would surround them with other objects emitting the honest aromas that make up American odor culture.

I have a few ideas of what these other objects should be. I got them from William Cain of Yale University and the John B. Pierce Foundation Laboratory in New Haven, Conn. Cain studies what he calls the smell game. He had people sniff 80 everyday things, and then he ranked the substances by how recognizable their odors were. His list is the place for the aroma preservationist to begin.

On it are Juicy Fruit gum and Vicks VapoRub (remember getting it rubbed on your chest?), Ivory soap, Johnson's baby powder and Lysol. Cain also tested Band-Aids, nail-polish remover, shoe polish (which reminds me of church) and bleach.

Crayons are on the list, ranked eighteenth in recognizability. Coffee was first, peanut butter second. Not on the list, but favorites of mine, are rubber cement (which I remember from my newspaper days) and Cutter Insect Repellent.

I know there will be judgment calls. Some people will want to preserve Brut after shave and Herbal Essence shampoo, numbers 35 and 53 on Cain's list, while I will not. Others won't want fresh cow manure in the museum. I think it's a must.

Whatever the choices, it's time to start paying attention to our odor culture. We're responsible for what posterity will smell, and like to smell. If we're not careful, we may end up with a country in which everyone thinks garden hoses are supposed to smell like cherries.

Idiosyncrasies, Anyone?

Bill Bryson

Seeking the Perfect Union Between Custom and Country, I recently discovered a phenomenon that I call the Copenhagen movie house syndrome. I call it that because it was in a Copenhagen movie house that I first thought of it. What I thought was this: Every country in the world does some things far better than every other country and some things far worse, and I began to wonder why that should be. Sometimes a nation's little practices and inventions are so instantly engaging that we associate them with that country alone—double-decker buses in Britain, windmills in Holland, sidewalk cafés in France. But at the same time, there are some things most countries do without difficulty that some can scarcely do at all. Consider the Copenhagen movie house.

When you went into a movie theater in Denmark, at least until recently, you were given a ticket for an assigned seat. On the occasion of my visit, I found that my ticket directed me to sit beside the only other people in the place, a young couple locked in the sort of impassioned embrace associated with dockside reunions at the end of very long wars. I could no more have sat right beside them than I could have asked to join in—it actually would have come to much the same thing—so I took a place a few discreet seats away.

People came into the theater, examined their tickets, and filled the adjacent seats. By the time the movie started, there were about thirty of us sitting together in a tight pack in the middle of a vast and otherwise empty auditorium. A woman laden with shopping bags came in and made her way with difficulty down my row, stopped beside me, and announced in a stern Danish voice, full of glottals and indignation, that I had taken her seat. This caused much play of flashlights by a corps of usherettes and fretful reexamining of tickets by everyone in the vicinity until it became generally realized that I was an American tourist with an evident inability

Example 81

to follow simple seating instructions and was escorted in some shame back to my assigned place.

So we sat all together, thirty or so of us, in crowded discomfort, like refugees in an overloaded lifeboat, rubbing shoulders and sharing small noises, and watched the movie. And I would submit, with all respect to Denmark and her long and noble history as a sovereign state, that that is a pretty nerdy way to run a movie house.

The phenomenon, I hasten to add, is not exclusive to the Danes, even with regard to the movies. The Germans can be equally insensate when it comes to the silver screen. Once, caught in a downpour in Munich, I spied a movie theater across the street showing a Charlie Chaplin silent picture. No language problems there, I thought brightly and dashed in. Barely had I seated myself and wiped the steamy mist from my glasses than the film concluded, and everyone departed.

An usherette came and told me that I must go too. I explained that I had only just arrived and would hang on for the next showing. The usherette indicated severely that this was against the rules. I explained again that I had only just arrived and showed her that the rain was even now dripping from my brow and chin. But this cut *kein* ice with the lady, who conducted me to the back door with the efficiency of a bouncer and left me standing blinking in an alleyway.

The Germans are, of course, famous for such officiousness. I've never been entirely sure whether we notice this streak of Teutonic inflexibility in them because we have been conditioned to look for it or because it genuinely exists. But I do know a couple renting a cottage in the Black Forest who were ordered by their landlady to take down their washing from the clothesline and rehang it in a more orderly and regimented manner before they were allowed to go out for the day.

The great British failing, on the other hand, is a strange uncomfortableness with regard to food, particularly mass catering, a fact that can become evident to the traveler almost from the moment he sets foot in the Country. In his book *Flying Visits*, the Australian critic Clive James describes the food at Heathrow Airport as not fit for a dog to eat. That is perhaps a little unfair—you could certainly feed it to a dog—but it is true that the most charitable thing that can be said of the food there, and at many other public gathering places like train stations and motorway service areas, is that it won't kill you.

More than that, there is among the British a curious inability to grasp the basic idea of many foods—as evidenced by the persistent British habit of eating hamburgers with a knife and fork. In fact, there isn't much to do with dining in Britain that isn't mildly odd to foreign eyes, from the types of food eaten (baked beans on toast) to the manner of their eating (holding the fork upside down and balancing the food precariously on its back). As I write, a commercial is running on British television that shows a man enthusiastically spreading his favorite brand of peanut butter across an ear of sweet corn. I would suggest that this alone is evidence of a kind of national dementia where eating is concerned.

On the credit side, however, the British are consummate queuers—so much so that during riots in Liverpool in 1981 looters formed a line outside the store. I swear it. This is in stark contrast to the French, who have never quite come to terms with the concept of queuing. Wherever you go in Paris, you see orderly lines waiting patiently at bus stops. But as soon as the bus arrives, the line instantly disintegrates into something reminiscent of a fire drill at an insane asylum as everyone scrambles to be the first aboard.

The most bewildering French custom, however, is the practice of putting timers on light switches in hotel corridors and staircases. These are designed, with uncanny precision, to plunge you into darkness the moment you get near your room, so that you must complete the last stages of the process—feeling your way along the walls, finding the door and doorknob, fumbling with the key—without benefit of vision.

To the casual observer there may seem little point in providing illumination if it's going to poop out at the critical moment, or in forming an orderly line at bus stops if it's just going to lead to anarchy once the bus heaves into view. But that is a crucial feature of the syndrome: The behavior must seem largely inexplicable to any rational outsider, yet be accepted without question by the natives. In its most extreme form, it can even take on a kind of bizarre logic.

Consider the matter of dining out in Norway. I once made the mistake in that country of not thinking about dinner until almost dinnertime. This, I discovered, was several hours too late. Finding myself in Bergen on a Sunday, I ventured out onto the streets at about 5:30 with that agreeable pang of anticipation that comes with having a large appetite in a strange city. I wandered through the empty lanes of the old town and far out into the suburbs, but at every restaurant I came across the windows showed only darkened premises with chairs stacked on the tables.

At one place, I turned forlornly from the window to find an elderly woman watching me. "There's no one there," I croaked in bewilderment. "Yes," she replied in perfect English, "I expect the staff have all gone home to eat. It *is* dinnertime, you know." But of course.

In Spain, the problem comes at the other extreme of the clock. The Spanish wait until all the visitors to the country have put on their pajamas and gone to bed before they eat. For a long time I supposed that this was so they could talk about us, but I am assured by a Spanish friend that it is an ancient practice and there's nothing personal in it. Nonetheless, it is a strange sensation to wander to the hotel desk in the small hours, half expecting to see the night clerk in his bathrobe and everyone else sensibly tucked up in bed, only to find the hotel restaurant packed with laughing people, with children running around and aged grannies plowing into large platters of paella.

Outbreaks of the Copenhagen movie house syndrome can be found in all countries. One of the most prolific, if improbable, sources is the automobile light. In most parts of the world, people work from the assumption that when it is dark you put your car lights on and when it is light you switch them off. This seems pretty basic to most of us. Yet in Sweden there is a law that all drivers must put their lights on all the time, even in brilliant sunshine.

You would think the Swedes would be embarrassed to have saddled themselves with such an ineffably silly law ("It was a bad week; we don't know what came over us"), but evidently not. It is equivalent to making pedestrians wear miners' helmets, yet the Swedes appear to see nothing strange in it.

The British, conversely, use their car lights as sparingly as possible, as if fearful of running up a large quarterly bill for their use. At dusk throughout Britain, you see the strange phenomenon of gray, unilluminated shapes sweeping at you out

—— *Example* ———————————————————— *83*

of the gloom, their drivers peering intently through the windshields, unable to see much of anything. Why, you wonder, don't they put their lights on? It is a mystery that no one can answer. The British, of course, are particularly skilled at doing silly things (viz., requiring their judges to wear little mops on their heads).

And as for us Americans, what are our national shortcomings? Since one of the requirements of the Copenhagen movie house syndrome is that we be blind to our own faults, I am not entirely sure. An informal survey among foreign friends elicited a host of suggested shortcomings, ranging from Tammy Bakker's eyelashes to a misguided affection for plaid pants. But in my view perhaps the most fundamental of all our faults is simply the complete inability to follow simple seating instructions in foreign movie houses.

Were Dinosaurs Dumb?

Stephen Jay Gould

When Muhammad Ali flunked his army intelligence test, he quipped (with a wit that belied his performance on the exam): "I only said I was the greatest; I never said I was the smartest." In our metaphors and fairy tales, size and power are almost always balanced by a want of intelligence. Cunning is the refuge of the little guy. Think of Br'er Rabbit and Br'er Bear; David smiting Goliath with a slingshot; Jack chopping down the beanstalk. Slow wit is the tragic flaw of a giant.

The discovery of dinosaurs in the nineteenth century provided, or so it appeared, a quintessential case for the negative correlation of size and smarts. With their pea brains and giant bodies, dinosaurs became a symbol of lumbering stupidity. Their extinction seemed only to confirm their flawed design.

Dinosaurs were not even granted the usual solace of a giant—great physical prowess. God maintained a discreet silence about the brains of behemoth, but he certainly marveled at its strength: "Lo, now, his strength is in his loins, and his force is in the navel of his belly. He moveth his tail like a cedar. . . . His bones are as strong pieces of brass; his bones are like bars of iron [Job 40:16–18]." Dinosaurs, on the other hand, have usually been reconstructed as slow and clumsy. In the standard illustration, *Brontosaurus* wades in a murky pond because he cannot hold up his own weight on land.

Popularizations for grade school curricula provide a good illustration of prevailing orthodoxy. I still have my third grade copy (1948 edition) of Bertha Morris Parker's *Animals of Yesterday*, stolen, I am forced to suppose, from P.S. 26, Queens (sorry Mrs. McInerney). In it, boy (teleported back to the Jurassic) meets brontosaur:

> It is huge, and you can tell from the size of its head that it must be
> stupid. . . . This giant animal moves about very slowly as it eats.
> No wonder it moves slowly! Its huge feet are very heavy and its
> great tail is not easy to pull around. You are not surprised that the

—— *Example* ———————————————————— 85

thunder lizard likes to stay in the water so that the water will help it hold up its huge body. . . . Giant dinosaurs were once the lords of the earth. Why did they disappear? You can probably guess part of the answer—their bodies were too large for their brains. If their bodies had been smaller, and their brains larger, they might have lived on.

Dinosaurs have been making a strong comeback of late, in this age of "I'm OK, you're OK." Most paleontologists are now willing to view them as energetic, active, and capable animals. The *Brontosaurus* that wallowed in its pond a generation ago is now running on land, while pairs of males have been seen twining their necks about each other in elaborate sexual combat for access to females (much like the neck wrestling of giraffes). Modern anatomical reconstructions indicate strength and agility, and many paleontologists now believe that dinosaurs were warm-blooded. . . .

The idea of warm-blooded dinosaurs has captured the public imagination and received a torrent of press coverage. Yet another vindication of dinosaurian capability has received very little attention, although I regard it as equally significant. I refer to the issue of stupidity and its correlation with size. The revisionist interpretation, which I support in this column, does not enshrine dinosaurs as paragons of intellect, but it does maintain that they were not small brained after all. They had the "right-sized" brains for reptiles of their body size.

I don't wish to deny that the flattened, minuscule head of large-bodied *Stegosaurus* houses little brain from our subjective, top-heavy perspective, but I do wish to assert that we should not expect more of the beast. First of all, large animals have relatively smaller brains than related, small animals. The correlation of brain size with body size among kindred animals (all reptiles, all mammals, for example) is remarkably regular. As we move from small to large animals, from mice to elephants or small lizards to Komodo dragons, brain size increases, but not so fast as body size. In other words, bodies grow faster than brains, and large animals have low ratios of brain weight to body weight. In fact, brains grow only about two-thirds as fast as bodies. Since we have no reason to believe that large animals are consistently stupider than their smaller relatives, we must conclude that large animals require relatively less brain to do as well as smaller animals. If we do not recognize this relationship, we are likely to underestimate the mental power of very large animals, dinosaurs in particular.

Second, the relationship between brain and body size is not identical in all groups of vertebrates. All share the same rate of relative decrease in brain size, but small mammals have much larger brains than small reptiles of the same body weight. This discrepancy is maintained at all larger body weights, since brain size increases at the same rate in both groups—two-thirds as fast as body size.

Put these two facts together—all large animals have relatively small brains, and reptiles have much smaller brains than mammals at any common body weight—and what should we expect from a normal, large reptile? The answer, of course, is a brain of very modest size. No living reptile even approaches a middle-sized dinosaur in bulk, so we have no modern standard to serve as a model for dinosaurs.

Fortunately, our imperfect fossil record has, for once, not severely disappointed us in providing data about fossil brains. Superbly preserved skulls have been found for many species of dinosaurs, and cranial capacities can be measured. (Since brains do not fill craniums in reptiles, some creative, although not unreasonable, manipulation must be applied to estimate brain size from the hole within a skull.) With these data, we have a clear test for the conventional hypothesis of dinosaurian stupidity. We should agree, at the outset, that a reptilian standard is the only proper one—it is surely irrelevant that dinosaurs had smaller brains than people or whales. We have abundant data on the relationship of brain and body size in modern reptiles. Since we know that brains increase two-thirds as fast as bodies as we move from small to large living species, we can extrapolate this rate to dinosaurian sizes and ask whether dinosaur brains match what we would expect of living reptiles if they grew so large.

Harry Jerison studied the brain sizes of ten dinosaurs and found that they fell right on the extrapolated reptilian curve. Dinosaurs did not have small brains; they maintained just the right-sized brains for reptiles of their dimensions. So much for Ms. Parker's explanation of their demise.

Jerison made no attempt to distinguish among various kinds of dinosaurs; ten species distributed over six major groups scarcely provide a proper basis for comparison. Recently, James A. Hopson of the University of Chicago gathered more data and made a remarkable and satisfying discovery.

Hopson needed a common scale for all dinosaurs. He therefore compared each dinosaur brain with the average reptilian brain we would expect at its body weight. If the dinosaur falls on the standard reptilian curve, its brain receives a value of 1.0 (called an encephalization quotient, or EQ—the ratio of actual brain to expected brain for a standard reptile of the same body weight). Dinosaurs lying above the curve (more brain than expected in a standard reptile of the same body weight) receive values in excess of 1.0, while those below the curve measure less than 1.0.

Hopson found that the major groups of dinosaurs can be ranked by increasing values of average EQ. This ranking corresponds perfectly with inferred speed, agility and behavioral complexity in feeding (or avoiding the prospect of becoming a meal). The giant sauropods, *Brontosaurus* and its allies, have the lowest EQ's—0.20 to 0.35. They must have moved fairly slowly and without great maneuverability. They probably escaped predation by virtue of their bulk alone, much as elephants do today. The armored ankylosaurs and stegosaurs come next with EQ's of 0.52 to 0.56. These animals, with their heavy armor, probably relied largely upon passive defense, but the clubbed tail of ankylosaurs and the spiked tail of stegosaurs imply some active fighting and increased behavioral complexity.

The ceratopsians rank next at about 0.7 to 0.9. Hopson remarks: "The larger ceratopsians, with their great horned heads, relied on active defensive strategies and presumably required somewhat greater agility than the tail-weaponed forms, both in fending off predators and in intraspecific combat bouts. The smaller ceratopsians, lacking true horns, would have relied on sensory acuity and speed to escape from predators." The ornithopods (duckbills and their allies) were the brainiest herbivores, with EQ's from 0.85 to 1.5. They relied upon "acute senses and relatively fast speeds" to elude carnivores. Flight seems to require more acuity and agility than standing defense. Among ceratopsians, small, hornless, and presumably fleeing *Protoceratops* had a higher EQ than great three-horned *Triceratops*.

Carnivores have higher EQ's than herbivores, as in modern vertebrates. Catching a rapidly moving or stoutly fighting prey demands a good deal more upstairs

—— *Example* ———————————————————————— 87

than plucking the right kind of plant. The giant theropods (*Tyrannosaurus* and its allies) vary from 1.0 to nearly 2.0. Atop the heap, quite appropriately at its small size, rests the little coelurosaur *Stenonychosaurus* with an EQ well above 5.0. Its actively moving quarry, small mammals and birds perhaps, probably posed a greater challenge in discovery and capture than *Triceratops* afforded *Tyrannosaurus*.

I do not wish to make a naive claim that brain size equals intelligence or, in this case, behavioral range and agility (I don't know what intelligence means in humans, much less in a group of extinct reptiles). Variation in brain size within a species has precious little to do with brain power (humans do equally well with 900 or 2,500 cubic centimeters of brain). But comparison across species, when the differences are large, seems reasonable. I do not regard it as irrelevant to our achievements that we so greatly exceed koala bears—much as I love them—in EQ. The sensible ordering among dinosaurs also indicates that even so coarse a measure as brain size counts for something.

If behavioral complexity is one consequence of mental power, then we might expect to uncover among dinosaurs some signs of social behavior that demand coordination, cohesiveness, and recognition. Indeed we do, and it cannot be accidental that these signs were overlooked when dinosaurs labored under the burden of a falsely imposed obtuseness. Multiple trackways have been uncovered, with evidence for more than twenty animals traveling together in parallel movement. Did some dinosaurs live in herds? At the Davenport Ranch sauropod trackway, small footprints lie in the center and larger ones at the periphery. Could it be that some dinosaurs traveled much as some advanced herbivorous mammals do today, with large adults at the borders sheltering juveniles in the center?

In addition, the very structures that seemed most bizarre and useless to older paleontologists—the elaborate crests of hadrosaurs, the frills and horns of ceratopsians, and the nine inches of solid bone above the brain of *Pachycephalosaurus*—now appear to gain a coordinated explanation as devices for sexual display and combat. Pachycephalosaurs may have engaged in head-butting contests much as mountain sheep do today. The crests of some hadrosaurs are well designed as resonating chambers; did they engage in bellowing matches? The ceratopsian horn and frill may have acted as sword and shield in the battle for mates. Since such behavior is not only intrinsically complex, but also implies an elaborate social system, we would scarcely expect to find it in a group of animals barely muddling through at a moronic level.

But the best illustration of dinosaurian capability may well be the fact most often cited against them—their demise. Extinction, for most people, carries many of the connotations attributed to sex not so long ago—a rather disreputable business, frequent in occurrence, but not to anyone's credit, and certainly not to be discussed in proper circles. But, like sex, extinction is an ineluctable part of life. It is the ultimate fate of all species, not the lot of unfortunate and ill-designed creatures. It is no sign of failure.

The remarkable thing about dinosaurs is not that they became extinct, but that they dominated the earth for so long. Dinosaurs held sway for 100 million years while mammals, all the while, lived as small animals in the interstices of their world. After 70 million years on top, we mammals have an excellent track record and good prospects for the future, but we have yet to display the staying power of dinosaurs.

People, on this criterion, are scarcely worth mentioning—5 million years perhaps since *Australopithecus*, a mere 50,000 for our own species, *Homo sapiens*. Try the ultimate test within our system of values: Do you know anyone who would wager a substantial sum, even at favorable odds, on the proposition that *Homo sapiens* will last longer than *Brontosaurus*?

Naming Names:
The Eponym Craze

Cullen Murphy

The 1996 elections had no sooner sloughed into despond than I came across the following sentence in an election-eve wrap-up by Michael Lewis in the *New Republic*. "There is no denying," Lewis wrote, in the finale to an antic "Campaign Journal" series that saw him parting the crowds around various presidential entourages with the prosthetic assistance of a television Steadycam on his shoulder, "that I was excited by working alongside Ted Koppel, driven less by a Fallovian desire to inform the public than a lust to become rich and famous."

The word popped out: *Fallovian*. Could I have been witnessing the birth of an eponym—as wondrous a sight in its way as our recent glimpse of an island-in-the-making off the coast of Hawaii? An eponym, of course, is a word that has been formed from the name of a person, place, or thing (*eponumos* is a Greek word meaning "named on"). For some eponymous terms, the eponymy is obvious, or famous: *Caesarean section; graham cracker; Molotov cocktail; boycott; leotard; Luddite; silhouette; volt*. Many more eponyms, though familiar, are not so obviously eponymous. *Maudlin,* for instance, comes from the name of Mary Magdalene, who in painted and sculpted form is typically shown weeping. *Masochism* comes from the name of the demented nineteenth-century novelist Leopold von Sacher-Masoch, who described the relevant eponymous practices in his writings. (Recently, a group in Ukraine has been attempting to raise a monument to Masoch in his native city, Lviv.)

And *Fallovian?* In this case, the contextual evidence suggested that Michael Lewis' coinage fell into the class of eponym known as a "derivative"—in this case, derived from a name, that of James Fallows, editor of *U.S. News & World Report,* who has championed an approach to reporting that emphasizes hard analysis of serious issues and eschews the cult of journalists as highly paid pundits, celebrities, or oddsmakers. Lewis confirmed that this meaning was precisely the one intended, and said that, as far as he knew, his use of it in the *New Republic* marked this proper noun's maiden voyage as an adjective. Fallows himself, affably abashed, was unaware of previous appearances of the term.

Eponymous words have never needed much tending or encouragement. There are about thirty-five thousand of them in the ordinary stock of the English language, a figure that does not include the many eponymous words in the specialized languages of science, engineering, and especially medicine. The use of eponyms in medicine is steeply on the decline, but ordinary eponyms, linguistic experts say, are enjoying a growth spurt these days. According to citations in recent newspapers and magazines, to *gump* through life is to make one's way by means of dumb luck To espouse two positions at once is to *pull a Clinton.* To adopt the hairstyle popularized by the actress Jennifer Aniston on *Friends* is to *get a Rachel* or to *get a* Friends *do*. A *sagan* is a unit of quantity equivalent to "billions and billions"— the quotation an unintentionally self-parodic trademark of the late astronomer Carl Sagan. *Imeldific,* made possible by Imelda Marcos, refers to ostentatious grandiosity and extravagant bad taste. An *Iraqi manicure* is torture. *Waldheimer's disease* is a convenient lapse of memory.

To *kevork* someone is to assist him in the commission of suicide—an eponym derived proximately, of course, from the work of Dr. Jack Kevorkian, but made possible by the prior success of the rhyming verb to *bork* (from the name Robert Bork, and meaning to use every means possible to sabotage a nominee to high office). An eponymous verb derived from the name O.J. Simpson— to *O.J.,* meaning "to slash"—shows some signs of acceptance among teenagers (O.J. had a previous life as an eponym, denoting a big car of the kind Simpson drove in his commercials for Hertz. "Drive off in a def O.J.," went a line in a 1979 rap song by the Sugar Hill Gang.)

The verb to *bobbitt,* with its well-known specific connotation under the household-amputation rubric, has become so widely used as to have now acquired metaphoric senses. For instance, the verb is used to mean "to deprive of vigor" in this sentence from a letter to the editor of the conservative *Washington Times:* "Bravo to Tony Snow for exposing the bobbi[t]ting of the GOP leadership when confronted with Democratic tirades." (Linguistic note from abroad: The practice of *bobbitting,* according to an Asia correspondent of some years—my sister Cait, as it happens—is relatively frequent in Thailand. The local name for the practice is a Thai word that, when translated into English, means "feeding the ducks.")

The surge in eponyms is no doubt related, in part, to the efflorescence of metanames* in general. Pseudonyms have never been more widely employed than they are today, when millions of invented, incorporeal identities are in play in all kinds of electronic communication. The married woman who takes her husband's family name as a surname yet keeps her own family name as a middle name— Hillary Rodham Clinton, Sandra Day O'Connor—has unwittingly introduced a new form of patronymic,** which takes its place alongside the more traditional (Slavic, Scandinavian, Islamic, Hispanic) versions. Even anonymity, owing to controversy [. . .] over the authorship of the novel *Primary Colors,* has had to endure an uncharacteristically high public profile [. . .]. I don't know what name future

—— *Example* —————————————————————————————— *91*

historians will bestow on our present age, but arguably the age deserves not a name but a nym.

Why more eponymy now? Some people, of course, have set out to make well-known eponymous terms of their names, as Donald Trump is doing with his new magazine *Trump Style*. The proliferation of commercial brand names is certainly a major factor: Consider *Nintendo neck*, the *Twinkie defense*, the *Teflon presidency*. For reasons that hardly need belaboring, it is easier today than ever before for any name—personal or commercial—to become widely known quickly, even if transiently. Memorable eponymous terms require memorable nominal roots and, in the English-speaking world, people's names are becoming more diverse and interesting as more cultures are demographically and linguistically annexed. Also, eponymous terms allow almost anyone to display competence, even brilliance, at coining useful and appropriate-sounding new words—thereby encouraging further attempts to do so.

Leona Helmsley. Mark Furhman. Alfonse D'Amato. Madonna. Roberto Alomar. Mother Teresa. Bill Gates. Oliver Stone. These and scores of other names cry out for eponyplasty. I look forward to your suggestions.

---

*The flowering of names that transcend their original meanings.

**Name derived from that of the father or paternal ancestor.

Bike Wear

Student

In order to get the best performance and most comfort out of serious bicycle riding, proper attire is necessary. A riding jersey is comfortable, and it has pockets sewn into the lower back which let you carry food or light snacks. The jersey can also hold small tools, such as a hex key or a spoke wrench, to make minor repairs to the rear derailleur or adjustments to a wheel that might twist out of true. Riding jerseys are aerodynamic and much more appropriate than a T-shirt or no shirt at all. In addition, it is important to wear riding shorts that are designed with a genuine deerskin chamois to help prevent chafing and irritation which can cause discomfort while riding. Purchasing superior bike wear with major names like Vigorrelli or Duigi can help to insure quality construction, contoured fit and reliable durability. Another important part of attire is cleated shoes made especially for bicycling. The cleats have a narrow notch that slip over the back stage of the pedals. This feature allows the rider to push down on one pedal while simultaneously pulling up on the other pedal. Cleated shoes tremendously affect the smoothness of the pedal stroke and the efficiency of the rider's power. Taking advantage of the specialized riding apparel available, the serious bicycle enthusiast can expect increased performance and comfort.

How to Save Fuel and Money

Student

Rising energy and fuel costs are forcing me to be very careful with my consumption of these expensive commodities. For example, during the winter months my thermostat is turned down as low as I can tolerate which is usually 68 degrees. I turn the thermostat down even lower when I'm not at home. I also wear sweaters and use heavy blankets when I sleep in the effort to not allow the heater to run continuously. My summer months are spent with the doors and windows open to let breezes help cool my home as much as possible. Therefore, the air conditioner is kept idle as much as possible. Moreover, I take shorter showers and do not turn the water temperature up as high as I used to. This helps to conserve on the electricity which is used to warm the water heater. When cooking, I use my microwave oven as much as possible because it is cheaper to run than the electric stove or oven. Also, I am careful to keep nonessential lights turned off, because wasted wattage is one of the main sources of my high electricity bills. Lastly, I have learned to step lighter on the accelerator pedal of my car when driving. I also take shorter trips when traveling in my car. By this practice, I save pocket money for the end of the month which helps to pay my electric bill. Since becoming more conscientious in my efforts to use energy sparingly, I am experiencing lower electric and gasoline expenses and also conserving energy.

How to Be a Successful Basketball Player

Student

When I was in high school, my Uncle Jack convinced me that dedication and hard work are the secret to the success of a basketball player. He first stressed the importance of conditioning. I worked hard getting myself into shape. I got up every morning at five o'clock just to run and stretch out. Every day I pushed myself further and further and soon found myself getting burnt out on the same old routine, but I was dedicated to basketball and continued to work hard. In his second step, he stressed how important it was to handle a basketball every day. I practiced on my dribbling and shooting skills every morning. Initially, I learned how to dribble with my left hand so that I could dribble in any direction with either hand. I would then shoot ten balls from selected spots on the court over and over again until I could hit nine out of ten from each spot. I worked hard at this every morning until basketball season arrived. The third step my uncle continued to stress was how important it was to take the game seriously and put forth my best effort. I did as he instructed, and to this day I'm still the leading scorer of Otis-Bison High School. My dedication and hard work really did pay off.

CHAPTER 5

Process Analysis

A process analysis describes something that occurs over a period of time, as opposed to description (see chapter two), which typically describes something as it stands still in time. The length of time could be a few seconds or a few centuries or anywhere in between. Often a process analysis describes a procedure in a series of steps. To analyze means to take something apart, to break it down into its basic components. Process analysis explains how something works, how an action occurs, and/or why something occurred, by breaking the process down into smaller parts and then describing each part. You might be writing about how to find a job, how to raise a child, how to perform an unpleasant task, the best ways to interview, or how to keep a girlfriend happy.

Process analysis has two different forms: directive and informative. When you give directions, such as how to deliver an effective speech, this is directive writing. When you analyze how something happened, this is informative writing. Informative process analysis is an excellent form of essay writing because it allows you to thoroughly analyze some subject step by step to let the reader see it in great detail. Directive process analysis is an extremely practical form of writing; all user manuals, for example, are based on the directive form of process analysis.

Why Write Using Process Analysis?

You will often need to explain a procedure or explain how or why something happened. In order to do so successfully, you will write a process analysis. Using process analysis in your essays can make you a stronger writer by developing your thinking analytically. You may know why something happened, but being able to explain that to a reader takes careful writing. Even the best writer often assumes that the reader knows something that only the writer could know because we easily let ourselves slip into a self-centered way of thinking. "If I know it, then everybody else probably knows it, too" is a convenient but intellectually sloppy attitude to adopt. By carefully writing an objective process analysis essay, you are guiding your audience to an understanding of the occurrence as a whole.

How to Write a Process Analysis Essay

Begin your essay with an introductory paragraph in which you state your topic and the number of procedural steps. This will give the essay a focus and direct the reader. For example, your thesis statement on how to mix a song using professional deejay equipment might read as follows: "To mix a song you need to do three major things: pick out the two songs to mix, match the beats per minute, and find the breaks and the thirty-twos."

These divisions in your thesis statement will then become the basis for the subsequent body paragraphs in which you will discuss the procedural steps using description, details, and examples. You need to follow a logical chronology that any reader can understand. Use a sufficient number of transitional words and phrases which suggest procedure, such as *first, second, third, moreover, next, therefore, subsequently, in consequence of, finally*. Within the body, as you explain the procedure, be sure to explain any terminology that is unique to your topic that your audience might not be familiar with.

Your conclusion should summarize all the parts of the procedure emphasizing the usefulness or uniqueness of the process or why you found it interesting enough to write about.

Criteria for Writing a Process Analysis Essay

1. Choose a topic that illustrates a meaningful process. (If you're writing an informative process analysis essay rather than a directive process analysis essay, you should avoid topics such as how to change oil, how to wallpaper a room, how to fix a tire. A more meaningful topic would be how to achieve success in college. You want to choose a topic that divides logically into three or four units—three or four body paragraphs.) With a directive topic, you'll end up with a series of sentences, each expressing a separate command. (Open the cap. Insert the funnel. Pour in the oil.) Be careful. A directive process analysis essay might prevent you from having sufficiently developed body paragraphs, one of the key aspects of expository writing, if you don't add sufficient explanation or illustration to each step.

2. Use a clever introduction that will capture and hold the reader's interest in your topic.

3. Include a precise thesis statement in the introduction that states the topic and the steps to be followed.

4. Include all necessary steps in your process. Failure to do so prevents your audience from accomplishing the task you're describing or grasping the overall procedure and how it is composed

of related smaller steps. Moreover, a detailed explanation of all parts of the process is essential.

5. Rely on analysis (breaking into components), description, and explanation to develop your essay. In an informative analysis essay, you're doing much more than just listing steps. You are analyzing and then explaining.

6. Follow a logical chronology. Inherent to all procedures is a process to follow that is unique to that procedure. If you neglect to adhere to the chronology, a reader couldn't duplicate the process.

7. Use a sufficient number of transitional words and phrases to create overall unity and coherence.

8. Employ active, vivid words that will enliven your procedure. Such wording will help sustain reader interest.

9. Include varied sentence constructions and different length sentences so that your style adds to reader interest in the essay.

10. Write a concluding paragraph that allows your reader to see the entire procedure, and reflect on the applicability of the procedure (if this is appropriate). When readers can see the importance or usefulness of a topic for them, they're more interested in the essay.

Topic Ideas for Process Analysis Essays

Planting a garden
Performing a search on the Internet
Firing or hiring an employee
Designing a web page
Overcoming insomnia
Writing an essay
Staying awake in class
Taking effective notes
Succeeding in the workplace
Finding a good job
Getting fired from a job
Making a bad impression on your date's parents
Performing an unpleasant task at work

Peer Evaluation for Process Analysis Essays

1. What process is being analyzed in the essay?
2. Is the topic meaningful and important?

3. Did the writer explain how something happened or how something worked?

4. Is the essay informative?

5. If not informative, did the writer write a directive process analysis essay?

6. Did the writer catch your interest in the introduction? Why or why not?

7. Did the writer introduce the process to be analyzed?

8. Did the writer divide the topic into recognizable steps? How many?

9. Is the process discussed in chronological order?

10. Did the writer use sufficient transitions that suggest process?

11. Does the writer pay attention to the audience and fully explain all parts of the process?

12. Has the writer been descriptive and analytical (with sufficient explanation)?

13. Has the writer maintained focus throughout the essay?

14. Do you see the process as a complete entity when the essay concludes?

15. Do you understand why the author chose this topic to write about?

A Hairy Experience

Dave Barry

Summer vacation is almost here. Soon it will be time for you parents to pile the kids into the car, show them how to work the ignition key, then watch them roar off down the street, possibly in reverse, as you head back into your house for two weeks of quiet relaxation.

I am pulling your leg, of course. You have to go with them. You also are required, by federal law, to take them to at least one historical or natural site featuring an educational exhibit with a little button that you're supposed to push, except that when you do, nothing happens, because all the little light bulbs which were supposed to light up in an educational manner and tell The Story Of Moss, burned out in 1973. But this does not matter. What matters is that this is a memorable and rewarding and, above all, enjoyable vacation experience that you are providing for your children whether they like it or not.

"DAMMIT YOU KIDS," you might find yourself explaining to them, "IF YOU DON'T TAKE THOSE LEGOS OUT OF YOUR LITTLE BROTHER'S NOSE AND COME LOOK AT THIS EDUCATIONAL EXHIBIT THIS INSTANT, I SWEAR, I WILL NOT TAKE YOU TO THE OYSTER KINGDOM THEME PARK."

This situation demonstrates why you should never set out on a family summer vacation without a complete set of parental threats. You cannot simply assume that when your children have, for example, locked somebody else's child inside the motel ice machine, you'll be able to come up with a good parental threat right there on the spot. You need to prepare your threats in advance and write them on a wallet card for easy reference.

You (sternly): "If you kids don't let that child out of the ice machine this instant, I'm going to (referring to wallet card). . . DONATE MY ORGANS."

First Child: "Huh?"

Second Child: "He's reading from his driver's license again."

You (referring to another wallet card): "OK, here we go: I'm going to TAKE AWAY YOUR GAMEBOY!"

First Child: "We don't have a Game Boy."

Second Child: "Jason threw it into the Water Whiz ride back at Pez Adventure."

You (in a very stern parental voice): "All right then, we'll just have to BUY ANOTHER ONE."

Yes, you need strict discipline on a family vacation. You also should have some kind of theme for your trip, and this year the theme that I am recommending is: Hairballs Across America. Your first stop is Garden City, Kan., home of the Finney County Historical Society Museum, which features, according to news reports sent in by many alert readers, the largest known hairball in captivity, not counting members of Congress. This hairball measures 37 inches in diameter and weighs 55 pounds. That is what we in professional journalism call "a big hairball."

I called up the historical society museum director, Mary Warren, who told me that the hairball was graciously donated by local meat packing plant, which found it inside the stomach of a cow. Cows develop interior hairballs from licking their own coats and swallowing fur, similar to the way cats do, except that cats can get rid of their hairballs by hawking them up onto your face while you sleep. Cows cannot do this, of course; they have no way of getting into your bedroom.

Anyway, the Finney County hairball is larger than the one that recently won a national hairball contest (I am not making any of this up) sponsored by Ripley's Believe It or Not. Mary Warren told me that another local meat-packing plant had recently offered the historical society an even LARGER hairball, but she turned it down. I think this was wise. You put two hairballs of that magnitude in one place, and crowd control becomes a problem.

Anyway, Warren confirmed that the original hairball will be on display this summer, along with other cow-related exhibits that I am sure will have your kids punching each other in the head with delight. After you tear them away, your next stop will be the nearby Midwestern state of Indiana (motto: "It's Also Pretty Flat"), where you will be visiting the city of Alexandria. This is the historic site where, according to a story written by Sarah Mawhorr for The Anderson (Ind.) Herald Bulletin, it took three men to pull a giant hairball out of a manhole last year.

"We thought we had a goat," a city sewer official was quoted as saying.

Needless to say, this hairball was not caused by a cow. Cows do not fare well in the sewer environment, because of the alligators. This hairball was formed by people taking showers, and having their hairs wash down the drain and clump together in a giant mass that would be a wonderful symbol of the Common Bond That Unites All Humanity if it weren't basically a big disgusting wad of sewage-drenched hair.

Tragically—and this is yet another argument for stricter federal guidelines—the giant hairball was left outside, and it disintegrated. But it had already become famous—it got mentioned in USA Today—and a replica hairball (I am still not making this up) appeared in Alexandria's annual Christmas parade. So even though there is, technically, nothing to see, I am recommending that you take your children to Alexandria and let them soak up the historic atmosphere.

"Just think, kids!" you should tell them. "Right here in this town, there was a hairball THE SIZE OF A GOAT! Isn't that amazing? Kids? HEY, YOU KIDS COME BACK HERE!"

You should never have left the keys in the car.

Foundation Waterproofing

Creative Homeowner Press

If regular inside wall waterproofing and crack patching don't solve a leaky foundation wall problem, the very best way to tackle it is to waterproof the exterior of the foundation wall. It is costly to do this, and it is time-consuming. However, it is within a do-it-yourselfer's skills if the job is approached with lots of patience.

Dig a trench around the foundation wide enough for you to fit into the trench and deep enough to reach under the foundation footing. Clean off the foundation wall: use a wide scraper for this such as an ice scraper or a flat tiling spade. Scrub the wall down with water from a garden hose and a stiff broom or brush.

Lay a 3-in. bed of medium-sized gravel in the trench. Then lay a row of field tile on the gravel around the bottom of the foundation. The tile should have a slight pitch.

At one corner of the house, where the tile comes together in the downward pitch, run a length of tile out into the lawn about 10 ft. You will need to dig a trench for this, too. Lay the tile on 3 ins. of gravel.

Coat the foundation walls, from the footing to grade level, with a thick application of asphalt roofing cement. You can apply this with a trowel and brush, Make sure all areas are covered thoroughly.

Embed a vapor barrier of black 4 mil polyethylene film into the asphalt roofing cement. Overlap the joints of the polyfilm about 4 ins., sticking the joints together with asphalt roofing cement.

Let the job dry for a couple of days. Then backfill the earth into the trench. Make sure the fill slopes away from the house at a rate of about 1 in. per foot. Save any leftover dirt. The ground will settle for some time, and you will need this dirt to fill depressions.

How to Open a CD Box

Tibor Kalman and Lulu Kalman

1. Remove the plastic wrap. How? With a knife? Better yet, buy a special 99-cent EZ-CD opener tool designed precisely for this purpose. Ain't America grand? (Now, where did you put that thing?)

2. Peel off the special sticker that seals the CD case. Don't bother with the little pull tab—it'll tear off and become useless if you dare touch it. Just start peeling the plastic off with your nails instead. The pieces are superglued, so they will stick to your fingers. Roll them into a ball and flick it against the wall. Then ask a neighbor to remove the little ball of sticky plastic and throw it away.

3. Open the plastic box. It's snapped tight on itself. Insert your index finger at the opening opposite the hinge and pry carefully. Try very hard not to break the box. The box, called a jewel box probably because of the jewels that the packaging executives were able to purchase with their profits, is five-sixteenths of an inch thick. You can fit about fifty into a foot of drawer space. A CD that is slipped into a cardboard sleeve the way LP's were packaged is about one-sixteenth of an inch thick. You can fit nearly two hundred in a foot of drawer space.

4. Ah. Now you can see the CD! Try to remove it. Go ahead. It's plugged onto that little plastic thing with the little plastic fingers—plugged on really tight to secure it for shipping. In the next two weeks, those little, tiny plastic fingers will break off, one at a time, and fall on the floor. Your dog will eat them. ("It might be food. If not, I'll just throw up.")

5. The CD itself has a colorful label with a stunning color photo of a boot. No artist's name, no title, no song list, just this beautiful, shiny boot. The back cover of the CD box has the other boot. To find the song list, you must try to remove the CD booklet. This will take considerable ingenuity because it is wedged into position by several cleverly designed plastic tabs and a special device that is a last-ditch attempt to block you when you try to remove it. This will cost you a cuticle.

6. Open the CD booklet. Turn to the last page. There, among the copyright notices, publishing credits and assistant tape-engineer credits, you'll find the song list. Isn't it fun reading with a magnifying glass?

7. Enjoy the CD.

8. Return the CD to its shelf. Since the boxes are slippery, carry them one at a time and never stack them, to avoid the consequences of No. 9. Make appointments with your optometrist and chiropractor if you amass a shelved collection.

9. In two weeks, you'll drop the plastic box while trying to open it. Its hinges will break, challenging you to find another solution to the problem of storing your now naked CD.

10. In a couple of years, you'll put them in the basement, next to your LP's, replacing them with mini-CCDVDCVDX's, the new state-of-the-art format. The guys with the jewels have the packaging already figured out. Just fourteen steps.

How to Poison the Earth

Linnea Saukko

Poisoning the earth can be difficult because the earth is always trying to cleanse and renew itself. Keeping this in mind, we should generate as much waste as possible from substances such as uranium-238, which has a half-life (the time it takes for half of the substance to decay) of one million years, or plutonium, which has a half-life of only 0.5 million years but is so toxic that if distributed evenly, ten pounds of it could kill every person on the earth. Because the United States generates about eighteen tons of plutonium per year, it is about the best substance for long-term poisoning of the earth. It would help if we would build more nuclear power plants because each one generates only 500 pounds of plutonium each year. Of course, we must include persistent toxic chemicals such as polychlorinated biphenyl (PCB) and dichlorodiphenyl trichloroethane (DDT) to make sure we have enough toxins to poison the earth from the core to the outer atmosphere. First, we must develop many different ways of putting the waste from these nuclear and chemical substances in, on, and around the earth.

Putting these substances in the earth is a most important step in the poisoning process. With deep-well injection we can ensure that the earth is poisoned all the way to the core. Deep-well injection involves drilling a hole that is a few thousand feet deep and injecting toxic substances at extremely high pressures so they will penetrate deep into the earth. According to the Environmental Protection Agency (EPA), there are about 360 such deep injection wells in the United States. We cannot forget the groundwater aquifers that are closer to the surface. These must also be contaminated. This is easily done by shallow-well injection, which operates on the same principle as deep-well injection, only closer to the surface. The groundwater that has been injected with toxins will spread contamination beneath the earth. The EPA estimates that there are approximately 500,000 shallow injection wells in the United States.

Burying the toxins in the earth is the next best method. The toxins from land-fills, dumps, and lagoons slowly seep into the earth, guaranteeing that contamination will last a long time. Because the EPA estimates there are only about 50,000 of these dumps in the United States, they should be located in areas where they will leak to the surrounding ground and surface water.

Applying pesticides and other poisons on the earth is another part of the poisoning process. This is good for coating the earth's surface so that the poisons will be absorbed by plants, will seep into the ground, and will run off into surface water.

Surface water is very important to contaminate because it will transport the poisons to places that cannot be contaminated directly. Lakes are good for long-term storage of pollutants while they release some of their contamination to rivers. The only trouble with rivers is that they act as a natural cleansing system for the earth. No matter how much poison is dumped into them, they will try to transport it away to reach the ocean eventually.

The ocean is very hard to contaminate because it has such a large volume and a natural buffering capacity that tends to neutralize some of the contamination. So in addition to the pollution from rivers, we must use the ocean as a dumping place for as many toxins as possible. The ocean currents will help transport the pollution to places that cannot otherwise be reached.

Now make sure that the air around the earth is very polluted. Combustion and evaporation are major mechanisms for doing this. We must continuously pollute because the wind will disperse the toxins while rain washes them from the air. But this is good because a few lakes are stripped of all living animals each year from acid rain. Because the lower atmosphere can cleanse itself fairly easily, we must explode nuclear tests bombs that shoot radioactive particles high into the upper atmosphere where they will circle the earth for years. Gravity must pull some of the particles to earth, so we must continue exploding these bombs.

So it is that easy. Just be sure to generate as many poisonous substances as possible and be sure they are distributed in, on, and around the entire earth at a greater rate than it can cleanse itself. By following these easy steps we can guarantee the poisoning of the earth.

How to Say Nothing in Five Hundred Words

Paul Roberts

It's Friday afternoon, and you have almost survived another week of classes. You are just looking forward dreamily to the weekend when the English instructor says: "For Monday you will turn in a five-hundred-word composition on college football."

Well, that puts a good big hole in the weekend. You don't have any strong views on college football one way or the other. You get rather excited during the season and go to all the home games and find it rather more fun than not. On the other hand, the class has been reading Robert Hutchins in the anthology and perhaps Shaw's "Eighty-Yard Run," and from the class discussion you have got the idea that the instructor thinks college football is for the birds. You are no fool. You can figure out what side to take.

After dinner you get out the portable typewriter that you got for high school graduation. You might as well get it over with and enjoy Saturday and Sunday. Five hundred words is about two double-spaced pages with normal margins. You put in a sheet of paper, think up a title, and you're off:

Why College Football Should Be Abolished

*College football should be abolished because it's bad for the school
and also bad for the players. The players are so busy practicing
that they don't have any time for their studies.*

This, you feel, is a mighty good start. The only trouble is that it's only thirty-two words. You still have four hundred and sixty-eight to go, and you've pretty well exhausted the subject. It comes to you that you do your best thinking in the morning, so you put away the typewriter and go to the movies. But the next morning you have to do your washing and some math problems, and in the afternoon you go to the game. The English instructor turns up too, and you wonder if you've taken the right side after all. Saturday night you have a date, and Sunday morning you have to go to church. (You can't let English assignments interfere with your religion.) What with one thing and another, it's ten o'clock Sunday night before you get out the typewriter again. You make a pot of coffee and start to fill out your views on college football. Put a little meat on the bones.

Why College Football Should Be Abolished

In my opinion, it seems to me that college football should be abolished. The reason why I think this to be true is because I feel that football is bad for the colleges in nearly every respect. As Robert Hutchins says in his article in our anthology in which he discusses college football, it would be better if the colleges had race horses and had races with one another, because then the horses would not have to attend classes. I firmly agree with Mr. Hutchins on this point, and I am sure that many other students would agree too.

One reason why it seems to me that college football is bad is that it has become too commercial. In the olden times when people played football just for the fun of it, maybe college football was all right, but they do not play football just for the fun of it now as they used to in the old days. Nowadays college football is what you might call a big business. Maybe this is not true at all schools, and I don't think it is especially true here at State, but certainly this is the case at most colleges and universities in America nowadays, as Mr. Hutchins points out in his very interesting article. Actually the coaches and alumni go around to the high schools and offer the high school stars large salaries to come to their colleges and play football for them. There was one case where a high school star was offered a convertible if he would play football for a certain college.

Another reason for abolishing college football is that it is bad for the players. They do not have time to get a college education, because they are so busy playing football. A football player has to practice every afternoon from three to six and then he is so tired that he can't concentrate on his studies. He just feels like dropping off to sleep after dinner, and then the next day he goes to his classes without having studied and maybe he fails the test.

(Good ripe stuff so far, but you're still a hundred and fifty-one words from home. One more push.)

Also I think college football is bad for the colleges and the universities because not very many students get to participate in it. Out of a college of ten thousand students only seventy-five or a hundred play football, if that many. Football is what you might call a spectator sport. That means that most people go to watch it but do not play it themselves.

(Four hundred and fifteen. Well, you still have the conclusion, and when you retype it, you can make the margins a little wider.)

> *These are the reasons why I agree with Mr. Hutchins that college football should be abolished in American colleges and universities.*

On Monday you turn it in, moderately hopeful, and on Friday it comes back marked "weak in content" and sporting a big "D."

This essay is exaggerated a little, not much. The English instructor will recognize it as reasonably typical of what an assignment on college football will bring in. He knows that nearly half of the class will contrive in five hundred words to say that college football is too commercial and bad for the players. Most of the other half will inform him that college football builds character and prepares one for life and brings prestige to the school. As he reads paper after paper all saying the same thing in almost the same words, all bloodless, five hundred words dripping out of nothing, he wonders how he allowed himself to get trapped into teaching English when he might have had a happy and interesting life as an electrician or a confidence man.

Well, you may ask, what can you do about it? The subject is one on which you have few convictions and little information. Can you be expected to make a dull subject interesting? As a matter of fact, this is precisely what you are expected to do. This is the writer's essential task. All subjects, except sex, are dull until somebody makes them interesting. The writer's job is to find the argument, the approach, the angle, the wording that will take the reader with him. This is seldom easy, and it is particularly hard in subjects that have been much discussed: College Football, Fraternities, Popular Music, Is Chivalry Dead?, and the like. You will feel that there is nothing you can do with such subjects except repeat the old bromides. But there are some things you can do which will make your papers, if not throbbingly alive, at least less insufferably tedious than they might otherwise be.

Avoid the Obvious Content

Say the assignment is college football. Say that you've decided to be against it. Begin by putting down the arguments that come to your mind: it is too commercial, it takes the students' minds off their studies, it is hard on the players, it makes the university a kind of circus instead of an intellectual center, for most schools it is financially ruinous. Can you think of any more arguments, just off hand? All right. Now when you write your paper, *make sure that you don't use any of the material on this list.* If these are the points that leap to your mind, they will leap to everyone else's too, and whether you get a "C" or a "D" may depend on whether the instructor reads your paper early when he is fresh and tolerant or late, when the sentence "In my opinion, college football has become too commercial," inexorably repeated, has brought him to the brink of lunacy.

Be against college football for some reason or reasons of your own. If they are keen and perceptive ones, that's splendid. But even if they are trivial or foolish or indefensible, you are still ahead so long as they are not everybody else's reasons too. Be against it because the colleges don't spend enough money on it to make it worthwhile, because it is bad for the characters of the spectators, because the players are forced to attend classes, because the football stars hog all the beautiful women, because it competes with baseball and is therefore un-American and possibly Communist inspired. There are lots of more or less unused reasons for being against college football.

Sometimes it is a good idea to sum up and dispose of the trite and conventional points before going on to your own. This has the advantage of indicating to the reader that you are going to be neither trite nor conventional. Something like this:

> *We are often told that college football should be abolished because it has become too commercial or because it is bad for the players. These arguments are no doubt very cogent, but they don't really go to the heart of the matter.*

Then you go to the heart of the matter.

Take the Less Usual Side

One rather simple way of getting into your paper is to take the side of the argument that most of the citizens will want to avoid. If the assignment is an essay on dogs, you can, if you choose, explain that dogs are faithful and lovable companions, intelligent, useful as guardians of the house and protectors of children, indispensable in police work—in short, when all is said and done, man's best friends. Or you can suggest that those big brown eyes conceal, more often than not, a vacuity of mind and an inconstancy of purpose; that the dogs you have known most intimately have been mangy, ill-tempered brutes, incapable of instruction; and that only your nobility of mind and fear of arrest prevent you from kicking the flea-ridden animals when you pass them on the street.

Naturally personal convictions will sometimes dictate your approach. If the assigned subject is "Is Methodism Rewarding to the Individual?" and you are a pious Methodist, you have really no choice. But few assigned subjects, if any, will fall in this category. Most of them will lie in broad areas of discussion with much to be said on both sides. They are intellectual exercises, and it is legitimate to argue now one way and now another, as debaters do in similar circumstances. Always take the side that looks to you hardest, least defensible. It will almost always turn out to be easier to write interestingly on that side.

This general advice applies where you have a choice of subjects. If you are to choose among "The Value of Fraternities" and "My Favorite High School Teacher" and "What I Think About Beetles," by all means plump for the beetles. By the time the instructor gets to your paper, he will be up to his ears in tedious tales about the French teacher at Bloombury High and assertions about how fraternities build character and prepare one for life. Your views on beetles, whatever they are, are bound to be a refreshing change.

Don't worry too much about figuring out what the instructor thinks about the subject so that you can cuddle up with him. Chances are his views are no stronger than yours. If he does have convictions and you oppose him, his problem is to keep from grading you higher than you deserve in order to show he is not biased. This doesn't mean that you should always cantankerously dissent from what the instructor says; that gets tiresome too. And if the subject assigned is "My Pet

Peeve," do not begin, "My pet peeve is the English instructor who assigns papers on 'my pet peeve.'" This was still funny during the War of 1812, but it has sort of lost its edge since then. It is in general good manners to avoid personalities.

Slip Out of Abstraction

If you will study the essay on college football [near the beginning of this essay], you will perceive that one reason for its appalling dullness is that it never gets down to particulars. It is just a series of not very glittering generalities: "football is bad for the colleges," "it has become too commercial," "football is a big business," "it is bad for the players," and so on. Such round phrases thudding against the reader's brain are unlikely to convince him, though they may well render him unconscious.

If you want the reader to believe that college football is bad for the players, you have to do more than say so. You have to display the evil. Take your roommate, Alfred Simkins, the second-string center. Picture poor old Alfy coming home from football practice every evening, bruised and aching, agonizingly tired, scarcely able to shovel the mashed potatoes into his mouth. Let us see him staggering up to the room, getting out his econ textbook, peering desperately at it with his good eye, falling asleep and failing the test in the morning. Let us share his unbearable tension as Saturday draws near. Will he fail, be demoted, lose his monthly allowance, be forced to return to the coal mines? And if he succeeds, what will be his reward? Perhaps a slight ripple of applause when the third-string center replaces him, a moment of elation in the locker room if the team wins, of despair if it loses. What will he look back on when he graduates from college? Toil and torn ligaments. And what will be his future? He is not good enough for pro football, and he is too obscure and weak in econ to succeed in stocks and bonds. College football is tearing the heart from Alfy Simkins and, when it finishes with him, will callously toss aside the shattered hulk.

This is no doubt a weak enough argument for the abolition of college football, but it is a sight better than saying, in three or four variations, that college football (in your opinion) is bad for the players.

Look at the work of any professional writer and notice how constantly he is moving from the generality, the abstract statement, to the concrete example, the facts and figures, the illustration. If he is writing on juvenile delinquency, he does not just tell you that juveniles are (it seems to him) delinquent and that (in his opinion) something should be done about it. He shows you juveniles being delinquent, tearing up movie theatres in Buffalo, stabbing high school principals in Dallas, smoking marijuana in Palo Alto. And more than likely he is moving toward some specific remedy, not just a general wringing of the hands.

It is no doubt possible to be *too* concrete, too illustrative or anecdotal, but few inexperienced writers err this way. For most the soundest advice is to be seeking always for the picture, to be always turning general remarks into seeable examples. Don't say, "Sororities teach girls the social graces." Say, "Sorority life teaches a girl how to carry on a conversation while pouring tea, without sloshing the tea into the saucer." Don't say, "I like certain kinds of popular music very much." Say, "Whenever I hear Gerber Sprinklittle play 'Mississippi Man' on the trombone, my socks creep up my ankles."

Get Rid of Obvious Padding

The student toiling away at his weekly English theme is too often tormented by a figure: five hundred words. How, he asks himself, is he to achieve this staggering total? Obviously by never using one word when he can somehow work in ten.

He is therefore seldom content with a plain statement like "Fast driving is dangerous." This has only four words in it. He takes thought, and the sentence becomes:

> *In my opinion, fast driving is dangerous.*

Better, but he can do better still:

> *In my opinion, fast driving would seem to be rather dangerous.*

If he is really adept, it may come out:

> *In my humble opinion, though I do not claim to be an expert on this complicated subject, fast driving, in most circumstances, would seem to be rather dangerous in many respects, or at least so it would seem to me.*

Thus four words have been turned into forty, and not an iota of content has been added.

Now this is a way to go about reaching five hundred words, and if you are content with a "D" grade, it is as good a way as any. But if you aim higher, you must work differently. Instead of stuffing your sentences with straw, you must try steadily to get rid of the padding, to make your sentences lean and tough. If you are really working at it, your first draft will greatly exceed the required total, and then you will work it down, thus:

> *It is thought in some quarters that fraternities do not contribute as much as might be expected to campus life.*
>
> *Some people think that fraternities contribute little to campus life.*
>
> *The average doctor who practices in small towns or in the country must toil night and day to heal the sick.*
>
> *Most country doctors work long hours.*
>
> *When I was a little girl, I suffered from shyness and embarrament in the presence of others.*
>
> *I was a shy little girl.*
>
> *It is absolutely necessary for the person employed as a marine fireman to give the matter of steam pressure his undivided attention at all times.*
>
> *The fireman has to keep his eye on the steam gauge.*

You may ask how you can arrive at five hundred words at this rate. Simple. You dig up more real content. Instead of taking a couple of obvious points off the surface of the topic and then circling warily around them for six paragraphs, you work in and explore, figure out the details. You illustrate. You say that fast driving is dangerous, and then you prove it. How long does it take to stop a car at forty and at eighty? How far can you see at night? What happens when a tire blows? What happens in a head-on collision at fifty miles an hour? Pretty soon your paper will be full of broken glass and blood and headless torsos, and reaching five hundred words will not really be a problem.

Call a Fool a Fool

Some of the padding in freshman themes is to be blamed not on anxiety about the word minimum but on excessive timidity. The student writes, "In my opinion, the principal of my high school acted in ways that I believe every unbiased person would have to call foolish." This isn't exactly what he means. What he means is, "My high school principal was a fool." If he was a fool, call him a fool. Hedging the thing about with "in-my-opinion's" and "it-seems-to-me's" and "as-I-see-it's" and "at-least-from-my-point-of-view's" gains you nothing. Delete these phrases whenever they creep into your paper.

The student's tendency to hedge stems from a modesty that in other circumstances would be commendable. He is, he realizes, young and inexperienced, and he half suspects that he is dopey and fuzzy-minded beyond the average. Probably only too true. But it doesn't help to announce your incompetence six times in every paragraph. Decide what you want to say and say it as vigorously as possible, without apology and in plain words.

Linguistic diffidence can take various forms. One is what we call *euphemism*. This is the tendency to call a spade "a certain garden implement" or women's underwear "unmentionables." It is stronger in some eras than others and in some people than others but it always operates more or less in subjects that are touchy or taboo: death, sex, madness, and so on. Thus we shrink from saying "He died last night" but say instead "passed away," "left us," "joined his Maker," "went to his reward." Or we try to take off the tension with a lighter cliché: "kicked the bucket," "cashed in his chips," "handed in his dinner pail." We have found all sorts of ways to avoid saying *mad*: "mentally ill," "touched," "not quite right upstairs," "feeble-minded," "innocent," "simple," "off his trolley," "not in his right mind." Even such a now plain word as *insane* began as a euphemism with the meaning "not healthy."

Modern science, particularly psychology, contributes many polysyllables in which we can wrap our thoughts and blunt their force. To many writers there is no such thing as a bad schoolboy. Schoolboys are maladjusted or unoriented or misunderstood or in the need of guidance or lacking in continued success toward satisfactory integration of the personality as a social unit, but they are never bad. Psychology no doubt makes us better men and women, more sympathetic and tolerant, but it doesn't make writing any easier. Had Shakespeare been confronted with psychology, "To be or not to be" might have come out, "To continue as a social unit or not to do so. That is the personality problem. Whether 'tis a better sign of integration at the conscious level to display a psychic tolerance toward the maladjustments and repressions induced by one's lack of orientation in one's environment or—" But Hamlet would never have finished the soliloquy.

Writing in the modern world, you cannot altogether avoid modern jargon. Nor, in an effort to get away from euphemism, should you salt your paper with four-letter words. But you can do much if you will mount guard against those roundabout phrases, those echoing polysyllables that tend to slip into your writing to rob it of its crispness and force.

Beware of Pat Expressions

Other things being equal, avoid phrases like "other things being equal." Those sentences that come to you whole, or in two or three doughy lumps, are sure to be bad sentences. They are no creation of yours but pieces of common thought floating in the community soup.

Pat expressions are hard, often impossible, to avoid, because they come too easily to be noticed and seem too necessary to be dispensed with. No writer avoids them altogether, but good writers avoid them more often than poor writers.

By "pat expressions" we mean such tags as "to all practical intents and purposes," "the pure and simple truth," "from where I sit," "the time of his life," "to the ends of the earth," "in the twinkling of an eye," "as sure as you're born," "over my dead body," "under cover of darkness," "took the easy way out," "when all is said and done," "told him time and time again," "parted the best of friends," "stand up and be counted," "gave him the best years of her life," "worked her fingers to the bone." Like other clichés, these expressions were once forceful. Now we should use them only when we can't possibly think of anything else.

Some pat expressions stand like a wall between the writer and thought. Such a one is "the American way of life." Many student writers feel that when they have said that something accords with the American way of life or does not they have exhausted the subject. Actually, they have stopped at the highest level of abstraction. The American way of life is the complicated set of bonds between a hundred and eighty million ways. All of us know this when we think about it, but the tag phrase too often keeps us from thinking about it.

So with many another phrase dear to the politician: "this great land of ours," "the man in the street," "our national heritage." These may prove our patriotism or give a clue to our political beliefs, but otherwise they add nothing to the paper except words.

Colorful Words

The writer builds with words, and no builder uses a raw material more slippery and elusive and treacherous. A writer's work is a constant struggle to get the right word in the right place, to find that particular word that will convey his meaning exactly, that will persuade the reader or soothe him or startle or amuse him. He never succeeds altogether—sometimes he feels that he scarcely succeeds at all—but such successes as he has are what make the thing worth doing.

There is no book of rules for this game. One progresses through everlasting experiment on the basis of ever-widening experience. There are few useful generalizations that one can make about words as words, but there are perhaps a few.

Some words are what we call "colorful." By this we mean that they are calculated to produce a picture or induce an emotion. They are dressy instead of plain, specific instead of general, loud instead of soft. Thus, in place of "Her heart beat," we may write, "Her heart *pounded, throbbed, fluttered, danced.*" Instead of "He sat in his chair," we may say, "He *lounged, sprawled, coiled.*" Instead of "It was hot," we may say, "It was *blistering, sultry, muggy, suffocating, steamy, wilting.*"

However, it should not be supposed that the fancy word is always better. Often it is as well to write "Her heart beat" or "It was hot" if that is all it did or all it was. Ages differ in how they like their prose. The nineteenth century liked it rich and smoky. The twentieth has usually preferred it lean and cool. The twentieth century writer, like all writers, is forever seeking the exact word, but he is wary of sounding feverish. He tends to pitch it low, to understate it, to throw it away. He knows that if he gets too colorful, the audience is likely to giggle.

See how this strikes you: "As the rich, golden glow of the sunset died away along the eternal western hills, Angela's limpid blue eyes looked softly and trustingly into Montague's flashing brown ones, and her heart pounded like a drum in time with the joyous song surging in her soul." Some people like that sort of thing, but most modern readers would say, "Good grief," and turn on the television.

Colored Words

Some words we would call not so much colorful as colored—that is, loaded with associations, good or bad. All words—except perhaps structure words—have associations of some sort. We have said that the meaning of a word is the sum of the contexts in which it occurs. When we hear a word, we hear with it an echo of all the situations in which we have heard it before.

In some words, these echoes are obvious and discussible. The word *mother,* for example, has for most people, agreeable associations. When you hear *mother* you probably think of home, safety, love, food, and various other pleasant things. If one writes, "She was like a mother to me," he gets an effect which he would not get in "She was like an aunt to me." The advertiser makes use of the associations of *mother* by working it in when he talks about his product. The politician works it in when he talks about himself.

So also with such words as *home, liberty, fireside, contentment, patriot, tenderness, sacrifice, childlike, manly, bluff, limpid.* All of these words are loaded with associations that would be rather hard to indicate in a straight-forward definition. There is more than a literal difference between "They sat around the fireside" and "They sat around the stove." They might have been equally warm and happy around the stove, but *fireside* suggests leisure, grace, quiet tradition, congenial company, and *stove* does not.

Conversely, some words have bad associations. *Mother* suggests pleasant things, but *mother-in-law* does not. Many mothers-in-law are heroically lovable and some mothers drink gin all day and beat their children insensible, but these facts of life are beside the point. The point is that *mother* sounds good and *mother-in-law* does not.

Or consider the word *intellectual.* This would seem to be a complimentary term, but in point of fact it is not, for it has picked up associations of impracticality and ineffectuality and general dopiness. So also such words as *liberal, reactionary, Communist, socialist, capitalist, radical, schoolteacher, truck driver, undertaker, operator, salesman, huckster, speculator.* These convey meaning on the literal level, but beyond that—sometimes, in some places—they convey contempt on the part of the speaker.

The question of whether to use loaded words or not depends on what is being written. The scientist, the scholar, try to avoid them; for the poet, the advertising writer, the public speaker, they are standard equipment. But every writer should take care that they do not substitute for thought. If you write, "Anyone who thinks that is nothing but a Socialist (or Communist or capitalist)," you have said nothing except that you don't like people who think that, and such remarks are effective only with the most naive readers. It is always a bad mistake to think your readers more naive than they really are.

Colorless Words

But probably most student writers come to grief not with words that are colorful or those that are colored but with those that have no color at all. A pet example is nice, a word we would find it hard to dispense with in casual conversation but which is no longer capable of adding much to a description. Colorless words are those of such general meaning that in a particular sentence they mean nothing. Slang adjectives like *cool* ("That's real cool") tend to explode all over the language. They are applied to everything, lose their original force, and quickly die.

Beware also of nouns of very general meaning, like *circumstances, cases, instances, aspects, factors, relationships, attitudes, eventualities,* etc. In most circumstances you will find that those cases of writing which contain too many instances of words like these will in this and other aspects have factors leading to unsatisfactory relationships with the reader resulting in unfavorable attitudes on his part and perhaps other eventualities, like a grade of "D." Notice also what "etc." means. It means "I'd like to make this list longer, but I can't think of any more examples."

How to Write with Style

Kurt Vonnegut

Newspaper reporters and technical writers are trained to reveal almost nothing about themselves in their writings. This makes them freaks in the world of writers, since almost all of the other ink-stained wretches in that world reveal a lot about themselves to readers. We call these revelations, accidental and intentional, elements of literary style.

These revelations are fascinating to us as readers. They tell us what sort of person it is with whom we are spending time. Does the writer sound ignorant or informed, crazy or sane, stupid or bright, crooked or honest, humorless or playful—? And on and on.

When you yourself put words on paper, remember that the most damning revelation you can make about yourself is that you do not know what is interesting and what is not. Don't you yourself like or dislike writers mainly for what they choose to show you or make you think about? Did you ever admire an empty-headed writer for his or her mastery of the language? No.

So your own winning literary style must begin with interesting ideas in your head. Find a subject you care about and which you in your heart feel others should care about. It is this genuine caring, and not your games with language, which will be the most compelling and seductive element in your style.

I am not urging you to write a novel, by the way—although I would not be sorry if you wrote one, provided you genuinely cared about something. A petition to the mayor about a pothole in front of your house or a love letter to the girl next door will do.

Do not ramble, though.

As for your use of language: Remember that two great masters of our language, William Shakespeare and James Joyce, wrote sentences which were almost

117

childlike when their subjects were most profound. "To be or not to be?" asks Shakespeare's Hamlet. The longest word is three letters long. Joyce, when he was frisky, could put together a sentence as intricate and glittering as a necklace for Cleopatra, but my favorite sentence in his short story "Eveline" is this one: "She was tired." At that point in the story, no other words could break the heart of a reader as those words do.

Simplicity of language is not only reputable, but perhaps even sacred. The Bible opens with a sentence well within the writing skills of a lively fourteen-year-old: "In the beginning God created the heavens and the earth."

It may be that you, too, are capable of making necklaces for Cleopatra, so to speak. But your eloquence should be the servant of the ideas in your head. Your rule might be this: If a sentence, no matter how excellent, does not illuminate my subject in some new and useful way, scratch it out. Here is the same rule paraphrased to apply to storytelling, to fiction: Never include a sentence which does not either remark on character or advance the action.

The writing style which is most natural for you is bound to echo speech you heard when a child. English was the novelist Joseph Conrad's third language, and much that seems piquant in his use of English was no doubt colored by his first language, which was Polish. And lucky indeed is the writer who has grown up in Ireland, for the English spoken there is so amusing and musical. I myself grew up in Indianapolis, Indiana, where common speech sounds like a band saw cutting galvanized tin, and employs a vocabulary as unornamental as a monkey wrench.

In some of the more remote hollows of Appalachia, children still grow up hearing songs and locutions of Elizabethan times. Yes, and many Americans grow up hearing a language other than English, or an English dialect a majority of Americans cannot understand.

All these varieties of speech are beautiful, just as the varieties of butterflies are beautiful. No matter what your first language, you should treasure it all your life. If it happens not to be standard English, and if it shows itself when you write standard English, the result is usually delightful, like a very pretty girl with one eye that is green and one that is blue.

I myself find that I trust my own writing most, and others seem to trust it most, too, when I sound most like a person from Indianapolis, which is what I am. What alternatives do I have? The one most vehemently recommended by teachers has no doubt been pressed on you, as well: that I write like cultivated Englishmen of a century or more ago.

I used to be exasperated by such teachers, but am no more. I understand now that all those antique essays and stories with which I was to compare my own work were not magnificent for their datedness or foreignness, but for saying precisely what their authors meant them to say. My teachers wished me to write accurately, always selecting the most effective words, and relating the words to one another unambiguously, rigidly, like parts of a machine. The teachers did not want to turn me into an Englishman after all. They hoped that I would become understandable—and therefore understood.

And there went my dream of doing with words what Pablo Picasso did with paint or what any number of jazz idols did with music. If I broke all the rules of punctuation, had words mean whatever I wanted them to mean, and strung them together higgledy-piggledy, I would simply not be understood. So you, too, had better avoid Picasso-style or jazz-style writing, if you have something worth saying and wish to be understood.

If it were only teachers who insisted that modern writers stay close to literary styles of the past, we might reasonably ignore them. But readers insist on the very same thing. They want our pages to look very much like pages they have seen before.

Why? It is because they themselves have a tough job to do, and they need all the help they can get from us. They have to identify thousands of little marks on paper, and make sense of them immediately. They have to *read*, an art so difficult that most people do not really master it even after having studied it all through grade school and high school—for twelve long years.

So this discussion, like all discussions of literary styles, must finally acknowledge that our stylistic options as writers are neither numerous nor glamorous, since our readers are bound to be such imperfect artists. Our audience requires us to be sympathetic and patient teachers, ever willing to simplify and clarify—whereas we would rather soar high above the crowd, singing like nightingales.

That is the bad news. The good news is that we Americans are governed under a unique Constitution, which allows us to write whatever we please without fear of punishment. So the most meaningful aspect of our styles, which is what we choose to write about, is unlimited.

Also: we are members of an egalitarian society, so there is no reason for us to write, in case we are not classically educated aristocrats, as though we were classically educated aristocrats.

For a discussion of literary style in a narrower sense, in a more technical sense, I commend to your attention *The Elements of Style* by William Strunk, Jr., and E. B. White (Macmillan, 1979). It contains such rules as this: "A participial phrase at the beginning of a sentence must refer to the grammatical subject," and so on. E. B. White is, of course, one of the most admirable literary stylists this country has so far produced.

You should realize, too, that no one would care how well or badly Mr. White expressed himself, if he did not have perfectly enchanting things to say.

Let's Get Vertical!

Beth Wald

Here I am, 400 feet up on the steep west face of Devil's Tower, a tiny figure in a sea of petrified rock. I can't find enough footholds and handholds to keep climbing. My climbing partner anxiously looks up at me from his narrow ledge. I can see the silver sparkle of the climbing devices I've jammed into the crack every eight feet or so.

I study the last device I've placed, a half-inch aluminum wedge 12 feet below me. If I slip, it'll catch me, but only after a 24-foot fall, a real "screamer." It's too difficult to go back; I have to find a way up before my fingers get too tired. I must act quickly.

Finding a tiny opening in the crack, I jam two fingertips in, crimp them, pull hard, and kick my right foot onto a sloping knob, hoping it won't skid off. At the same time, I slap my right hand up to what looks like a good hold. To my horror, it's round and slippery.

My fingers start to slide. Panic rivets me for a second, but then a surge of adrenalin snaps me back into action. I scramble my feet higher, lunge with my left hand, and catch a wider crack. I manage to get a better grip just as my right hand pops off its slick hold. My feet find edges, and I regain my balance, whipping a chock (wedge) off my harness, I slip it into the crack and clip my rope through a carabiner (oblong metal snaplink). After catching my breath, I start moving again, and the rest of the climb flows upward like a vertical dance.

The Challenges and Rewards

I've tried many sports, but I haven't found any to match the excitement of rock climbing. It's a unique world, with its own language, communities, controversies, heroes, villains, and devoted followers. I've lived in vans, tepees, tents, and caves; worked three jobs to save money for expenses; driven 24 hours to spend a weekend at a good rock; and lived on beans and rice for months at a time—all of this to be able to climb. What is it about scrambling up rocks that inspires such a passion? The answer is, no other sport offers so many challenges and so many rewards.

The physical challenges are obvious. You need flexibility, balance, and strength. But climbing is also a psychological game of defeating your fear, and it demands creative thinking. It's a bit like improvising a gymnastic routine 200 feet in the air while playing a game of chess.

Climbers visit some of the most spectacular places on earth and see them from a unique perspective—the top! Because the sport is so intense, friendships between climbers tend to be strong and enduring.

Anyone Can Climb

Kids playing in trees or on monkey bars know that climbing is a natural activity, but older people often have to relearn to trust their instincts. This isn't too hard, though. The ability to maintain self-control in difficult situations is the most important trait for a beginning climber to have. Panic is almost automatic when you run out of handholds 100 feet off the ground. The typical reaction is to freeze solid until you fall off. But with a little discipline, rational thinking, and/or distraction tactics such as babbling to yourself, humming, or even screaming, fear can change to elation as you climb out of a tough spot.

Contrary to popular belief, you don't have to be superhumanly strong to climb. Self-confidence, agility, a good sense of balance, and determination will get you farther up the rock than bulging biceps. Once you've learned the basics, climbing itself will gradually make you stronger, though many dedicated climbers speed up the process by training at home or in the gym.

Nonclimbers often ask, "How do the ropes get up there?" It's quite simple; the climbers bring them up as they climb. Most rock climbers today are "free climbers." In free climbing, the rope is used only for safety in case of a fall, *not* to help pull you up. (Climbing without a rope, called "free soloing," is a *very* dangerous activity practiced only by extremely experienced—and crazy—climbers.)

First, two climbers tie into opposite ends of a 150-foot-long nylon rope. Then one of them, the belayer, anchors himself or herself to a rock or tree. The other, the leader, starts to climb, occasionally stopping to jam a variety of aluminum wedges or other special gadgets, generically referred to as protection, into cracks in the rock. To each of these, he or she attaches a snaplink, called a carabiner, and clips the rope through. As the leader climbs, the belayer feeds out the rope, and it runs through the carabiners. If the leader falls, the belayer holds the rope, and the highest piece of protection catches the leader. The belayer uses special techniques and equipment to make it easy to stop falls.

When the leader reaches the end of a section of rock—called the pitch—and sets an anchor, he or she becomes the belayer. This person pulls up the slack of the rope as the other partner climbs and removes the protection. Once together again, they can either continue in the same manner or switch leaders. These worldwide techniques work on rock formations, cliffs, peaks, even buildings.

Rocks, Rocks Everywhere

Some of the best climbing cliffs in the country are in the Shawangunk Mountains, only two hours from New York City. Seneca Rocks in West Virginia draws climbers from Washington, D.C., and Pittsburgh, Pennsylvania. Chattanooga, Tennessee, has a fine cliff within the city limits. Most states in the U.S. and provinces in Canada offer at least one or two good climbing opportunities.

Even if there are no large cliffs or rock formations nearby, you can climb smaller rocks to practice techniques and get stronger. This is called bouldering. Many climbers who live in cities and towns have created climbing areas out of old stone walls and buildings. Ask someone at your local outdoor shop where you can go to start climbing.

Get a Helping Hand

There's no substitute for an expert teacher when it comes to learning basic techniques and safety procedures. One of the best (and least expensive) ways to learn climbing is to convince a veteran climber in your area to teach you. You can usually meet these types at the local crag or climbing shop.

As another option, many universities and colleges, some high schools, and some YMCAs have climbing clubs. Their main purpose is to introduce people to climbing and to teach the basics. Other clubs, such as the Appalachian Mountain Club in the eastern U.S. and the Mountaineers on the West Coast, also provide instruction. Ask at your outdoor shop for the names of clubs in your area.

If you live in a place completely lacking rocks and climbers, you can attend one of the fine climbing schools at the major climbing area closest to you. Magazines like *Climbing, Rock & Ice,* and *Outside* publish lists of these schools. Once you learn the basics, you're ready to get vertical.

In rock climbing, you can both lose yourself and find yourself. Life and all its troubles are reduced to figuring out the puzzle of the next section of cliff or forgotten in the challenge and delight of moving through vertical space. And learning how to control anxiety, how to piece together a difficult sequence of moves, and how to communicate with a partner are all skills that prove incredibly useful back on the ground!

How Not to Kill
Yourself Water-skiing

Student

"Hit it!" I yelled. My brother-in-law opened the throttle on his boat and I popped up out of the water like a submerged cork coming to the surface. This was the first time I had water-skied in over twelve years. Everything I had been taught came back to me pretty fast once I was up. My skis kept trying to split apart, my legs wouldn't stay together, and I had to deal with rough water. I think I managed to stay up for about one hundred yards before I went down. The four main points that you have to remember about water-skiing are keeping your skis straight, bending your knees, releasing the rope just before you crash, and if you do crash, try rolling onto your back.

"Keep your skis straight," my father told me as I was trying to learn how to water-ski. It may sound easy, but believe me it isn't. Trying to keep your skis straight with the front third sticking out of the water, waves moving you around, and a rope running out in front of you is definitely not the easiest thing. Your skis want to start pointing outward and spreading apart with the waves rolling over them. You feel like an idiot floating in the water in a squatting position waiting for the rope to tighten up. Once the rope is tight, it's a bit easier to control the skis, but only while you are in the water. When you are skimming across the surface of the water, you still have to keep the skis straight. It hurts when your skis start to split apart, and you end up falling. That's when the second rule of skiing comes into play.

"Keep your knees slightly bent," said my father as I looked over at him, smiled and nodded my understanding. Little did I realize that this is one of the most important rules to know, since you can use your legs as shock absorbers. It doesn't hurt as much when you have to go across the wakes of other boats if you can use your legs for this purpose. Another reason for keeping your knees bent, that I figured out on my own, is it's easier to sit down rather than land hard. Believe me; hitting the water hurts more than you would think, especially if you land on your front. There's nothing fun about doing a belly flop at high speed. There is one flaw with this rule; if you keep your knees bent too much, your legs tire out a lot faster. After my third try at skiing, my legs felt like rubber, and I was breathing like I had just run a couple of miles.

Third, and just as important as the first two, is as soon as you know you're going to fall, release the rope! This is important because as soon as you let go you start to slow down, thus making your landing that much easier on your body. After losing my balance going over the first set of boat wakes, I recovered nicely, managing to stay upright. I was caught by surprise with the next set of waves and completely lost it. Just before I lost my balance, I was thinking to myself, "Yes, I can keep my feet under me. It's like riding a bike or walking." Truthfully though, it's nothing like that. You don't move your feet or legs; the boat does the moving for you. Imagine your feet stuck in cement and leaning forward or backward; you have that sense that your feet aren't going to move. Unfortunately, with skiing your feet do not stay under you as you lean. They may start getting behind you or in front of you, and you may be able to recover a slight difference between your body and your feet, but if your feet get too far out from under you, that's it; you're going down. If your feet are in front of you, consider yourself lucky; all you have to do is sit down. If, on the other hand, your feet are in back of you, release that rope quickly because more than likely you are going to go down hard and at full speed. If this happens, try to lose the skis as well; to do this make like you are stepping out of boots; this usually works to get the skis off before you hit the water. If they don't come off, don't worry; as soon as you hit the water, they will.

Finally, once you know you're going to fall on your front, if you can lose the skis, try to roll to your side or back to land. The reason I say this is, hitting the water with your face hurts more than hitting your back. I have landed on my front one time, many years ago, and the next day I could barely stand, much less walk. After that one fall I quickly decided to twist my body as much as possible so I would land on my back instead. Another reason for this is you can make a bigger splash if you land on your back and that is always more impressive to onlookers. It's also great for getting some sympathy out of the onlookers as well.

These pointers of keeping your skis straight, bending your knees, releasing the rope, and rolling or twisting to land on your back are definitely things you want to try to remember. They will help the beginner as well as the more accomplished skier survive water-skiing. I thoroughly enjoyed my weekend of pain and suffering all in the cause of water-skiing and would gladly do that again.

How to Mix a Song Using Professional Deejay Equipment

Student

"What song do I play next?" I said to my partner. He told me to put in a song that is around 124 bpms, beats per minute, and is being played on the radio a lot. I decided to play a new rap remix of a popular song. This song was 126 bpms, and the song I was playing was 124 bpms. I started the new song on a thirty-two like normal and slowed it down just a bit until it sounded like the beats were on top of each other. Then I stopped the new song and waited for a break in the vocals. When my break came I counted thirty-two beats and started the next song. I moved the fader over very slowly until the first song started to get back in the vocals and then I cut it out to play the second song. If you are not a Deejay, you're asking yourself, "Huh?" To mix a song you need to do three major things: pick out the two songs to mix, match the bpms, and find the breaks and thirty-twos.

Picking two songs to mix is a very easy thing to do if one is familiar with their CD catalog. If you don't know your catalog, this can get tricky. A normal deejay will carry about seventy CDs, each with fifteen to twenty songs each. This fact makes it hard for a deejay to choose a song to go with another one. The first thing you want to look for is compatibility of the songs. By this I mean, if you are playing eighties music, the next song should be eighties until you are done with your retro section of the night. Then you should move on to a different type of music. The second thing a deejay deals with is choosing a song that people will dance to.

Without dancing, the position of a deejay is pointless. The best dance songs are the common songs played on the radio, or have been played many times in the past. A major obstacle deejays have to watch when they are preparing a mix is if they play one musical group too much during the evening and then play the same group later on, someone in the crowd will get mad. The best thing to do if you want to play two songs by the same group is to cut into the middle of the first song during the break and mix in the second song. This way everyone will get to hear the two songs and it will just take up nearly the same time one song would have.

The second phase of mixing a song is the most technical. Matching the beats per minute, also known as "bpms," is one of the hardest parts about deejaying. This part takes lots of practice and concentration. Some mixers, like the Pioneer 300s, have automatic bpm counters built in. This counter will give you the average bpm of the song during the section that is playing. This is a very helpful tool but it doesn't do all the work for you. When one is matching bpms they will need three things. One of those is a mixer. The other is a CD catalog, and the third is a set of headphones. The headphone must be large to cover your ears completely and have the proper connector for the mixer. Most deejays wear their headphones around their neck and have only one ear on the headphones. This makes them able to hear the music coming from the next song and the song actually playing. Each song playing has thirty-two beat sections, which means when a thirty-two starts you must start the second song on that beat to keep the song congruent. It is like having two people walking at the same speed, side-by-side, and having the same feet land on the ground at the same time. The beats are never matched up perfectly at this point due to the delay on the CD player. Now one must speed up the song with the pitch by touching the pitch control forward or backward quickly. It is like setting the cruise control on your car. You set the speed how you want it at first and then push the accelerate button to speed up or the coast button to slow down. During this process, you should be moving the cross fader over slowly until your break is through.

Finding the thirty-twos and the breaks can be very easy or the most difficult thing during a mix. Almost every song you listen to starts at beat one and goes to beat thirty-two, where the song will distinctly change and start over the cycle. There is one good way you can find the thirty-twos and determine when you should be starting your next song. Listen to the beat in the song, not the words, and find where the song reaches a dramatic point. After the highest point is reached, there is usually a drop-off. This is the thirty-second beat. Breaks can be found in the beginning, middle, or end of a song. The beginning break is called the intro, while the ending break is the outro. This is the best place to start or end a song because of its lack of lyrics. The breaks usually last for sixty-four beats and have a thirty-two still in the middle. If you are mixing during this period, you will want to finish the mix before the next song has started its lyrics. Mixing on the break is the most efficient way of mixing, because of its casualness in starting the next song. By this I mean it starts the next song without the crowd really noticing it.

Deejaying is one of the most difficult things a person can do; it is also a lot of fun and should be experienced at least once by everybody to see if they could actually do it. If you want to deejay professionally, you must practice everyday for several hours. Mixing a song is an art, there are some people who can paint a mix like Van Gogh. Picking out the song, matching the beats, and finding the breaks and thirty-twos is the main things a deejay looks at during a mix. I think that everyone should be able to deejay if they put their hearts to it, and try hard. There is not much talent involved; it is mostly skill that you have learned by practicing.

CHAPTER 6

Division / Classification

Division and classification go hand in hand. Division is similar to process analysis; in both types of analysis you take apart something to discuss it. When you classify, however, after you break your topic down into smaller parts, you then group them together according to their common or similar traits. In other words, when you classify, you bring things back together, categorizing them logically. You might decide to classify types of coaches you have had, for example. After recalling all of your coaches and considering their similarities and differences, you might then classify them into the following categories: "the helpful coaches," "the yellers," and "the winner take all" coaches.

Why Learn How to Write Division/Classification Essays?

Learning how to write an essay of division/classification will help you to become more logical and organized in your thinking. By analyzing a complex system and looking for logical, related divisions, you exercise a part of your intellect that you might later use in a number of different types of academic and business decisions.

Criteria for Writing Division/Classification Essays

1. State an overall purpose for your classification. If the topic is types of coaches, for example, what is the purpose of such a classification? Are you trying to help your younger sister learn about coaches before she starts a soccer season? Are you trying to learn from your coaches' personalities and attitudes and how these helped motivate your performance? Are you trying to entertain your reader with illustrations of coaches' eccentric behavior?

2. Divide your classification. Coaches can be classified into categories such as "coaches who just put in their time," "coaches who tried," and "coaches who really made a difference in my

life." These divisions can then become the basis for your body paragraphs. Be careful that you divide your topic into like things. For example, you wouldn't find "coaches who always helped me win" and "coaches who chewed tobacco" within the same classification system.

3. Use a logical arrangement for your divisions. You might want to save the best type of coach for last in your essay because many readers remember this part of an essay the most.

4. State your division/classification in a thesis statement such as the following: Soccer coaches fall into three basic categories: "the helpful coach," "the yeller," and "the winner takes all."

5. Determine that your classifications don't overlap. The same coach can't appear in two different categories. If this is the case, then you need to reexamine the criteria you have used.

6. Develop your classifications in body paragraphs using examples, descriptive details, and explanations. When you use examples, rely on both short and extended examples. You'll be drawing on your experiences with coaches to develop your ideas.

7. Use transitions to emphasize examples or features such as *for example, for instance, in fact, in other words, on the other hand, in contrast, to illustrate,* etc.

8. Balance your development so that each classification gets approximately one third of the essay.

Topic Suggestions for Division/Classification

Different approaches to building web pages

Bosses you have had

The three different types of effective employees

Different types of children's personalities

Different teaching styles

Different types of shoppers

Your three favorite types of movies

Different types of students according to where they sit in the classroom

Different types of students according to the cars they drive

Different types of students according to how they react to bad grades on exams

Reasons for attending school

Reasons for quitting school

Peer Evaluation Guide for Division/Classification Essays

1. Has the writer divided the topic into at least three parts?

2. Are the different classifications logically related?

3. Do any of the classifications overlap?

4. Does the writer use a thesis statement?

5. Does the writer use transitions to begin each body paragraph and within the body paragraphs?

6. Does the writer use examples both extended and short to develop the paragraphs?

7. Does the writer also use explanations and descriptive details in the body paragraphs?

8. What is the writer's purpose for writing on this topic?

9. Has the writer employed sentence variety?

10. Did the writer vary his or her words?

11. Did the writer check for correctness of grammar, punctuation, and spelling?

The Big Five Fears of Our Time

Stephanie Brush

In a recent survey, 1,000 Americans were asked to name the fear that torments them the most. They're listed here in no particular order-of-fearsomeness, but most everyone has a personal favorite on this list.

1. Fear of Gradual Hysteria

Gradual hysteria is what happens when you feel your life is completely out of control.

Many of us attempt to exert control by redecorating our homes, for example. We move a picture and find that there is a rectangular spot on the wall where the picture used to be. Then we move the TV stand and find that there are four identical indentations in the rug. Then we move the TV stand back and find that there are now eight identical indentations in the rug. Then someone starts drilling into the pavement outside the window, and the phone rings exactly once, and stops, and we run to answer it, and hear only a metallic click and start to scream, very quietly. We feel that God is talking to us. "Just try it," He is saying, "Just try and make something out of your life."

Gradual hysteria happens in this way to just about everybody. It is usually triggered by loud noises, helplessness, and cumulative stress, and yes, it has the power to destroy everything in its path. But you'd rather have that happening to you than to someone else, wouldn't you?

2. Fear of People Who Have Had Too Much Assertiveness Training

There was a movement back in the seventies in which thousands of ineffectual nebbishes decided that they were not standing firm where it counted in life, and they went out and shelled out $300 at adult-education classes around the country, so that they could Learn to Say No! To Get Their Needs Met! To Not Take a Lot of BS From the Guy at the Auto Body Shop!

They walk among us now, and the threat they pose is inestimable.

Have they become, in fact, "assertive" people? Let's be serious. Assertiveness comes from being *born* knowing you're going to get the goods in life, whatever they may be. You don't have to take *courses* in this stuff, okay? And the reason an assertiveness-trained nebbish is a dangerous commodity is that he suspects he is still a nebbish but he's not sure whether it shows or not. It *shows*, all right?

He starts to breathe heavily at the cleaners' because he's just found a spot on his jacket that wasn't there before, and now he is trying to remember his "lines" for the big confrontation to come.

Sometimes, Assertiveness-Trained Nebbishes get the heady feeling of "being honest" and "owning their feelings"—and they do embarrassing things like embrace you and say, "I hate your rug, but the honesty of this moment feels beautiful."

Whatever we do, it is essential for us to impress on our friends that we liked them better when they were obsequious, waffling little toadies. At least then we knew what we were dealing with. At least life had some kind of structure.

There is some work being done to "de-program" these people, sort of like former members of cults. But it is too soon to tell whether this technique is going to have any effect.

3. Insomnia: Fear of Consciousness

"Consciousness" is a state of awareness of all the realities of life. If we had to live in a state of total awareness all the time, if we had to dwell on realities like crime and war and what happens to the members of "Menudo" after they turn fifteen, then we should all surely become mad and highly depressed.

So sleep was invented to spare us from total consciousness. But the more we can't sleep, the more conscious—and therefore *anxious*—we become. The same scientists who have clocked things like REM cycles and muscle-activity cycles have also clocked pre-sleep anxiety cycles.

- Cycle I usually involves WORK ANXIETY. Did I remember to turn off my office light? Does my boss like me? Would my boss recognize me if he saw me in a small crowd?
- Cycle II involves CURRENT-EVENTS ANXIETY. Is there plutonium in my drinking water? Will the world be safe for my children? With street crime in the state it's in, would it be all right if I asked my dog to walk himself at night?
- Cycle III occurs when the mind drifts off to a netherworld of halfformed dreads and sinister potentialities. What if my family got sick and died? What if they were tied to a stake in the Amazon rain forest and eaten by termites? What if I were on a quiz show and had to know the Gross National Product of Burma?

Some of these fears, unfortunately, have more than a little merit (although for what it's worth, the GNP of Burma is 657,000 Bwenzii a year, and there are no termites in the Amazon rain forest. Then again, there's nothing to stop them from being flown in.)

It is estimated that over 45 percent of the population suffers from insomnia on any given night; which means that on any given night YOU ARE ALONE WITH 150 MILLION OTHER AMERICANS. So when you think about it, it would make sense if you were given these people's phone numbers, so you'd at least have someone to talk to. (And yet, paradoxically, if you called them, they would scream into the receiver, "What are you, *crazy*? It's *three o'clock in the morning*!" And they would call the police.)

4. Fear of Amnesia

There are really three varieties of amnesia we need to talk about here: "Random" amnesia strikes about 5 million Americans a year, including an undisclosed number of dental patients who "forget" to floss between meals, and a number of hotel guests who "forget" to return the towels, stationery, and light fixtures to the rooms where they found them. Also every year, twelve or thirteen natives of Florence, Oregon, fall victim to *group* amnesia and awaken and imagine themselves to be natives of Florence, Italy. They immediately start painting frescoes all over the sides of municipal buildings, and each year the frescoes have to be sandblasted off, at the expense of thousands to the taxpayers, since no one in Oregon is known to have any artistic talent.

By far the most virulent form of amnesia is SOAPSTAR amnesia, which occurs relentlessly in daytime television. Hardly a day goes by when someone on one of the major networks is not suffering from a complete memory loss—"*What do you mean 'Nicki Matuszak'? I've never heard of a 'Nicki Matuszak' in my life! I'm a beekeeper! Stay away from me!*"

These poor doomed sufferers are destined to wander around strange towns in brunette wigs and unattractive clothing, marry people they have never met before, and ignore the pleas of their husbands and wives on television ("Nicki! It's me, Stefano! I never meant to shoot you in the brain! Please come home!").

Naturally, if we watch a lot of daytime TV, we are afraid that this fate could befall us (although we secretly wonder how TV amnesiacs can use their American Express cards for months at a time, pay the finance charge, and still not have a clue to their identity).

5. Fear of Major Brain-Loss

Many people are afraid of appearing helpless, foolish, and "brainless." For example, of being in serious car crashes and becoming "vegetables." (Although if you get incinerated in a *plane* crash, you get to become a "mineral," which is probably much, much worse.)

A far greater threat than this, however, is that of having a song you really hate running through your head that you just can't get rid of. It certainly happens more frequently. No one ever has a song they like running through their head. Large numbers of college graduates still hear "Yummy, Yummy, Yummy," by the Ohio

Express, and some people have gone nearly insane with a continual rendition of "Hey! You! Get Offa My Cloud!" as performed by the Ray Conniff Singers.

Add to the dangers of brain-loss the persistent lure of religious cults, lurking tantalizingly with "all the answers" around every corner. Beyond even the Hare Krishnas and the Unification Church lies the "Pepsi Generation," a dangerous cult headed by singer LIONEL RICHIE. Instead of working regular hours and contributing to the Gross National Product, the Pepsi Generation spends hours taking dancing lessons and having their teeth professionally polished. They venerate organized volleyball and drive dune buggies to all their major appointments. Fortunately, they are closely watched and monitored by a number of federal agencies.

The Plot Against People

Russell Baker

WASHINGTON, JUNE 17—Inanimate objects are classified scientifically into three major categories—those that don't work, those that break down and those that get lost.

The goal of all inanimate objects is to resist man and ultimately to defeat him, and the three major classifications are based on the method each object uses to achieve its purpose. As a general rule, any object capable of breaking down at the moment when it is most needed will do so. The automobile is typical of the category.

With the cunning typical of its breed, the automobile never breaks down while entering a filling station with a large staff of idle mechanics. It waits until it reaches a downtown intersection in the middle of the rush hour, or until it is fully loaded with family and luggage on the Ohio turnpike.

Thus it creates maximum misery, inconvenience, frustration and irritability among its human cargo, thereby reducing its owner's life span.

Washing machines, garbage disposals, lawn mowers, light bulbs, automatic laundry dryers, water pipes, furnaces, electrical fuses, television tubes, hose nozzles, tape recorders, slide projectors—all are in league with the automobile to take their turn at breaking down whenever life threatens to flow smoothly for their human enemies.

Many inanimate objects, of course, find it extremely difficult to break down. Pliers, for example, and gloves and keys are almost totally incapable of breaking down. Therefore, they have had to evolve a different technique for resisting man.

They get lost. Science has still not solved the mystery of how they do it, and no man has ever caught one of them in the act of getting lost. The most plausible theory is that they have developed a secret method of locomotion which they are able to conceal the instant a human eye falls upon them.

It is not uncommon for a pair of pliers to climb all the way from the cellar to the attic in its single-minded determination to raise its owner's blood pressure. Keys have been known to burrow three feet under mattresses. Women's purses, despite their great weight, frequently travel through six or seven rooms to find hiding space under a couch.

Scientists have been struck by the fact that things that break down virtually never get lost, while things that get lost hardly ever break down.

A furnace, for example, will invariably break down at the depth of the first winter cold wave, but it will never get lost. A woman's purse, which after all does have some inherent capacity for breaking down, hardly ever does; it almost invariably chooses to get lost.

Some persons believe this constitutes evidence that inanimate objects are not entirely hostile to man, and that a negotiated peace is possible. After all, they point out, a furnace could infuriate a man even more thoroughly by getting lost than by breaking down, just as a glove could upset him far more by breaking down than by getting lost.

Not everyone agrees, however, that this indicates a conciliatory attitude among inanimate objects. Many say it merely proves that furnaces, gloves and pliers are incredibly stupid.

The third class of objects—those that don't work—is the most curious of all. These include such objects as barometers, car clocks, cigarette lighters, flashlights and toy-train locomotives. It is inaccurate, of course, to say that they never work. They work once, usually for the first few hours after being brought home, and then quit. Thereafter, they never work again.

In fact, it is widely assumed that they are built for the purpose of not working. Some people have reached advanced ages without ever seeing some of these objects—barometers, for example—in working order.

Science is utterly baffled by the entire category. There are many theories about it. The most interesting holds that the things that don't work have attained the highest state possible for an inanimate object, the state to which things that break down and things that get lost can still only aspire.

They have truly defeated man by conditioning him never to expect anything of them, and in return they have given man the only peace he receives from inanimate society. He does not expect his barometer to work, his electric locomotive to run, his cigarette lighter to light or his flashlight to illuminate, and when they don't it does not raise his blood pressure.

He cannot attain that peace with furnaces and keys, and cars and women's purses as long as he demands that they work for their keep.

What Are Friends For?

Marion Winik

I was thinking about how everybody can't be everything to each other, but some people can be something to each other, thank God, from the ones whose shoulder you cry on to the ones whose half-slips you borrow to the nameless ones you chat with in the grocery line.

Buddies, for example, are the workhorses of the friendship world, the people out there on the front lines, defending you from loneliness and boredom. They call you up, they listen to your complaints, they celebrate your successes and curse your misfortunes, and you do the same for them in return. They hold out through innumerable crises before concluding that the person you're dating is no good, and even then understand if you ignore their good counsel. They accompany you to a movie with subtitles or to see the diving pig at Aquarena Springs. They feed your cat when you are out of town and pick you up from the airport when you get back. They come over to help you decide what to wear on a date. Even if it is with that creep.

What about family members? Most of them are people you just got stuck with, and though you love them, you may not have very much in common. But there is that rare exception, the Relative Friend. It is your cousin, your brother, maybe even your aunt. The two of you share the same views of the other family members. Meg never should have divorced Martin. He was the best thing that ever happened to her. You can confirm each other's memories of things that happened a long time ago. Don't you remember when Uncle Hank and Daddy had that awful fight in the middle of Thanksgiving dinner? Grandma always hated Grandpa's stamp collection; she probably left the windows open during the hurricane on purpose.

While so many family relationships are tinged with guilt and obligation, a relationship with a Relative Friend is relatively worry-free. You don't even have to hide your vices from this delightful person. When you slip out Aunt Joan's back door for a cigarette, she is already there.

Then there is that special guy at work. Like all the other people at the job site, at first he's just part of the scenery. But gradually he starts to stand out from the crowd. Your friendship is cemented by jokes about coworkers and thoughtful favors around the office. Did you see Ryan's hair? Want half my bagel? Soon you know the names of his turtles, what he did last Friday night, exactly which model CD player he wants for his birthday. His handwriting is as familiar to you as your own.

Though you invite each other to parties, you somehow don't quite fit into each other's outside lives. For this reason, the friendship may not survive a job change. Company gossip, once an infallible source of entertainment, soon awkwardly accentuates the distance between you. But wait. Like School Friends, Work Friends share certain memories which acquire a nostalgic glow after about a decade.

A Faraway Friend is someone you grew up with or went to school with or lived in the same town as until one of you moved away. Without a Faraway Friend, you would never get any mail addressed in handwriting. A Faraway Friend calls late at night, invites you to her wedding, always says she is coming to visit but rarely shows up. An actual visit from a Faraway Friend is a cause for celebration and binges of all kinds. Cigarettes, Chips Ahoy, bottles of tequila.

Faraway Friends go through phases of intense communication then may be out of touch for many months. Either way, the connection is always there. A conversation with your Faraway Friend always helps to put your life in perspective: When you feel you've hit a dead end, come to a confusing fork in the road, or gotten lost in some subdivision of your life, the advice of the Faraway Friend—who has the big picture, who is so well acquainted with the route that brought you to this place—is indispensable.

Another useful function of the Faraway Friend is to help you remember things from a long time ago, like the name of your seventh-grade history teacher, what was in that really good stir-fry, or what happened that night on the boat with the guys from Florida.

Ah, the Former Friend. A sad thing. At best a wistful memory, at worst a dangerous enemy who is in possession of many of your deepest secrets. But what was it that drove you apart? A misunderstanding, a betrayed confidence, an unrepaid loan, an ill-conceived flirtation. A poor choice of spouse can do in a friendship just like that. Going into business together can be a serious mistake. Time, money, distance, cult religions: all noted friendship killers. You quit doing drugs, you're not such good friends with your dealer anymore.

And lest we forget, there are the Friends You Love to Hate. They call at inopportune times. They say stupid things. They butt in, they boss you around, they embarrass you in public. They invite themselves over. They take advantage. You've done the best you can, but they need professional help. On top of all this, they love you to death and are convinced they're your best friend on the planet.

So why do you continue to be involved with these people? Why do you tolerate them? On the contrary, the real question is, What would you do without them? Without Friends You Love to Hate, there would be nothing to talk about with your other friends. Their problems and their irritating stunts provide a reliable source of conversation for everyone they know. What's more, Friends You Love to Hate make you feel good about yourself, since you are obviously in so much better shape than they are. No matter what these people do, you will never get rid of them. As much as they need you, you need them too.

At the other end of the spectrum are Hero Friends. These people are better than the rest of us, that's all there is to it. Their career is something you wanted to be when you grew up—painter, forest ranger, tireless doer of good. They have beautiful homes filled with special handmade things presented to them by villagers in the remote areas they have visited in their extensive travels. Yet they are modest. They never gossip. They are always helping others, especially those who have suffered a death in the family or an illness. You would think people like this would just make you sick, but somehow they don't.

A New Friend is a tonic unlike any other. Say you meet her at a party. In your bowling league. At a Japanese conversation class, perhaps. Wherever, whenever, there's that spark of recognition. The first time you talk, you can't believe how much you have in common. Suddenly, your life story is interesting again, your insights fresh, your opinion valued. Your various shortcomings are as yet completely invisible.

It's almost like falling in love.

Predictable Crises of Adulthood

Gail Sheehy

We are not unlike a particularly hardy crustacean. The lobster grows by developing and shedding a series of hard, protective shells. Each time it expands from within, the confining shell must be sloughed off. It is left exposed and vulnerable until, in time, a new covering grows to replace the old.

With each passage from one stage of human growth to the next we, too, must shed a protective structure. We are left exposed and vulnerable—but also yeasty and embryonic again, capable of stretching in ways we hadn't known before. These sheddings may take several years or more. Coming out of each passage, though, we enter a longer and more stable period in which we can expect relative tranquillity and a sense of equilibrium regained.

As we shall see, each person engages the steps of development in his or her own characteristic *step-style*. Some people never complete the whole sequence. And none of us "solves" with one step—by jumping out of the parental home into a job or marriage, for example—the problems in separating from the caregivers of childhood. Nor do we "achieve" autonomy once and for all by converting our dreams into concrete goals, even when we attain those goals. The central issues or tasks of one period are never fully completed, tied up, and cast aside. But when they lose their primacy and the current life structure has served its purpose, we are ready to move on to the next period.

Can one catch up? What might look to others like listlessness, contrariness, a maddening refusal to face up to an obvious task may be a person's own unique detour that will bring him out later on the other side. Developmental gains won can later be lost—and rewon. It's plausible, though it can't be proven, that the mastery of one set of tasks fortifies us for the next period and the next set of challenges. But its important not to think too mechanistically. Machines work by units. The bureaucracy (supposedly) works step by step. Human beings, thank God, have an individual inner dynamic that can never be precisely coded.

Although I have indicated the ages when Americans are likely to go through each stage, and the differences between men and women where they are striking, do not take the ages too seriously. The stages are the thing, and most particularly the sequence.

Here is the briefest outline of the developmental ladder.

Pulling Up Roots

Before 18, the motto is loud and clear: "I have to get away from my parents." But the words are seldom connected to action. Generally still safely part of our families, even if away at school, we feel our autonomy to be subject to erosion from moment to moment.

After 18, we begin Pulling Up Roots in earnest. College, military service, and short-term travels are all customary vehicles our society provides for the first round trips between family and a base of ones own. In the attempt to separate our view of the world from our family's view, despite vigorous protestations to the contrary—"I know exactly what I want!"—we cast about for any beliefs we can call our own. And in the process of testing those beliefs we are often drawn to fads, preferably those most mysterious and inaccessible to our parents.

Whatever tentative memberships we try out in the world, the fear haunts us that we are really kids who cannot take care of ourselves. We cover that fear with acts of defiance and mimicked confidence. For allies to replace our parents, we turn to our contemporaries. They become conspirators. So long as their perspective meshes with our own, they are able to substitute for the sanctuary of the family. But that doesn't last very long. And the instant they diverge from the shaky ideals of "our group," they are seen as betrayers. Rebounds to the family are common between the ages of 18 and 22.

The tasks of this passage are to locate ourselves in a peer group role, a sex role, an anticipated occupation, an ideology or world view. As a result, we gather the impetus to leave home physically and the identity to *begin* leaving home emotionally.

Even as one part of us seeks to be an individual, another part longs to restore the safety and comfort of merging with another. Thus one of the most popular myths of this passage is: We can piggyback our development by attaching to a Stronger One. But people who marry during this time often prolong financial and emotional ties to the family and relatives that impede them from becoming self-sufficient.

A stormy passage through the Pulling Up Roots years will probably facilitate the normal progression of the adult life cycle. If one doesn't have an identity crisis at this point, it will erupt during a later transition, when the penalties may be harder to bear.

The Trying Twenties

The Trying Twenties confront us with the question of how to take hold in the adult world. Our focus shifts from the interior turmoils of late adolescence—"Who am I?" "What is truth?"—and we become almost totally preoccupied with working out the externals. "How do I put my aspirations into effect?" "What is the best way to start?" "Where do I go?" "Who can help me?" "How did you do it?"

In this period, which is longer and more stable compared with the passage that leads to it, the tasks are as enormous as they are exhilarating: To shape a Dream, that vision of ourselves which will generate energy, aliveness, and hope. To prepare for a lifework, to find a mentor if possible. And to form the capacity for intimacy, without losing in the process whatever consistency of self we have thus far mustered. The first test structure must be erected around the life we choose to try.

Doing what we "should" is the most pervasive theme of the twenties. The "shoulds" are largely defined by family models, the press of the culture, or the prejudices of our peers. If the prevailing cultural instructions are that one should get married and settle down behind one's own door, a nuclear family is born. If instead the peers insist that one should do one's own thing, the 25-year-old is likely to harness himself onto a Harley-Davidson and burn up Route 66 in the commitment to have no commitments.

One of the terrifying aspects of the twenties is the inner conviction that the choices we make are irrevocable. It is largely a false fear. Change is quite possible, and some alteration of our original choices is probably inevitable.

Two impulses, as always, are at work. One is to build a firm, safe structure for the future by making strong commitments, to "be set." Yet people who slip into a ready-made form without much self-examination are likely to find themselves *locked in.*

The other urge is to explore and experiment, keeping any structure tentative and therefore easily reversible. Taken to the extreme, these are people who skip from one trial job and one limited personal encounter to another, spending their twenties in the *transient* state.

Although the choices of our twenties are not irrevocable, they do set in motion a Life Pattern. Some of us follow the locked-in pattern, others the transient pattern, the wunderkind pattern, the caregiver pattern, and there are a number of others. Such patterns strongly influence the particular questions raised for each person during each passage. . . .

Buoyed by powerful illusions and belief in the power of the will, we commonly insist in our twenties that what we have chosen to do is the one true course in life. Our backs go up at the merest hint that we are like our parents, that two decades of parental training might be reflected in our current actions and attitudes.

"Not me," is the motto, "I'm different."

Catch-30

Impatient with devoting ourselves to the "shoulds," a new vitality springs from within as we approach 30. Men and women alike speak of feeling too narrow and restricted. They blame all sorts of things, but what the restrictions boil down to are the outgrowth of career and personal choices of the twenties. They may have been choices perfectly suited to that stage. But now the fit feels different. Some inner aspect that was left out is striving to be taken into account. Important new choices must be made, and commitments altered or deepened. The work involves great change, turmoil, and often crisis—a simultaneous feeling of rock bottom and the urge to bust out.

One common response is the tearing up of the life we spent most of our twenties putting together. It may mean striking out on a secondary road toward a new vision or converting a dream of "running for president" into a more realistic goal. The single person feels a push to find a partner. The woman who was previously content at home with children chafes to venture into the world. The childless couple reconsiders children. And almost everyone who is married, especially those married for seven years, feels a discontent.

If the discontent doesn't lead to a divorce, it will, or should, call for a serious review of the marriage and of each partner's aspirations in their Catch-30 condition. The gist of that condition was expressed by a 29-year-old associate with a Wall Street law firm:

> *"I'm considering leaving the firm. I've been there four years now; I'm getting good feedback, but I have no clients of my own. I feel weak. If I wait much longer, it will be too late, too close to that fateful time of decision on whether or not to become a partner. I'm success-oriented. But the concept of being 55 years old and stuck in a monotonous job drives me wild. It drives me crazy now, just a little bit. I'd say that 85 percent of the time I thoroughly enjoy my work. But when I get a screwball case, I come away from court saying, 'What am I doing here?' It's a visceral reaction that I'm wasting my time. I'm trying to find some way to make a social contribution or a slot in city government. I keep saying, 'There's something more.'"*

Besides the push to broaden himself professionally, there is a wish to expand his personal life. He wants two or three more children. "The concept of a home has become very meaningful to me, a place to get away from troubles and relax. I love my son in a way I could not have anticipated. I never could live alone."

Consumed with the work of making his own critical life-steering decisions, he demonstrates the essential shift at this age: an absolute requirement to be more self-concerned. The self has new value now that his competency has been proved.

His wife is struggling with her own age-30 priorities. She wants to go to law school, but he wants more children. If she is going to stay home, she wants him to make more time for the family instead of taking on even wider professional commitments. His view of the bind, of what he would most like from his wife, is this:

> *"I'd like not to be bothered. It sounds cruel, but I'd like not to have to worry about what she's going to do next week. Which is why I've told her several times that I think she should do something. Go back to school and get a degree in social work or geography or whatever. Hopefully that would fulfill her, and then I wouldn't have to worry about her line of problems. I want her to be decisive about herself."*

The trouble with his advice to his wife is that it comes out of concern with *his* convenience, rather than with *her* development. She quickly picks up on this lack of goodwill: He is trying to dispose of her. At the same time, he refuses her the same latitude to be "selfish" in making an independent decision to broaden her own horizons. Both perceive a lack of mutuality. And that is what Catch-30 is all about for the couple.

Rooting and Extending

Life becomes less provisional, more rational and orderly in the early thirties. We begin to settle down in the full sense. Most of us begin putting down roots and sending out new shoots. People buy houses and become very earnest about climbing career ladders. Men in particular concern themselves with "making it." Satisfaction with marriage generally goes downhill in the thirties (for those who have remained together) compared with the highly valued, vision-supporting marriage of the twenties. This coincides with the couple's reduced social life outside the family and the in-turned focus on raising their children.

The Deadline Decade

In the middle of the thirties we come upon a crossroads. We have reached the halfway mark. Yet even as we are reaching our prime, we begin to see there is a place where it finishes. Time starts to squeeze.

The loss of youth, the faltering of physical powers we have always taken for granted, the fading purpose of stereotyped roles by which we have thus far identified ourselves, the spiritual dilemma of having no absolute answers—any or all of these shocks can give this passage the character of crisis. Such thoughts usher in a decade between 35 and 45 that can be called the Deadline Decade. It is a time of both danger and opportunity. All of us have the chance to rework the narrow identity by which we defined ourselves in the first half of life. And those of us who make the most of the opportunity will have a full-out authenticity crisis.

To come through this authenticity crisis, we must reexamine our purposes and reevaluate how to spend our resources from now on. "Why am I doing all this? What do I really believe in?" No matter what we have been doing, there will be parts of ourselves that have been suppressed and now need to find expression. "Bad" feelings will demand acknowledgment along with the good.

It is frightening to step off onto the treacherous footbridge leading to the second half of life. We can't take everything with us on this journey through uncertainty. Along the way, we discover that we are alone. We no longer have to ask permission because we are the providers of our own safety. We must learn to give ourselves permission. We stumble upon feminine or masculine aspects of our natures that up to this time have usually been masked. There is grieving to be done because an old self is dying. By taking in our suppressed and even our unwanted parts, we prepare at the gut level for the reintegration of an identity that is ours and ours alone—not some artificial form put together to please the culture or our mates. It is a dark passage at the beginning. But by disassembling ourselves, we can glimpse the light and gather our parts into a renewal.

Women sense this inner crossroads earlier than men do. The time pinch often prompts a woman to stop and take an all-points survey at age 35. Whatever options she has already played out, she feels a "my last chance" urgency to review those options she has set aside and those that aging and biology will close off in the *now foreseeable* future. For all her qualms and confusion about where to start looking for a new future, she usually enjoys an exhilaration of release. Assertiveness begins rising. There are so many firsts ahead.

Men, too, feel the time push in the mid-thirties. Most men respond by pressing down harder on the career acceleration. It's "my last chance" to pull away from the pack. It is no longer enough to be the loyal junior executive, the promising young novelist, the lawyer who does a little *pro bono* work on the side. He wants now to become part of top management, to be recognized as an established writer, or an active politician with his own legislative program. With some chagrin, he discovers that he has been too anxious to please and too vulnerable to criticism. He wants to put together his own ship.

During this period of intense concentration on external advancement, it is common for men to be unaware of the more difficult, gut issues that are propelling them forward. The survey that was neglected at 35 becomes a crucible at 40. Whatever rung of achievement he has reached, the man of 40 usually feels stale, restless, burdened, and unappreciated. He worries about his health. He wonders, "Is this all there is?" He may make a series of departures from well established lifelong base lines, including marriage. More and more men are seeking second careers in midlife. Some become self-destructive. And many men in their forties experience a major shift of emphasis away from pouring all their energies into their own advancement. A more tender, feeling side comes into play. They become interested in developing an ethical self.

Renewal or Resignation

Somewhere in the mid-forties, equilibrium is regained. A new stability is achieved, which may be more or less satisfying.

If one has refused to budge through the midlife transition, the sense of staleness will calcify into resignation. One by one, the safety and supports will be withdrawn from the person who is standing still. Parents will become children; children will become strangers; a mate will grow away or go away; the career will become just a job—and each of these events will be felt as an abandonment. The crisis will probably emerge again around 50. And although its wallop will be greater, the jolt may be just what is needed to prod the resigned middle-ager toward seeking revitalization.

On the Other Hand . . .

If we have confronted ourselves in the middle passage and found a renewal of purpose around which we are eager to build a more authentic life structure, these may well be the best years. Personal happiness takes a sharp turn upward for partners who can now accept the fact: "I cannot expect *anyone* to fully understand me." Parents can be forgiven for the burdens of our childhood. Children can be let go without leaving us in collapsed silence. At 50, there is a new warmth and mellowing. Friends become more important than ever, but so does privacy. Since it is so often proclaimed by people past midlife, the motto of this stage might be "No more bullshit."

DeVry Students and Financial Aid

Student

We routinely accept that DeVry students are *serious about success*. They vary in their diligence; however, student financial aid demands their attention. Most of the institute's patrons regularly receive some form of fiduciary assistance that allows them to finance their education. Their management of the associated responsibility categorizes them as financial aid angels, financial aid users, and financial aid nightmares.

A select few of the student body are angels in the eyes of the Financial Aid Office. Scholarship winners and independently wealthy students whose files are thin and free of excess paperwork require little effort by advisors. Advisors look fondly even upon students who require loans and grants when the students actually read directions and complete their paperwork flawlessly every time.

The vast majority of DeVry students are financial aid users. Financial aid is important to their educational careers but occupies only a minuscule portion of their thoughts. Users are the students who bring their partially completed paperwork into the Financial Aid Office and say, "I have a few questions." Although an advisor may occasionally need to call the student or add a name to the Call List, the user responds to the requests made of him and his problems are quickly resolved. Even students whose files are complex, such as those who attended previous colleges, defaulted on but paid back a prior student loan, or left school for a term are users because their financial aid processing generally follows a well-defined path that is quickly traversed. Delays or mistakes with financial aid administration occasionally frustrate them, but they recognize these obstacles as part of life, and move on without any genuine contempt for the financial aid office.

Angels and users are the majority at DeVry, and the administration designs the processes of financial aid primarily for them. But there are a few students who add dark flair to financial assistance.

The nightmare is the student whose file is considered to be possessed by financial aid demons. Their contact logs overflow from the many times they have entered the financial aid office with complex problems they have created for themselves—seemingly on purpose, for these problems are not the natural results of daily events. Their six-inch-thick files bulge out of the file cabinets as evidence of the times they have abandoned their classes only to enroll again. They ignore the letters, calls, and signs that demand their attention to financial aid, then enter the Financial Aid Office and ask, "Why don't I have any money this term?" They take advantage of DeVry's lenient deadline policies, then return their required documents months late while still expecting immediate action. They apply for federal assistance, and when an advisor requests their absent tax information, they don puzzled looks and declare, "I didn't know I had to file taxes last year." They request that thousands of dollars be loaned to them and sign their promissory notes, only to exclaim in surprise months later, "I have to pay that money back?" Some even come to our school from foreign lands; they practice their limited grasp of our language as the painful sounds of the last crash of the INS, IRS, and Department of Education still echo through their advisors' memories. Financial aid workers throw the nightmares' names about as insults and expletives as their stories become the urban legends of financial aid.

Every day, hordes of students parade through the financial aid office. As financial aid angels, financial aid users, and financial aid nightmares, they add variety and challenge to the otherwise redundant and tedious work of managing student financial assistance.

Spare Time at DeVry

Student

Break time is really when students exercise their options, rather than simply a time to relax from a typical day's demands. Really anywhere, but particularly at DeVry, students or employees have a number of choices for break, and what they do says a lot about themselves. Generally, one finds people either sleeping, relaxing/sleeping, studying, playing, or feeding their addictions.

It's not a very big group of people, but the "nodders and dozers" are unique, so I've got to include them. Occasionally, we see them strewn about the floor like so much debris, or on a makeshift cot, or even slumped over in one of our Hezbollah-designed chairs. Oddly, these are not the most agreeable of people, but that may be because they only talk after you trip over them. Maybe they've been deprived of sleep recently, or perhaps they would just as soon sleep as to do anything productive or enjoyable—that's not for me to say, but I know as long as I don't bother them, they won't bother me.

The polar opposites of the sleepers are, horror of horrors, the studiers. These academic warriors not only use their time, but they use it judiciously. What possesses them to spend what little time they can enjoy or at least waste, doing work is beyond my capacity to understand. Whenever I walk by one of these heathens, I am almost overcome by the need to spread the gospel of good news: "Gather ye rosebuds while ye may," man, join the fold.

Thus far, what we have dealt with are the anti-social types, but I know of at least two other groups (not necessarily only two others) which could really stand examination. Now, these two related groups don't actually mix much, mostly because of the nature of their addiction, so we can deal with them separately. I'm talking about the addicts and the free-recreators—two groups that probably form the majority of DeVry students.

The arcade is packed at break time almost every day with people who are, whether quickly or slowly, surely relieved of their pocket money. Really, it costs

149

enough, don't you think, to come to DeVry without being hypnotized and pick-pock-eted daily by school sanctioned no-armed bandits? I'm trying to cut back myself, but this school doesn't make it easy; and come to think of it, why should it?

Smokers have nothing on the gamers, even though they don't overtly stand there pumping quarters into a mindless machine of evil—they just spend it else-where. The tobacco industry is some kind of racket, I've got to tell you, because not only do they addict you endlessly to this thing, they make sure it kills you s-l-o-w-l-y, so as to milk you for everything they can, no doubt. (Who invented these things anyway, Satan?) But as long as they're smoking, smokers are *very* easy to get along with, even if they make an ashtray of whatever is handy, like your WHOLE FREAKING PORCH.

I guess what I've proved is that we can be defined by our free time, and our free time is defined by our problems, so we can be defined in part by our problems—a flawless syllogism. Furthermore, we all have problems, so at least we must all have free time. I can only hope this has been educational, and in closing, please get help!

CHAPTER 7

Comparison / Contrast

A comparison-contrast reveals similarities and differences between two things. You can compare two people, two places, two activities, two jobs, two colleges, etc. You should pick two topics which interest you and about which you have adequate information.

Why Learn How to Write a Comparison-Contrast Essay?

Writing in other college classes could require you to compare and contrast. For example, you might have to write such a paper in history, comparing two generals' strategies for fighting a battle, the ways in which two countries were affected by a war, or the ways in which two political candidates campaigned for office. In a computer class, you might have to compare two types of software. Later on when you finish undergraduate school and enter the business world, your division could ask you to compare and contrast two operating systems or two types of computers to recommend one for purchase. Learning how to write essays of comparison and contrast will be helpful to you in many writing situations.

Criteria for Writing Comparison-Contrast Essays

1. Pick two comparable topics. You need to compare two things which are similar yet possess dissimilarities. For example, although a lawn mower and a computer are both pieces of equipment, they could not be logically compared. However, you could compare the advantages and disadvantages of ink-jet printers versus laser printers, or the level of violence depicted in movies of the 90s versus movies of the 70s. Write a thesis sentence that presents these two topics, the criteria by which you will compare and contrast them (see item 2 below), and how you will present the comparison-contrast (item 4). Use this structure implied in your thesis sentence to organize your body paragraphs.

2. Choose suitable criteria for your comparison-contrast that pertain to both topics.

For example, let's say you choose to compare your high school education with your college education. These are easily comparable topics that have both similarities and differences. You could compare any number of criteria such as teachers, course offerings, classrooms, students, testing methods, discipline, etc.

3. Limit the number of criteria for comparison. In other words, determined by the length of the assignment, such as an essay of 750 words, you should probably limit yourself to three criteria. For example, from the criteria listed above in item 2, choose the three that are the strongest and that you have the most to say about. Let's say that you choose to compare high school education with college education based on teachers, course offerings, and students. These three are your criteria for comparison-contrast.

4. Decide on a logical method of organization. You can organize either *topic to topic* or *point to point*. In *topic to topic* organization, you analyze one topic entirely before you analyze the second topic. Following is a typical *topic to topic* outline:

    I. High school
       A. Teachers
       B. Course offerings
       C. Students
    II. College
       A. Teachers
       B. Course offerings
       C. Students

In the *point to point* method of organization, you discuss one topic and then immediately compare it to the second topic, as shown in the following:

    I. Teachers
       A. High school
       B. College
    II. Course offerings
       A. High school
       B. College
    III. Students
       A. High school
       B. College

5. Use transitional words or phrases that suggest comparison-contrast, such as *likewise, the same as, too, also, similarly, but, yet, thus, however, on the other hand, on the contrary, in contrast, nevertheless, the opposite of,* etc.

6. Assure a balanced comparison-contrast by devoting 50 percent of the essay to one topic and 50 percent of the essay to the second topic.

7. Draw a logical conclusion based on the facts you compared and contrasted. For example, you could say that college is giving you a better education than high school gave you because of the teachers, the classrooms, and the students—but only if your essay's development has proven this.

Topic Suggestions

The school you currently attend vs. another college or university you've attended

Compact discs vs. vinyl

Liberal arts vs. a technical education

Two movies by your favorite director

Two television sitcoms

High school teachers vs. college professors

PCs vs. Macs

Two restaurants

Your family vs. another family

Being married with being single

Your two best friends

Two cities in which you've lived

Two countries you've lived in or visited

Your new girlfriend vs. your old girlfriend

How your parents raised you versus how you're raising your children

Peer Evaluation Guide for Comparison-Contrast Essays

1. Does the writer use a thesis statement in the introduction?

2. Is the introduction an attention getter?

3. Is the essay organized either topic to topic or point to point?

4. Has the writer used good, logical criteria for the comparison?

5. Is there logic to the placement of the criteria?

6. Does the student employ transitions?

7. How has the writer developed the body paragraphs? Does the writer use example, description, analysis, etc?

8. Does the conclusion seem to be based on the comparison?

9. Is the essay free of grammar, punctuation and spelling errors?

10. Does the writer sustain reader interest throughout the essay?

Neat People vs. Sloppy People

Susan Britt

I've finally figured out the difference between neat people and sloppy people. The distinction is, as always, moral. Neat people are lazier and meaner than sloppy people.

Sloppy people, you see, are not really sloppy. Their sloppiness is merely the unfortunate consequence of their extreme moral rectitude. Sloppy people carry in their mind's eye a heavenly vision, a precise plan, that is so stupendous, so perfect, it can't be achieved in this world or the next.

Sloppy people live in Never-Never-Land. Someday is their metier. Someday they are planning to alphabetize all their books and set up home catalogues. Someday they will go through their wardrobes and mark certain items for tentative mending and certain items for passing on to relatives of similar shape and size. Someday sloppy people will make family scrapbooks into which they will put newspaper clippings, postcards, locks of hair, and the dried corsage from their senior prom. Someday they will file everything on the surface of their desks, including the cash receipts from coffee purchases at the snack shop. Someday they will sit down and read all the back issues of *The New Yorker*.

For all these noble reasons and more, sloppy people never get neat. They aim too high and wide. They save everything, planning someday to file, order, and straighten out the world. But while these ambitious plans take clearer and clearer shape in their heads, the books spill from the shelves onto the floor, the clothes pile up in the hamper and closet, the family mementos accumulate in every drawer, the surface of the desk is buried under mounds of paper, and the unread magazines threaten to reach the ceiling.

Sloppy people can't bear to part with anything. They give loving attention to every detail. When sloppy people say they're going to tackle the surface of the desk, they really mean it. Not a paper will go unturned; not a rubber band will go unboxed. Four hours or two weeks into the excavation, the desk looks exactly the

154

same, primarily because the sloppy person is meticulously creating new piles of papers with new headings and scrupulously stopping to read all the old book catalogues before he throws them away. A neat person would just bulldoze the desk.

Neat people are bums and clods at heart. They have cavalier attitudes toward possessions, including family heirlooms. Everything is just another dust-catcher to them. If anything collects dust, it's got to go and that's that. Neat people will toy with the idea of throwing the children out of the house just to cut down the clutter.

Neat people don't care about process. They like results. What they want to do is get the whole thing over with so they can sit down and watch the rasslin' on TV. Neat people operate on two unvarying principles: Never handle any item twice, and throw everything away.

The only thing messy in a neat person's house is the trash can. The minute something comes to a neat person's hand, he will look at it, try to decide if it has immediate use and, finding none, throw it in the trash.

Neat people are especially vicious with mail. They never go through their mail unless they are standing directly over a trash can. If the trash can is beside the mailbox, even better. All ads, catalogues, pleas for charitable contributions, church bulletins, and money-saving coupons go straight into the trash can without being opened. All letters from home, postcards from Europe, bills and paychecks are opened, immediately responded to, then dropped in the trash can. Neat people keep their receipts only for tax purposes. That's it. No sentimental salvaging of birthday cards or the last letter a dying relative ever wrote. Into the trash it goes.

Neat people place neatness above everything, even economics. They are incredibly wasteful. Neat people throw away several toys every time they walk through the den. I knew a neat person once who threw away a perfectly good dish drainer because it had mold on it. The drainer was too much trouble to wash. And neat people sell their furniture when they move. They will sell a La-Z-Boy recliner while you are reclining in it.

Neat people are no good to borrow from. Neat people buy everything in expensive little single portions. They get their flour and sugar in two-pound bags. They wouldn't consider clipping a coupon, saving a leftover, reusing plastic nondairy whipped cream containers, or rinsing off tin foil and draping it over the unmoldy dish drainer. You can never borrow a neat person's newspaper to see what's playing at the movies. Neat people have the paper all wadded up and in the trash by 7:05 A.M.

Neat people cut a clean swath through the organic as well as the inorganic world. People, animals, and things are all one to them. They are so insensitive. After they've finished with the pantry, the medicine cabinet, and the attic, they will throw out the red geranium (too many leaves), sell the dog (too many fleas), and send the children off to boarding school (too many scuff marks on the hardwood floors).

Grant and Lee:
A Study in Contrasts

Bruce Catton

When Ulysses S. Grant and Robert E. Lee met in the parlor of a modest house at Appomattox Court House, Virginia, on April 9, 1865, to work out the terms for the surrender of Lee's Army of Northern Virginia, a great chapter in American life came to a close, and a great new chapter began.

These men were bringing the Civil War to its virtual finish. To be sure, other armies had yet to surrender, and for a few days the fugitive Confederate government would struggle desperately and vainly, trying to find some way to go on living now that its chief support was gone. But in effect it was all over when Grant and Lee signed the papers. And the little room where they wrote out the terms was the scene of one of the poignant, dramatic contrasts in American history.

They were two strong men, these oddly different generals, and they represented the strengths of two conflicting currents that, through them, had come into final collision.

Back of Robert E. Lee was the notion that the old aristocratic concept might somehow survive and be dominant in American life.

Lee was tidewater Virginia, and in his background were family, culture, and tradition . . . the age of chivalry transplanted to a New World which was making its own legends and its own myths. He embodied a way of life that had come down through the age of knighthood and the English country squire. America was a land that was beginning all over again, dedicated to nothing much more complicated than the rather hazy belief that all men had equal rights and should have an equal chance in the world. In such a land Lee stood for the feeling that it was somehow of advantage to human society to have a pronounced inequality in the social structure. There should be a leisure class, backed by ownership of land; in turn, society itself should be keyed to the land as the chief source of wealth and influence.

It would bring forth (according to this ideal) a class of men with a strong sense of obligation to the community; men who lived not to gain advantage for themselves, but to meet the solemn obligations which had been laid on them by the very fact that they were privileged. From them the country would get its leadership; to them it could look for the higher values—of thought, of conduct, of personal deportment—to give it strength and virtue.

Lee embodied the noblest elements of this aristocratic ideal. Through him, the landed nobility justified itself. For four years, the Southern states had fought a desperate war to uphold the ideals for which Lee stood. In the end, it almost seemed as if the Confederacy fought for Lee; as if he himself was the Confederacy . . . the best thing that the way of life for which the Confederacy stood could ever have to offer. He had passed into legend before Appomattox. Thousands of tired, under-fed, poorly clothed Confederate soldiers, long since past the simple enthusiasm of the early days of the struggle, somehow considered Lee the symbol of everything for which they had been willing to die. But they could not quite put this feeling into words. If the Lost Cause, sanctified by so much heroism and so many deaths, had a living justification, its justification was General Lee.

Grant, the son of a tanner on the Western frontier, was everything Lee was not. He had come up the hard way and embodied nothing in particular except the eternal toughness and sinewy fiber of the men who grew up beyond the mountains. He was one of a body of men who owed reverence and obeisance to no one, who were self-reliant to a fault, who cared hardly anything for the past but who had a sharp eye for the future.

These frontier men were the precise opposites of the tidewater aristocrats. Back of them, in the great surge that had taken people over the Alleghenies and into the opening Western country, there was a deep, implicit dissatisfaction with a past that had settled into grooves. They stood for democracy, not from any reasoned conclusion about the proper ordering of human society, but simply because they had grown up in the middle of democracy and knew how it worked. Their society might have privileges, but they would be privileges each man had won for himself. Forms and patterns meant nothing. No man was born to anything, except perhaps to a chance to show how far he could rise. Life was competition.

Yet along with this feeling had come a deep sense of belonging to a national community. The Westerner who developed a farm, opened a shop, or set up in business as a trader, could hope to prosper only as his won community prospered—and his community ran from the Atlantic to the Pacific and from Canada down to Mexico. If the land was settled, with towns and highways and accessible markets, he could better himself. He saw his fate in terms of the nation's own destiny. As its horizons expanded, so did his. He had, in other words, an acute dollars-and-cents stake in the continued growth and development of his country.

And that, perhaps, is where the contrast between Grant and Lee becomes most striking. The Virginia aristocrat, inevitably, saw himself in relation to his own region. He lived in a static society which could endure almost anything except change. Instinctively, his first loyalty would go to the locality in which that society existed. He would fight to the limit of endurance to defend it, because in defending it he was defending everything that gave his own life its deepest meaning.

The Westerner, on the other hand, would fight with an equal tenacity for the broader concept of society. He fought so because everything he lived by was tied to growth, expansion, and a constantly widening horizon. What he lived by would survive or fall with the nation itself. He could not possibly stand by unmoved in the face of an attempt to destroy the Union. He would combat it with everything he had, because he could only see it as an effort to cut the ground out from under his feet.

So Grant and Lee were in complete contrast, representing two diametrically opposed elements in American life. Grant was the modern man emerging; beyond him, ready to come on the stage, was the great age of steel and machinery, of crowded cities and a restless burgeoning vitality. Lee might have ridden down from the old age of chivalry, lance in hand, silken banner fluttering over his head. Each man was the perfect champion of his cause, drawing both his strengths and his weaknesses from the people he led.

Yet it was not all contrast, after all. Different as they were—in background, in personality, in underlying aspiration—these two great soldiers had much in common. Under everything else, they were marvelous fighters. Furthermore, their fighting qualities were really very much alike.

Each man had, to begin with, the great virtue of utter tenacity and fidelity. Grant fought his way down the Mississippi Valley in spite of acute personal discouragement and profound military handicaps. Lee hung on in the trenches at Petersburg after hope itself had died. In each man there was an indomitable quality . . . the born fighter's refusal to give up as long as he can still remain on his feet and lift his two fists.

Daring and resourcefulness they had, too; the ability to think faster and move faster than the enemy. These were the qualities which gave Lee the dazzling campaigns of Second Manassas and Chancellorsville and won Vicksburg for Grant.

Lastly, and perhaps greatest of all, there was the ability, at the end, to turn quickly from war to peace once the fighting was over. Out of the way these two men behaved at Appomattox came the possibility of a peace of reconciliation. It was a possibility not wholly realized, in the years to come, but which did, in the end, help the two sections to become one nation again . . . after a war whose bitterness might have seemed to make such a reunion wholly impossible. No part of either man's life became him more than the part he played in this brief meeting in the McLean house at Appomattox. Their behavior there put all succeeding generations of Americans in their debt. Two great Americans, Grant and Lee—very different, yet under everything very much alike. Their encounter at Appomattox was one of the great moments of American history.

Second Thoughts on the Information Highway

Cliff Stoll

Surely you've heard the predictions of our future digital age: "Multimedia will revolutionize the classroom," "Interactive electronic information will make books obsolete," "Businesses will flock to the computer networks for instant, low cost information." Visionaries see a future of telecommuting office workers, interactive libraries, and multimedia classrooms. They speak of electronic town meetings and virtual communities. Commerce and business will shift from offices and malls to networks and modems. Electronic mail will replace slow and inefficient snail mail. And thanks to the freedom of electronic networks, government will become profoundly democratic and efficient.

Such claims are utterly bogus. These glowing predictions of a digital nirvana make me wonder if some lemming-like madness has cursed our technologists. Do our computer pundits lack all common sense? I'm astonished at the wide gulf between their utopian dreams and the dreary reality that pours into my modem.

The truth is that no online database will replace your daily newspaper, no CD-ROM can take the place of a competent teacher, and no computer network will change the way government works. Work has never been easy; learning isn't painless, and bureaucracies have never been quick to change. The computer ain't gonna do it for you.

Consider today's online world. The Usenet, a worldwide bulletin board, allows anyone to post messages across the globe. Your word gets out, leapfrogging editors and publishers. Every voice can be heard cheaply and instantly. The result is that every voice is heard. The resultant cacophony more closely resembles Citizen Band Radio, complete with handles, harassment, and anonymous threats. When most everyone shouts, few listen.

How about electronic publishing? Try reading a book on your monitor. At best, it's an unpleasant chore: the myopic glow of a clunky computer replaces the friendly pages of a book. And you can't tote that laptop to the beach or leave it in your car—it'll get stolen. Yet Nicholas Negroponte, director of the MIT Media Center, predicts that we'll soon buy books straight over the Internet. Uh, sure.

What the Internet hucksters won't tell you is that the World Wide Web is an ocean of unedited data, without any pretense of completeness. Lacking editors, reporters, reviewers, or critics, the Internet has become a wasteland of unreviewed, unedited, unfiltered data. You don't know what to ignore and what's worth reading.

Logged onto the World Wide Web, I hunt for the date of the battle of Trafalgar. Hundreds of files show up, including Napoleon.txt, Trafalg.zip, and J41N32.gif. It takes fifteen minutes to unravel them—one's a biography written by an 8th grader, the second is a computer game that doesn't work, and the third is an image of a London monument. None answer my question, and my search is periodically interrupted by messages like, "Too many connections, try again later." This searching is a great way to waste time but hardly an efficient research tool.

Won't the Internet be useful in governing? Internet addicts clamor for government reports to be uploaded to the networks. But when Andy Speno ran for County Executive in Westchester County, NY, he put every press release and position paper onto a bulletin board. In that affluent county, with plenty of computer companies, how many voters logged in? Fewer than thirty did. This is hardly a good omen for the electronic democracy.

The strongest hype comes from those who are forcing computers into schools. We're told that multimedia and interactive video systems will make learning easy and schoolwork fun. Students will happily learn from animated characters while being taught by expertly tailored software. Teachers won't be as essential when we have computer-aided education.

Bah. These expensive toys are difficult to use in classrooms, require extensive teacher preparation, and waste what few dollars trickle into schools. Sure, kids love to play video games—but think of your own experience: Can you recall even one educational filmstrip of decades past? I'll bet you remember the two or three great teachers who made a difference in your life.

Cyberbusiness? We're promised instant catalog shopping—just point and click for great deals. We'll order airline tickets over the network, make restaurant reservations, and negotiate sales contracts. Stores will become obsolete. So how come my local mall does more business in an afternoon than the entire Internet handles in a month? Even if there were a trustworthy way to send money over the network— which there isn't—the networks are missing a most essential ingredient of capitalism: salespeople. Without the personal attention and human interactions of good salesfolk, the Internet can't blossom into an electronic shopping mail.

What's missing from this electronic wonderland? Human contact. Discount the fawning technoburble about virtual communities—computers and networks isolate us from each other. A network chat line is a limp substitute for meeting friends over coffee. No interactive multimedia display comes close to the excitement of a live concert. And who'd prefer cybersex to the real thing?

Is it likely that you can enjoy a rich online world and a plentiful personal life? Nope. Every hour that you spend linked through your modem is sixty minutes that you're not visiting with your friends or shagging fly balls with the kid down the block. While the Internet beckons brightly, seductively flashing an icon of knowledge-as-power, this non-place lures us to surrender our time on Earth. A poor substitute it is, this virtual reality where frustration is legion and where—in the holy names of Education and Progress—important aspects of human interactions are relentlessly devalued.

Get a Life?

Nicholas Negroponte

Any significant social phenomenon creates a backlash. The Net is no exception. It is odd, however, that the loudest complaints are shouts of "Get a life!"—suggesting that online living will dehumanize us, insulate us, and create a world of people who won't smell flowers, watch sunsets, or engage in face-to-face experiences. Out of this backlash comes a warning to parents that their children will "cocoon" and metamorphose into social invalids.

Experience tells us the opposite. So far, evidence gathered by those using the Net as a teaching tool indicates that kids who go online gain social skills rather than lose them. Since the distance between Athens, Georgia, and Athens, Greece, is just a mouse click away, children attain a new kind of worldliness. Young people on the Net today will intevitably experience some of the sophistication of Europe. In earlier days, only children from élite families could afford to interact with European culture during their summer vacations abroad.

I know that visiting Web pages in Italy or interacting with Italians via e-mail isn't the same as ducking the pigeons or listening to music in Piazza San Marco— but it sure beats never going there at all. Take all the books in the world, and they won't offer the real-time global experience a kid can get on the Net: here a child becomes the driver of the intellectual vehicle, not the passenger.

Mitch Resnick of the MIT Media Lab recently told me of an autistic boy who has great difficulty interacting with people, often giving inappropriate visual cues (like strange facial expressions) and so forth. But this child has thrived on the Net. When he types, he gains control and becomes articulate. He's an active participant in chat rooms and newsgroups. He has developed strong online friendships, which have given him greater confidence in face-to-face situations.

It's an extreme case, but isn't it odd how parents grieve if their child spends six hours a day on the Net but delight if those same hours are spent reading books? With the exception of sleep, doing anything six hours a day, every day, is not good for a child.

Adults on the Net enjoy even greater opportunity, as more people discover they can work from almost anywhere. Granted, if you make pizzas you need to be close to the dough; if you're a surgeon you must be close to your patients (at least for the next two decades). But if your trade involves bits (not atoms), you probably don't need to be anywhere specific—at least most of the time. In fact, it might be beneficial all around if you were in the Caribbean or Mediterranean—then your company wouldn't have to tie up capital in expensive downtown real estate.

Certain early users of the Net (bless them!) are now whining about its vulgarization, warning people of its hazards as if it were a cigarette. If only these whiners were more honest, they'd admit that it was they who didn't have much of a life and found solace on the Net, they who woke up one day with midlife crises and discovered there was more to living than what was waiting in their e-mail boxes. So, what took you guys so long? Of course there's more to life than e-mail, but don't project your empty existence onto others and suggest "being digital" is a form of virtual leprosy for which total abstinence is the only immunization.

My own lifestyle is totally enhanced by being online. I've been a compulsive e-mail user for more than 25 years; more often than not, it's allowed me to spend more time in scenic places with interesting people. Which would you prefer: two weeks' vacation totally offline or four to six weeks online? This doesn't work for all professions, but it is a growing trend among so-called "knowledge workers."

Once, only the likes of Rupert Murdoch or Aga Khan could cut deals from their satellite-laden luxury yachts off the coast of Sardinia. Now all sorts of people from Tahoe to Telluride can work from the back seat of a Winnebago if they wish.

I don't know the statistics, but I'm willing to guess that the executives of corporate America spend 70 to 80 percent of their time in meetings. I *do* know that most of those meetings, often a canonical one hour long, are 70 to 80 percent posturing and leveling (bringing the others up to speed on a common subject). The posturing is gratuitous, and the leveling is better done elsewhere—online, for example. This alone would enhance US productivity far more than any trade agreement.

I am constantly astonished by just how offline corporate America is. Wouldn't you expect executives at computer and communications companies to be active online? Even household names of the high-tech industry are *offline* human beings, sometimes more so than execs in extremely low-tech fields. I guess this is a corollary to the shoemaker's children having no shoes.

Being online not only makes the inevitable face-to-face meetings so much easier—it allows you to look outward. Generally, large companies are so inwardly directed that staff memorandums about growing bureaucracy get more attention than the dwindling competitive advantage of being big in the first place. David, who has a life, needn't use a slingshot. Goliath, *who doesn't*, is too busy reading office memos.

In the mid-1700s, mechanical looms and other machines forced cottage industries out of business. Many people lost the opportunity to be their own bosses and to enjoy the profits of hard work. I'm sure I would have been a Luddite under those conditions.

But the current sweep of digital living is doing exactly the opposite. Parents of young children find exciting self-employment from home. The "virtual corporation" is an opportunity for tiny companies (with employees spread across the world) to work together in a global market and set up base wherever they choose. If you don't like centralist thinking, big companies, or job automation, what better place to go than the Net? Work for yourself and get a life.

Gender Gap in Cyberspace

Deborah Tannen

I was a computer pioneer; but I'm still something of novice. That paradox is telling.

I was the second person on my block to get a computer. The first was my colleague Ralph. It was 1980. Ralph got a Radio Shack TRS-80; I got a used Apple IIt. He helped me get started and went on to become a maven, reading computer magazines, hungering for the new technology he read about, and buying and mastering it as quickly as he could afford. I hung on to old equipment far too long because I dislike giving up what I'm used to, fear making the wrong decision about what to buy and resent the time it takes to install and learn a new system.

My first Apple came with videogames: I gave them away. Playing games on the computer didn't interest me. If I had free time I'd spend it talking on the telephone to friends.

Ralph got hooked. His wife was often annoyed by the hours he spent at his computer and the money he spent upgrading it. My marriage had no such strains—until I discovered e-mail. Then I got hooked. E-mail draws me the same way the phone does: it's a souped-up conversation.

E-mail deepened my friendship with Ralph. Though his office was next to mine, we rarely had extended conversations because he is shy. Face to face he mumbled so, I could barely tell he was speaking. But when we both got on e-mail, I started receiving long, self-revealing messages; we poured our hearts out to each other. A friend discovered that e-mail opened up that kind of communication with her father. He would never talk much on the phone (as her mother would), but they have become close since they both got online.

Why I wondered, would some men find it easier to open up on e-mail? It's a combination of the technology (which they enjoy) and the obliqueness of the written word, just as many men will reveal feelings in dribs and drabs while riding in the car or doing something, which they'd never talk about sitting face to face. It's too intense, too bearing-down on them, and once you start you have to keep going. With a computer in between, it's safer.

It was on e-mail, in fact, that I described to Ralph how boys in groups often struggle to get the upper hand whereas girls tend to maintain an appearance of cooperation. And he pointed out that this explained why boys are more likely to be captivated by computers than girls are. Boys are typically motivated by a social structure that says if you don't dominate you will be dominated. Computers, by their nature, balk: you type a perfectly appropriate command and it refuses to do what it should. Many boys and men are incited by this defiance: "I'm going to whip this into line and teach it who's boss! I'll get it to do what I say!" (and if they work hard enough, they always can). Girls and women are more likely to respond, "This thing won't cooperate. Get it away from me!"

Although no one wants to think of herself as "typical"—how much nicer to be sui generis—my relationship to my computer is—gulp—fairly typical for a woman. Most women (with plenty of exceptions) aren't excited by tinkering with the technology, grappling with the challenge of eliminating bugs or getting the biggest and best computer. These dynamics appeal to many men's interest in making sure they're on the top side of the inevitable who's-up-who's-down struggle that life is for them. E-mail appeals to my view of life as a contest for connections to others. When I see that I have messages I feel loved.

I once posted a technical question on a computer network for linguists and was flooded with long dispositions, some pages long, I was staggered by the generosity and the expertise, but wondered where these guys found the time—and why all the answers I got were from men.

Like coed classrooms and meetings, discussions on e-mail networks tend to be dominated by male voices, unless they're specifically women-only; like single-sex schools. On line, women don't have to worry about getting the floor (you just send a message when you feel like it), but, according to linguists Susan Herring and Laurel Sutton, who have studied this, they have the usual problems of having their messages ignored or attacked. The anonymity of public networks frees a small number of men to send long, vituperative, sarcastic messages that many other men either can tolerate or actually enjoy, but turn most women off.

The anonymity of networks leads to another sad part of the e-mail story: there are men who deluge women with questions about their appearance and invitations to sex. On college campuses, as soon as women students log on, they are bombarded by references to sex, like going to work and finding pornographic posters adorning the walls.

Taking Time

Most women want one thing from a computer—to work. This is significant counterevidence to the claim that men want to focus on information while women are interested in rapport. That claim I found was often true in casual conversation, in which there is no particular information to be conveyed. But with computers, it is often women who are more focused on information, because they don't respond to the challenge of getting equipment to submit.

Once I had learned the basics, my interest in computers waned. I use it to write books (though I never mastered having it do bibliographies or tables of contents) and write checks (but not balance my checkbook). Much as I'd like to use it to do more, I begrudge the time it would take to learn.

Ralph's computer expertise costs him a lot of time. Chivalry requires that he rescue novices in need, and he is called upon by damsel novices far more often than knaves. More men would rather study the instruction booklet than ask directions, as it were, from another person. "When I do help men," Ralph wrote (on e-mail, of course), "they want to be more involved. I once installed a hard drive for a guy, and he wanted to be there with me, wielding the screwdriver and giving his own advice where he could." Women, he finds, usually are not interested in what he's doing; they just want him to get the computer to the point where they can do what they want.

Which pretty much explains how I managed to be a pioneer without becoming an expert.

Kansas vs. Hawaii

Student

Imagine you are lying in bed. It is a warm and humid night. You feel a faint breeze and hear a distant rhythmic roar. Where could you be? You could be in a beach front home with the seaward house vents open, listening to the distant pulsating of the Pacific Ocean on the shore. Or, you could be in a suburban home in the middle of the heartland with the ceiling fans on, listening to the distant roar of a nearby busy road in late spring. From personal experience, it is amazing how similar these two sensations are. Even though Kansas and Hawaii do share some similar attributes, when it comes to comparing their overall sceneries, cultures, and weather patterns, their vast differences become apparent.

For instance, Kansas and Hawaii's sceneries contrast in quality and physical attributes. Kansas stands out with its vast flat lands, many lakes, and seasonally varied vegetation. In particular, the flat lands and rolling hills of Kansas allow you to drive long scenic distances and view beautiful multi-colored sunsets. You can travel in all directions for hundreds and thousands of miles viewing the countryside before even reaching an ocean. In addition, the flat lands provide an excellent stage in displaying the gorgeous Kansas sunsets. Specifically, prairie sunsets are more dramatic than ocean sunsets because of the increase of dust particles in the air that intensify the brilliant colors of the sun's final rays. Another feature Kansas has is its many fresh water lakes that are available for recreational purposes. Furthermore, Kansas distinctively stands out with the ability to naturally support the growth of grass and deciduous trees due to having a season where they can die and regenerate. The growth of grass is widespread and naturally common along most roadways. Also, deciduous leaf trees are abundant in Kansas which provides a dynamic array of beautiful colors to enjoy in the Fall season.

Meanwhile, Hawaii's scenery is distinctively different from Kansas with its island attributes, volcanic mountains, and tropical vegetation. Since Hawaii is made up of several small islands, the road systems are limited and the chances of coming across a beach or ocean cliff shore is inevitable. In Hawaii, it is hard to become lost on the roads because typically there is only one main artery that circles the island along with a few internal public roadways. Due to the island attributes, there are no shortages of beautiful beaches and majestic ocean cliffs to view. The beaches provide a relaxing setting for observing the hypnotizing waves on the sand or the crashing breakers against the reefs. The many remnants of volcanoes are another unique and contrasting aspect of the Hawaiian islands. Hawaii is spotted with gorgeous volcanic ridges, craters and mountains that have in turn created additional scenic wonders, such as, natural waterfalls. Also, Hawaii consists of large exotic tropical forests that are wondrous to experience. The lush, thick vegetation, that includes palm trees and unbelievably beautiful and aromatic flowers, is abundant because of Hawaii's climate. This same climate, however, hampers Hawaii from growing grass on any large scale since there is no distinct change of season for it to repopulate.

Along with the scenic differences, Kansas and Hawaii culturally differ in their ethnic demographics, traditional activities, and native foods. First, the ethnic demographics of Kansas do not vary dramatically due to its geographical location. Approximately 90% of the population in Kansas are White. Since Kansas is in the middle of the United States, it is not prone to large settlement of differing nationalities. In addition, some of the activities that typify the culture of Kansas can be seen in the large number of rodeos and barbecues Kansas entertains. The rodeo events carry a historic heritage of the Old West which Kansas appears to take pride in identifying with, as evident in one particular event, the American Royal. Furthermore, the barbecue events are a way of life for Kansans. In the summertime, it is rare to go one week without hearing of a formal barbecuing contest or a friendly barbecue gathering. Another way in which Kansas differs is in the types of food that it can abundantly produce. In Kansas, there are a large number of ranches and farms that raise beef and grow various kinds of grains and vegetables.

In contrast, Hawaii's cultural aspects differ from Kansas. Demographically, Hawaii's population is over 60% Asian. This large Asian population is mainly due to Hawaii's location in the western part of the Pacific Ocean. Besides the ethnic structure, Hawaii's culture differs in the activities that are typified by their tribal dance performances and beach activities. A large portion of the native population appears to take pride in sharing the Hawaiian culture through the various island tribe dances. In the two weeks I stayed in Hawaii, I did not come across a day that I was not eagerly given instructions or had not viewed a demonstration of the various Pacific tribe dances. In addition, Hawaii is renowned for its treacherous surfs on the North Shore. According to a prior Hawaiian roommate of mine, spending time at the beach, both in and out of the water, is a way of life for many native Hawaiians. Moreover, Hawaii's culture differs in the types of native foods that can be abundantly produced and harvested. In Hawaii, the main native foods come from either plantations, which harvest all types of tropical fruits; or the ocean, where fishermen are able to catch large quantities of seafood.

Furthermore, Kansas and Hawaii's weather differ in their climatic features, such as temperatures, precipitations, and severest storm types. In Kansas, for example, you will experience a seasonal change in temperature. In one day, it is not uncommon for the temperature to change up to thirty degrees. These fluctuations, both daily and seasonally, open up the need for Kansans to keep a varied wardrobe to meet the possible hundred degree heats of summer to the sub-zero cold of winter. Similarly, the types of precipitation and their duration appear more extreme in Kansas. In Kansas you can have rain, sleet, hail, and snow. Also, the storms that produce these various degrees of precipitations are typically more intense and last longer. In fact, there are times when I remember having not seen the sun and sky for weeks on end. Typically, the worst storms Kansans have to face are tornadoes. Tornadoes and their destructive funnel clouds are a factor that is typical of flat expanses of land mixed with high winds and violent storm conditions. Tornadoes are erratic and do not provide much advance notice to those in its path. Because of the characteristics of tornadoes, most homes in Kansas have basements that serve the dual purpose as shelters from these potentially deadly storms.

On the other hand, if you reside in Hawaii, you will experience moderate temperatures. The temperature fluctuates little throughout the year unless you travel between the leeward and windward side of the islands; even then, you may only experience about a five to ten degree change in temperature. Typically, the temperature on the islands averages around seventy to eighty degrees. Since the temperature does not vary widely, there is less of a need for Hawaiians to maintain a large seasonal wardrobe. Besides the temperature differences between the two states, the patterns of precipitation are not as extreme for Hawaii but do occur more often. On most given days, if you venture outside and you do not like the weather, there is hope. I have learned first hand that rain does not particularly mean a wasted day. Most of the time, you only have to wait about ten to fifteen minutes for a storm to move on and the sun to come out again. Or else, you can often drive from a cloudy windward coast to find sun at a leeward beach. The precipitation variances come into play because of the mixture of volcanic mountains and wind currents from the Pacific Ocean that often create sporadic rain showers.

In Hawaii, the severest storms you have to guard against are hurricanes. Even though these storms can approach the islands at a very fast pace, typically hurricanes provide the residents with some advance warning. Basements are not practical to guard against severe storms in Hawaii. In actuality, high ground is to a Hawaiian in a hurricane as a basement is to a Kansan in a tornado.

On the whole, I have grown to appreciate both Kansas and Hawaii for the unique qualities and the exciting contrasts they have provided in my life experiences. If I had to choose between living in either Kansas or Hawaii, I would have to choose Kansas because I have grown to love the natural beauty, culture and dramatic weather it has to offer.

A Comparison Between Business and the Life of the Non-Traditional Student

Student

I returned to college from a business career as a training manager in California, for a variety of reasons. During my year's time at DeVry, I've noticed many similarities and dissimilarities between business life and existence, a la DeVry. However, it is in the realms of responsibilities, management of time, and how others view me, that the differences and similarities seem most clear.

Perhaps the most crucial difference in responsibility between business and the student life is to whom you ultimately answer. All moralistic yearnings and sky high wishes aside, in business, the person who comes around every two weeks with that envelope filled with pictures of Presidents is your ultimate responsibility. He/she does rule your life, and by their nature and management style can dictate everything from the tone of your workday to the pace of your advancement, if any. In comparison, many students have only themselves to own up to. However, my situation is more akin to business. The millstones of pressure, lack of time and financial burdens are also around my wife's neck. Though not ultimately responsible to her, I am to us as a family. In this respect my situation is not all that dissimilar to the business arena.

The management of one's time may be the area that contains the most similarities between business and student life. This applies even more so to DeVry which is designed, it seems, to simulate business conditions. Business is fast paced and so is DeVry. I worked as a computer trainer and manager of a Customer Service district. Serving over 3,000 on-line customers in meetings, trainings, answering their questions and traveling all required diligent planning of my day-to-day schedule. I see no difference in my present life as a student. To try to get the massive amount of reading, projects, etc. done takes the same coordinating. In business you must set aside time for customers. Playing their games, courting them, buttering them up takes lots of time. It's the political side of business. Here my life as a student has no equivalent. However, one area where the two comparisons almost merge is the projects required. Though they're not the same type, the volume stayed the same. In business I had training manuals to write, or computer works to prepare for my bosses' meetings. They all took careful management of time and the management of my projects here is no different. The major disparity between the two in time allocation is the weekends. In my business, you could mostly count the weekends as your own. I have had very few of them since hoisting the student's banner. At least 75 percent of these dubiously named weekends are spent studying, preparing projects, etc. Though responsibilities and management of time strike a balance between differences and similarities, it is not so with the way I believe I'm seen by my peers.

Where I worked in California I was the baby. This even held true in my job before I started school. Everyone, including my co-workers, the secretaries, etc. was older. Now my associates weren't exactly museum pieces, but usually five years more advanced, at the least. To lightly understate the matter, this is not the case at DeVry. With two or three exceptions, I'm the oldest member of my class. This difference was and is a great jolt to me. I don't see myself as ready to be measured for the pine box, but some of my peers probably firmly believe I personally knew Abraham Lincoln, or at latest Franklin Roosevelt. In my first term, a student, obviously direct from wherever high school, seriously asked me if I wouldn't be too old to work after graduating. I never experienced this attitude in business. Usually if you can contribute to the bottom line you're accepted. I've known many business people who have followed this same course of returning to school for a second career. My experience from California says it's not frowned upon, but accepted. The line between this attitude and the student's view is different yet subtle. They accept it, but I sense because they are too young to have had a first career, they see returning, older students as ones who couldn't cut it in their first.

I don't have a preference between these two lifestyles. Business and the real world can honestly be the most exciting, boring and mundane existence imaginable, all in the same day. But, the life of learning, and experimentation of a student possesses the same blood pulsing and snore inducing qualities. The numbers of non-traditional students (that is what they call us now) will grow for social, economic and demographic reasons. Life and business in this country move and change with the pace of a Cheetah chasing prey. Learning and studying will likely be a constant for all American professionals from now on. Since I am equally adept at both lifestyles, I might have a jump on the competition.

My Two Sons

Student

Every person who has experienced life into adulthood has passed through the stage of childhood. Children can bring out the best and the worst in anyone. All children seem to share common oddities no matter what race or culture. Two children from the same parents can also share these characteristics, and at the same time be as different as night and day. My sons Kevin and Kyle are comparable in physical attributes, personality characteristics, and social behaviors.

While Kevin and Kyle are from the same gene pool, their physical attributes are comparably different. Kevin is six years old and stands as tall as a ten-year-old. He has a stocky build with large bones. In fact, in his first grade class, he is a head taller than most of the other children. In addition to height he has a square-shaped head with multiple cowlicks making his head appear nest-like. With his thick, light-olive skin, platinum-blonde hair, big toothy smile, and grayish-blue eyes, he stands out like a steely in a sack of ordinary marbles. His shoulders are broad with a v-shaped back and a little potbelly. He has proportional sized hands and feet. On the other hand, Kyle is five years old and slightly above the average height. He has a slender, lanky build with long bones. In the animal kingdom, he mostly resembles a spider monkey. His head is round like a coconut with one cowlick that creates a bird-like image. With thin, pale, transparent skin, sandy blonde hair and giant, sea-blue eyes, he could blend with the best of Hallmark's precious moments. Furthermore, his back is slender and straight, his shoulders are bony, and his tummy is soft and flat. While his teeth are unusually small and square, he has large hands and feet.

Besides Kevin and Kyle having contrasting appearances, their personality characteristics are also different. Kevin is gentle with a soft touch, sweet with a protective nature, and innocently clumsy. For example, after Kyle crashed and burned on his bike, it was Kevin to the rescue. Wrapping his arms around the crash victim and asking if he was okay, Kevin helped Kyle up the stairs. He is loud by design, gracious at heart, and instinctively sneaky. Along with his sense of humor, it only takes a hint of music, from any source, to trigger his endless rhythm and creative imagination. Conversely, Kyle is fickle with a temperamental touch, compassionate with a survivalist nature, and mildly graceful. A light switch would be an accurate description when his temper is the topic. He is soft-spoken, yet insistently announced, stingy by nature, and tremendously bold. On his first day at summer camp, Kyle took inventory of friends and strangers, room by room, with no sign of fear or intimidation. He has passionate patience, high self-esteem, and a sadistic sense of humor. Explosions, guns and ninja warriors produce laughter and excitement, but if anyone is hurt, the tears begin to flow.

In addition to their personality characteristics, Kevin and Kyle are comparable in social behaviors, too. Kevin usually needs outside stimulation. Playing alone quietly is out of the question, unless he is drawing. In a classroom environment, he is a leader. When entering the classroom in the morning, some children greet him, another takes his bag, while others smile and wave around the room. However, at the store, Kevin is a terrorist looking for a hostage. Running down the aisles, crawling under the grocery carts, and hiding in and sneaking through racks of clothing are priority one. On the other hand, Kyle is perfectly content to sit with a book, play with blocks or solve a puzzle alone. In the classroom, Kyle is the parent, making up rules as the day goes on to keep everything fair. While at the store, he is the baby. "I want a new toy!" or "Can you carry me?" is the chorus whined throughout the shopping torture.

Kevin and Kyle are inseparable brothers to the end. Because of their contrasts, they constantly argue and fight, but, at the same time, their differences bring them closer together. While they both were raised the same way by the same parents, and each will go through similar childhood experiences, individualism will prevail.

Cause / Effect

To write a cause and effect essay, you analyze what makes something happen or determine why something happened.

Why Write an Essay of Causal Analysis?

Learning how to write a cause and effect essay can help you understand and discuss the connections between two things—such as why and how your financial status was affected when you began college, or the causes of global warming, or the effects of the Viet Nam War on college-age students in the 1960s and early 1970s. By learning how to discern the connections, you develop your ability to analyze and think logically. Causal analytical writing is much more complex than simple analytical writing. In analytical writing, you are taking a topic and discussing its components. In causal analysis writing, you are concerned with the components of both causes and effects. You could find that you have multiple causes and multiple effects. This type of essay, therefore, helps you to develop as a critical thinker.

In the business world, we often have to determine causes and effects. For example, your division might be having excess expenditure on automobile expenses. Your boss might ask you to determine what the problem or problems are and find out what will happen if they are not solved. This requires cause and effect reasoning. When you have to write a report about the problem to your boss and include possible recommendations, this requires cause and effect writing.

Learning how to write a cause and effect essay in college will help to prepare you to write on the job. Causal relationships are rarely simple. Any given effect is likely to have several causes, some more immediate than others. Each of these causes may have produced a variety of effects besides the one under consideration. In assigning causes to effects, you must be not only objective but also rational, following a logical sequence from causes to effects.

When to Write a Cause and Effect Essay

When you want to determine the results of something or to determine the causes, you can write cause and effect essays. Be sure to determine the focus of the essay before you begin writing so that your analysis is logical and the correct causes show the correct effects.

Criteria to Follow When You Write Cause and Effect Essays

1. Establish a precise focus involving both a cause(s) and an effect(s).

2. Write an introduction which presents the subject and expresses the purpose of the analysis in the essay.

3. Include a thesis statement in the introduction which states both the cause(s) and the effect(s).

4. Rely on the body of the essay to analyze the causes and the effects. A logical pattern of organization might be one-third cause and two-thirds effects, or you might have one-fourth cause and three-fourths effects, etc.

5. Analyze all possible causes and all possible effects in a logical, rational manner.

6. Use transitional words and phrases which suggest cause and effect relationships: *as the result of, in conclusion, because, on the other hand, besides, the consequence of, in addition,* etc.

7. Rely on concrete evidence and examples to support your comments. By using some extended examples, you will be able to have thorough development of both causes and effects.

8. Remain objective so that you look at all issues fairly. If you aren't objective, often the audience will be unable to understand or accept your reasoning.

9. Use the conclusion to summarize the different causes and the various effects. State any conclusions that can be drawn from your analysis.

10. Avoid oversimplifying your analysis or stating effects which could not have been logically caused.

11. When analyzing your topic, don't confuse events that happened before something else as necessarily being the cause(s) of what happened. You might find a logical link between event A and event B, which occurs later, but perhaps the link is only chronological.

Topic Ideas for Cause and Effect Writing

Why you quit your last job

Why you chose to attend this college

The effect of growing up in the country

The effect of growing up in the city

The effect of joining the military after high school rather than attending college

The effect having children has had on your marriage

The effect of your parents' divorcing

The effect of a bad relationship

Why movies have become more violent

Why you decided on your particular academic major

Why a particular person is your best friend/worst enemy

Peer Evaluation for Cause and Effect Essays

1. Does the writer use a thesis statement?
2. Does he or she show a logical relationship between cause and effects?
3. Is each main point in the body of the essay sufficiently developed?
4. Are the body paragraphs written in the same order as stated in the thesis?
5. Does each body paragraph begin with a topic sentence?
6. Does the writer use a sufficient number of transitions which suggest cause-effect?
7. What is the main cause and its effects?
8. Does the writer use sufficient examples to prove points?
9. Is the essay informative?
10. Do you believe the writer was objective?

Children and Violence in America

Dudley Erskine Devlin

Violence seems to be everywhere in America, but increasingly both the victims and the perpetrators are likely to be children and teenagers. According to a recent Department of Education study, 81 percent of the victims of violent crimes are now preteens and teenagers. Teenagers also lead adults in the number of serious crimes committed. As if to prove this point, recently a stray bullet from gang violence in Denver struck a 10-month-old child who was visiting the zoo. In another incident, a 13-year-old boy accidently shot his friend, and then in despair shot and killed himself. Even this morning's newspaper carries the story of a 15-year-old boy who accidently shot his 9-year-old sister while showing her how to load and unload his father's .22 semi-automatic handgun. The gun went off, and the bullet shattered her spine. The 9-year-old girl is now paralyzed. When people read these shocking and unbelievable stories, they begin to wonder about the causes of the problem. Why are children so frequently the victims or the perpetrators of violence?

The debate in America today is about the causes of violence involving children. But what exactly is the basic, underlying cause? Conventional explanations take an either/or approach: Either the cause lies in TV programs which promote violence or the cause is a society riddled with family instability, drugs, and poverty. It's a classic chicken-or-the-egg question: Does TV and movie violence promote social violence, or is social violence merely reflected in violent movies and television programs?

I believe that we should not be fooled by this either/or logic. There is, after all, a third possible answer. Instead of the primary cause being TV violence or the decline in family values, I believe that the news media themselves are the underlying cause of our crisis. The truth is that the liberal media—particularly newspapers and network TV news—have cleverly staged this crisis of violence by hyping a few statistics and isolated cases of violence. To prove this claim, I need to review the conventional arguments.

First, let's analyze the belief that violence on TV and in the movies is causing increased violence among children and teenagers. The self-appointed liberal reformers usually trot out a bunch of statistics and examples like the following:

- By the age of 18, the average American child will have seen 200,000 violent acts on television, including 40,000 murders. By the time an American child has left elementary school, he or she has witnessed 8,000 murders on TV.

- Today, television programs and films strive for high body counts, not high morals. *Terminator 2* seems like one long machine-gunning. In *RoboCop*, 32 people are killed. *Die Hard 2* may have the unofficial record with 264 people killed.

- In 1950, approximately 15 percent of America's homes had television; by 1990, 93 percent of America's homes had television. In that 40-year period, the murder rate per 100,000 people jumped from 5.3 to 10.2. That's almost a 100 percent increase in murders.

Using examples like these, the TV and media critics like Tipper Gore argue that children confuse images on TV with the real world, that they become desensitized to repeated acts of violence, and that they say that "it's fun" to do violence to others. Researchers like University of Illinois psychologists Leonard Eron and Rowell Huesmann argue that violence on TV does cause violent behavior: "Television violence affects youngsters of all ages, of both genders, at all socioeconomic levels. It cannot be denied or explained away."

On the other side of this either/or argument are those who believe that social violence causes violent behavior in children and teenagers. Those who make this argument point to drug use, poverty, and the decline in family values. Their best evidence is that violence already exists in our children's public schools. They like to cite figures released by the National Education Association (NEA) that show that violence is an everyday part of every child's education. Every school day, the NEA claims, at least 100,000 students bring guns to school; 40 are hurt or killed by firearms; 6,250 teachers are threatened with bodily injury; and 260 teachers are physically assaulted. Everywhere, schools are installing metal detectors and police are stationed in the hallways.

Obviously, each of these arguments represents a half-truth. Possibly there is some TV and movie violence that adds to the culture of violence in America. And yes, we can believe that there are a few, isolated pockets of violence in society and schools. But the real truth is that the newspaper media and the network news have actually invented this epidemic of violence in order to promote their product and frighten the public. Every day, reporters search for a few examples of violence to teens and children, plaster them on the front page, and blow the whole thing out of proportion.

To be sure, there are violent TV shows and movies that a few people watch, but there are also family shows like *Home Improvement* and *Home Alone* that don't get the publicity of *RoboCop* or *Terminator 2*. There are, of course, one or two cities in America, like Los Angeles and Washington, D.C., where there is occasional violence on the streets and in children's schools. But the liberal establishment press has done its thing again, trying to scare the daylights out of the public in order to sell newspapers and raise their Neilsen ratings.

So when you pick up your paper in the morning or turn on the TV news and see another story about teenage violence, take it with a big lump of salt and don't believe everything you read. As they say, one swallow doesn't make a summer, and one infant shot in the Denver Zoo does not mean that we have this huge crisis of violence. In terms of "telling it like it is," you'll find more truth if you turn to the comics and check out "Peanuts." When Lucy hits Charlie Brown, at least you know it's make-believe.

Fall of the Legends

Mike Lupica

Once it was common—the most normal thing in the world to put the stars of sports up on pedestals. Now the national pastime seems to be watching them fall one after another.

The memorable pictures in sports no longer catch Emmit Smith running for a touchdown or Barry Bonds at the plate, another baseball on its way out of the park. They show O.J. Simpson's mug shot or Mike Tyson in handcuffs or Magic Johnson announcing his retirement from basketball because he has contracted the AIDS virus after years of promiscuity. You can put Michael Jordan, the most famous athlete in the world, on that list, too: Jordan in sunglasses on national television, addressing allegations of million-dollar gambling losses; Jordan on the golf course, wagering a thousand dollars per hole; Jordan on ESPN's SportsCenter almost every night of the summer, striking out as a Double-A baseball player struggling to hit .200.

We are not talking about real heroes here, policemen or firemen or soldiers fighting for something important. The great heroes of sports are more like those of movies or fiction. They are larger than life. In a way, Babe Ruth was no more real than Beowulf. But now, forty years after Ruth's death, even the idea of the sports hero in this country is dead, as dead as the Game of the Week in baseball or the Friday Night Fights, dead as the Polo Grounds or Ebbets Field. The list of casualties is long and storied, from blue-collar champion Pete Rose to Hall of Fame ace Steve Carlton. In 1994 alone, Dwight Gooden, the most luminous baseball pitcher since Sandy Koufax, tested positive for drugs (his second offense); Darryl Strawberry, one of Gooden's closest friends, checked himself into rehab (his second visit); Scottie Pippen refused to take the court in an NBA playoff game; Jack Nicklaus served up a few uncensored thoughts on race and golf; Tonya Harding, one of America's darling figure skaters, looked the other way while her husband planned an assault on her closest rival; and John Daly, a golfer who came out of nowhere to win the PGA a few years ago, capturing the imagination of everyone who follows sports, updated his troubled history of alcohol abuse and domestic disputes to include a parking-lot scuffle with an elderly man.

Legends are not made by game footage or file tape. They are born in memory and imagination and by word of mouth. Mickey Mantle is a legend. In his playing days and beyond, he was the kind of mythical star Ruth had been. He played the second half of his career on ruined knees, but he always seemed larger than life. Now the Mantle of legend, the Mantle of memory, has been replaced by Mantle the recovering alcoholic, a February graduate of the Betty Ford Clinic. Looking frail and human, more so than he was ever supposed to look, Mantle admitted this year that he had a drinking problem. After he returned from rehab, I sent a note to his New York hotel, wishing him luck, telling him I was rooting harder for him now than I ever did as a kid. At the bottom of the note, I asked Mantle to give me a call. I thought I might write a column about his experience.

Later that night, I was watching the Yankees on television when the phone rang.

"Mike?"

I smiled. "Hey, Mickey, thanks for calling."

There was a pause at the other end of the line, and then in a quiet voice Mantle said, "How'd you know it was me?"

If you grew up in Upstate New York in the fifties and sixties—as I did—you rooted for the Yankees, listened to them on the radio, and watched them on television. Mel Allen and Red Barber and Phil Rizzuto brought you the games. Mantle was the sports hero. I tried to explain that to him. "If I don't know your voice by now . . ." I said, letting the thought drift away, back toward the time when Mantle hit those balls out of sight, the ones Mel Allen described as going . . . going . . . gone.

There was another pause. "Thanks for the note," Mantle said.

I told him I meant it.

"I get a lot of notes just like it these days," he said. "My mail's so different now you wouldn't believe it. You can't even call it fan mail anymore. It's more like letters from close friends. It's so unbelievable it touches my heart. It makes me cry."

Cheers never did that.

There is no one thing that killed the American sports hero. Some got sick and some were arrested. Some got drunk and some got high. Some of them beat up women. And some blew it all on gambling. The only real culprit, it seems, is time. In a different age, Magic Johnson would have been able to face no physical consequences. In another era of sports and life, Desiree Washington might not have had the courage to charge Mike Tyson with rape. Still, it's hard to imagine Roberto Clemente charging fifteen bucks for an autograph or Y. A. Tittle skipping camp to up his paycheck.

If the athletes have changed, it's because the landscape has changed. Today's players come to the big time with their wallets full and some preconceived idea of what a sports hero should be, how they should play things, and how they should be marketed. They are handed $60 million contracts when they leave college. You have to wonder how many of the heroes of the past could have taken that kind of hit and had the same careers. Would it have gone as well for Willie Mays if he had been rich beyond imagination at the age of twenty? Or Jack Kramer? Or even Jack Nicklaus?

There is more to this than money, though. The fan has changed as well. He wants to know too much. And those of us in the media are only too willing to give him what he wants. With each passing year, it seems the fan gets closer to the field. He gets into the action, then all the way into the locker room. And soon he discovers what I found out a long time ago: A seat in the stands is still the best seat in sports. The athletes may look small from high up in the stadium, but you can still make them out to be big. It's safe to assume, though, that Willie Mays's public relations would have been no beter today than those of his godson Barry Bonds, who is known to be prickly himself. . . . And I do not believe Joe DiMaggio, one of the few enduring sports heroes, would have stood up to the day-to-day scrutiny that modern ballplayers face. He would not enjoy being staked out by autograph hunters in a hotel lobby; he would not like hiding from the reporters and talk-show producers who stalk today's stars.

It's true. Sports heroes have destroyed themselves, but we have helped them off the pedestal. We love their skills but hate the money they make. We demand that they reveal themselves, and then when we see them as they really are, we blame *them* for letting us down. That is why most fans react with such viciousness when one of their heroes turns out to be a drunk or an addict. We don't ever want to hear how sick these guys are. After all they are rich and talented and, by God, they should know better

The best chance an athlete has is to be someone from the past. Mantle, who comes from a time when sports heroes were still gods, was greeted warmly as ever when he showed himself to the world as just another aging beat-up ex-drunk. He was celebrated for his recovery from alcoholism at the very time that Gooden was vilified by the angry children of sports journalism for having the nerve to act like an addict.

When Mantle and I spoke on the telephone, I told him that he might hear the biggest cheer of his life when he returned to Yankee Stadium for Oldtimer's Day.

"If that is true," Mantle said, "it would have to be some cheer, wouldn't it?"

As it turned out, the reception he got was not the greatest of his life. Just another one. They cheered Mickey Mantle at Yankee Stadium because he is still around. In a time when the sports hero is dead, he is a survivor.

My Wood

E. M. Forster

A few years ago I wrote a book which dealt in part with the difficulties of the English in India. Feeling that they would have had no difficulties in India themselves, the Americans read the book freely. The more they read it the better it made them feel, and a cheque to the author was the result. I bought a wood with the cheque. It is not a large wood—it contains scarcely any trees, and it is intersected, blast it, by a public footpath. Still, it is the first property that I have owned, so it is right that other people should participate in my shame, and should ask themselves, in accents that will vary in horror, this very important question. What is the effect of property upon the character? Don't let's touch economics; the effect of private ownership upon the community as a whole is another question—a more important question, perhaps, but another one. Let's keep to psychology. If you own things, what's their effect on you? What's the effect on me of my wood?

In the first place, it makes me feel heavy. Property does have this effect. Property produces men of weight, and it was a man of weight who failed to get into the Kingdom of Heaven. He was not wicked, that unfortunate millionaire in the parable, he was only stout; he stuck out in front, not to mention behind, and as he wedged himself this way and that in the crystalline entrance and bruised his well-fed flanks, he saw beneath him a comparatively slim camel passing though the eye of a needle and being woven into the robe of God. The Gospels all through couple stoutness and slowness. They point out what is perfectly obvious, yet seldom realized: that if you have a lot of things you cannot move about a lot, that furniture requires dusting, dusters require servants, servants require insurance stamps, and the whole tangle of them makes you think twice before you accept an invitation to dinner or go for a bathe in the Jordan. Sometimes the Gospels proceed further and say with Tolstoy that property is sinful; they approach the difficult ground of asceticism here, where I cannot follow them. But as to the immediate effects of property on people, they just show straightforward logic. It produces men of weight. Men of weight cannot, by definition, move like the lightning from the East unto the West, and the ascent of a fourteen-stone bishop into a pulpit is thus the exact antithesis of the coming of the Son of Man. My wood makes me feel heavy.

In the second place, it makes me feel it ought to be larger.

The other day I heard a twig snap in it. I was annoyed at first, for I thought that someone was blackberrying, and depreciating the value of the undergrowth. On coming nearer, I saw it was not a man who had trodden on the twig and snapped it, but a bird, and I felt pleased. My bird. The bird was not equally pleased. Ignoring the relation between us, it took fright as soon as it saw the shape of my face, and flew straight over the boundary hedge into a field, the property of Mrs. Henessy, where it sat down with a loud squawk. It had become Mrs. Henessy's bird. Something seemed grossly amiss here, something that would not have occurred had the wood been larger. I could not afford to buy Mrs. Henessy out, I dared not murder her, and limitations of this sort beset me on every side. Ahab did not want that vineyard—he only needed it to round off his property, preparatory to plotting a new curve—and all the land around my wood has become necessary to me in order to round off the wood. A boundary protects. But—poor little thing—the boundary ought in its turn to be protected. Noises on the edge of it. Children throw stones. A little more, and then a little more, until we reach the sea. Happy Canute! Happier Alexander! And after all, why should even the world be the limit of possession? A rocket containing a Union Jack, will, it is hoped, be shortly fired at the moon. Mars. Sirius. Beyond which . . . But these immensities ended by saddening me. I could not suppose that my wood was the destined nucleus of universal dominion—it is so very small and contains no mineral wealth beyond the blackberries. Nor was I comforted when Mrs. Henessy's bird took alarm for the second time and flew clean away from us all, under the belief that it belonged to itself.

In the third place, property makes its owner feel that he ought to do something to it. Yet he isn't sure what. A restlessness comes over him, a vague sense that he has a personality to express—the same sense which, without any vagueness, leads the artist to an act of creation. Sometimes I think I will cut down such trees as remain in the wood, at other times I want to fill up the gaps between them with new trees. But impulses are pretentious and empty. They are not honest movements towards money-making or beauty. They spring from a foolish desire to express myself and from an inability to enjoy what I have got. Creation, property, enjoyment form a sinister trinity in the human mind. Creation and enjoyment are both very, very good, yet they are often unattainable without a material basis, and at such moments property pushes itself in as a substitute, saying, "Accept me instead—I'm good enough for all three." It is not enough. It is, as Shakespeare said of lust, "the expense of spirit in a waste of shame"; it is "Before, a joy proposed; behind, a dream." Yet we don't know how to shun it. It is forced on us by our economic system as the alternative to starvation. It is forced on us by an internal defect in the soul, by the feeling that in property may lie the germs of self-development and of exquisite or heroic deeds. Our life on earth is, and ought to be, material and carnal. But we have not learned to manage our materialism and carnality properly; they are still entangled with the desire for ownership, where (in the words of Dante) "Possession is one with loss."

And this brings us to our fourth and final point: the blackberries.

Blackberries are not plentiful in the meagre grove, but they are easily seen from the public footpath which traverses it, and all too easily gathered. Foxgloves, too—people will pull up the foxgloves, and ladies of an educational tendency even grub for toadstools to show them on the Monday in class. Other ladies, less educated, roll down the bracken in the arms of their gentlemen friends. There is paper, there are tins. Pray, does my wood belong to me or doesn't it? And, if it does, should I not own it best by allowing no one else to walk there? There is a wood near Lyme Regis, also cursed by a public footpath, where the owner has not hesitated on this point. He has built high stone walls on each side of the path, and has spanned it by bridges, so that the public circulate like termites while he gorges on the black-berries unseen. He really does own his wood, this able chap. Dives in Hell did pretty well, but the gulf dividing him from Lazarus could be traversed by vision, and nothing traverses it here. And perhaps I shall come to this in time. I shall wall in and fence out until I really taste the sweets of property. Enormously stout, end-lessly avaricious, pseudocreative, intensely selfish, I shall weave upon my forehead the quadruple crown of possession until those nasty Bolshies come and take it off again and thrust me aside into the outer darkness.

Why We Crave Horror Movies

Stephen King

I think that we're all mentally ill; those of us outside the asylums only hide it a little better—and maybe not all that much better, after all. We've all known people who talk to themselves, people who sometimes squinch their faces into horrible grimaces when they believe no one is watching, people who have some hysterical fear—of snakes, the dark, the tight place, the long drop . . . and, of course, those final worms and grubs that are waiting so patiently underground.

When we pay our four or five bucks and seat ourselves at tenth-row center in a theater showing a horror movie, we are daring the nightmare.

Why? Some of the reasons are simple and obvious. To show that we can, that we are not afraid, that we can ride this roller coaster. Which is not to say that a really good horror movie may not surprise a scream out of us at some point, the way we may scream when the roller coaster twists through a complete 360 or plows through a lake at the bottom of the drop. And horror movies, like roller coasters, have always been the special province of the young; by the time one turns 40 or 50, one's appetite for double twists or 360-degree loops may be considerably depleted.

We also go to reestablish our feelings of essential normality; the horror movie is innately conservative, even reactionary. Freda Jackson as the horrible melting woman in *Die, Monster, Die!* confirms for us that no matter how far we may be removed from the beauty of a Robert Redford or a Diana Ross, we are still lightyears from true ugliness.

And we go to have fun.

Ah, but this is where the ground starts to slope away, isn't it? Because this is a very peculiar sort of fun, indeed. The fun comes from seeing others menaced—sometimes killed. One critic has suggested that if pro football has become the voyeur's version of combat, then the horror film has become the modern version of the public lynching.

It is true that the mythic, "fairy-tale" horror film intends to take away the shades of gray. . . . It urges us to put away our more civilized and adult penchant for analysis and to become children again, seeing things in pure blacks and whites. It may be that horror movies provide psychic relief on this level because this invitation to lapse into simplicity, irrationality, and even outright madness is extended so rarely. We are told we may allow our emotions a free rein . . . or no rein at all.

If we are all insane, then sanity becomes a matter of degree. If your insanity leads you to carve up women, like Jack the Ripper or the Cleveland Torso Murderer, we clap you away in the funny farm (but neither of those two amateur-night surgeons was ever caught, heh-heh-heh); if, on the other hand, your insanity leads you only to talk to yourself when you're under stress or to pick your nose on your morning bus, then you are left alone to go about your business . . . though it is doubtful that you will ever be invited to the best parties.

The potential lyncher is in almost all of us (excluding saints, past and present; but then, most saints have been crazy in their own ways), and every now and then, he has to be let loose to scream and roll around in the grass. Our emotions and our fears form their own body, and we recognize that it demands its own exercise to maintain proper muscle tone. Certain of these emotional muscles are accepted— even exalted—in civilized society; they are, of course, the emotions that tend to maintain the status quo of civilization itself. Love, friendship, loyalty, kindness— these are all the emotions that we applaud, emotions that have been immortalized in the couplets of Hallmark cards and in the verses (I don't dare call it poetry) of Leonard Nimoy.

When we exhibit these emotions, society showers us with positive reinforcement; we learn this even before we get out of diapers. When, as children, we hug our rotten little puke of a sister and give her a kiss, all the aunts and uncles smile and twit and cry, "Isn't he the sweetest little thing?" Such coveted treats as chocolate-covered graham crackers often follow. But if we deliberately slam the rotten little puke of a sister's fingers in the door, sanctions follow—angry remonstrance from parents, aunts and uncles; instead of a chocolate-covered graham cracker, a spanking.

But anticivilization emotions don't go away, and they demand periodic exercise. We have such "sick" jokes as, "What's the difference between a truckload of bowling balls and a truckload of dead babies?" (You can't unload a truckload of bowling balls with a pitchfork . . . a joke, by the way, that I heard originally from a ten-year-old.) Such a joke may surprise a laugh or a grin out of us even as we recoil, a possibility that confirms the thesis: If we share a brotherhood of man, then we also share an insanity of man. None of which is intended as a defense of either the sick joke or insanity but merely as an explanation of why the best horror films, like the best fairy tales, manage to be reactionary, anarchistic, and revolutionary all at the same time.

The mythic horror movie, like the sick joke, has a dirty job to do. It deliberately appeals to all that is worst in us. It is morbidity unchained, our most base instincts let free, our nastiest fantasies realized . . . , and it all happens, fittingly enough, in the dark. For those reasons, good liberals often shy away from horror films. For myself, I like to see the most aggressive of them—*Dawn of the Dead*, for instance—as lifting a trap door in the civilized forebrain and throwing a basket of raw meat to the hungry alligators swimming around in that subterranean river beneath.

Why bother? Because it keeps them from getting out, man. It keeps them down there and me up here. It was Lennon and McCartney who said that all you need is love, and I would agree with that.

As long as you keep the gators fed.

Fear of Dearth

Carl Tucker

I hate jogging. Every dawn, as I thud around New York City's Central Park reservoir, I am reminded of how much I hate it. It's so tedious. Some claim jogging is thought conducive: others insist the scenery relieves the monotony. For me, the pace is wrong for contemplation of either ideas or vistas. While jogging, all I can think about is jogging—or nothing. One advantage of jogging around a reservoir is that there's no dry shortcut home.

From the listless looks of some fellow trotters, I gather I am not alone in my unenthusiasm: Bill-paying, it seems, would be about as diverting. Nonetheless, we continue to jog; more, we continue to *choose* to jog. From a practically infinite array of opportunities, we select one that we don't enjoy and can't wait to have done with. Why?

For any trend, there are as many reasons as there are participants. This person runs to lower his blood pressure. That person runs to escape the telephone or a cranky spouse or a filthy household. Another person runs to avoid doing anything else, to dodge a decision about how to lead his life or a realization that his life is leading nowhere. Each of us has his carrot and stick. In my case, the stick is my slackening physical condition, which keeps me from beating opponents at tennis whom I overwhelmed two years ago. My carrot is to win.

Beyond these disparate reasons, however, lies a deeper cause. It is no accident that now, in the last third of the twentieth century, personal fitness and health have suddenly become a popular obsession. True, modern man likes to feel good, but that hardly distinguishes him from his predecessors.

With zany myopia, economists like to claim that the deeper cause of everything is economic. Delightfully, there seems no marketplace explanation for jogging. True, jogging is cheap, but then not jogging is cheaper. And the scant and skimpy equipment which jogging demands must make it a marketer's least favored form of recreation.

Some scout-masterish philosophers argue that the appeal of jogging and other body-maintenance programs is the discipline they afford. We live in a world in which individuals have fewer and fewer obligations. The work week has shrunk. Weekend worship is less compulsory. Technology gives us more free time. Satisfactorily filling free time requires imagination and effort. Freedom is a wide and risky river; it can drown the person who does not know how to swim across it. The more obligations one takes on, the more time one occupies, the less threat freedom poses. Jogging can become an instant obligation. For a portion of his day, the jogger is not his own man; he is obedient to a regimen he has accepted.

Theologists may take the argument one step further. It is our modern irreligion, our lack of confidence in any hereafter, that makes us anxious to stretch our mortal stay as long as possible. We run, as the saying goes, for our lives, hounded by the suspicion that these are the only lives we are likely to enjoy.

All of these theorists seem to me more or less right. As the growth of cults and charismatic religions and the resurgence of enthusiasm for the military draft suggest, we do crave commitment. And who can doubt, watching so many middle-aged and older persons torturing themselves in the name of fitness, that we are unreconciled to death, more so perhaps than any generation in modern memory?

But I have a hunch there's a further explanation of our obsession with exercise. I suspect that what motivates us even more than a fear of death is a fear of dearth. Our era is the first to anticipate the eventual depletion of all natural resources. We see wilderness shrinking; rivers losing their capacity to sustain life; the air, even the stratosphere, being loaded with potentially deadly junk. We see the irreplaceable being squandered, and in the depths of our consciousness we are fearful that we are creating an uninhabitable world. We feel more or less helpless and yet, at the same time, desirous to protect what resources we can. We recycle soda bottles and restore old buildings and protect our nearest natural resource—our physical health—in the almost superstitious hope that such small gestures will help save an earth that we are blighting. Jogging becomes a sort of penance for our sins of gluttony, greed, and waste. Like a hair shirt or a bed of nails, the more one hates it, the more virtuous it makes one feel.

That is why *we* jog. Why *I* jog is to win at tennis.

My Decision to Attend DeVry

Student

With only a week's forethought, I found myself sitting in the office of a DeVry recruitment counselor discussing what DeVry may have to offer for me. Prior to that week, I would have never thought that I would have ever stepped foot back into a formal educational environment. I entered the interview with high skepticism, but I slowly came to the realization that this was where I belonged. All of my excuses of why formal education was no longer applicable to me lost their validity. "Student" was now going to become my identity for the next two years. As a result of my decision to attend DeVry, my personal, financial, and educational life has changed dramatically.

For instance, my resolve to return to school personally altered my independence, my self-esteem, and my family relationships. Basically, I had to let go of the self-sufficient independence I had embraced over the last nine years. In order for me to attend school, it became necessary for me to move back in with my parents. Then, my employer of the last three years was unable to retain me on a part-time basis, so I lost my job. Also, due to my accelerated class schedule and studies, I had to modify my social activities. Even with losing some of my independence, the decision to attend DeVry personally provided me with a deeper sense of self-esteem. I was now imagining a future with a wealth of possibilities. I, also, grew more confident after realizing I would acquire new skills. Furthermore, I felt a sense of pride in coming to terms with my half-completed education, receiving satisfaction at the prospect of possessing a usable degree in the near future. Surprisingly, my decision to attend DeVry even enhanced my relationship with my family. Moving back in with my parents provided me the opportunity to interact with my family on a daily basis. Besides conversing with my parents more, I was also sharing many of my meals and helping them with their 40-acre horse farm.

In addition to the personal changes I have experienced from my decision to attend DeVry, financially I have increased my debt liabilities, eliminated the last of my long term investments, and provided a future potential for increased income. Attending DeVry exposed me to a whole new world of incurring long term debts to support both personal and educational obligations. Financial creativity and loans have become a necessity in order to support my various personal expenses. Little experiences of joy have occurred every once in a while, such as when I realized for the first time in my life that I would actually receive a tax refund for this next year. Unfortunately, tax refunds alone will not support both my personal and educational expenses incurred while at DeVry. Once I made the decision to attend, I was quickly introduced to the confusing world of student loans and the ever growing debt that follows. As a result of my decision to become a student, I had to sacrifice my present day financial security. Regular employment was no longer feasible with the twenty credit hour terms I carried. Also, the mounting expenses caused me to sell the last of my long term investments. On the other hand, the projected financial rewards of increasing my skills and marketability by attending DeVry compensates for any present day sacrifices. The skills and knowledge I will acquire at DeVry will give me an edge on having more of a choice on my future employment and salary level. In addition, receiving my education from DeVry will increase my ability to secure employment sooner because of DeVry's reputation and its placement program.

Moreover, the decision to attend DeVry reminded me of the value of gaining an education, opened up to me new knowledge and skills, and provided me the ability to visualize the application of this education. I discovered how much I missed the awe of learning, the moment when a completely foreign idea formulates into a comprehensible concept. In addition, I received a reawakened desire to seek out knowledge and not to be satisfied with only the status quo. Also, DeVry has enhanced my knowledge base through the various courses they offer with the Telecommunication Management Bachelors of Science degree. The telecommunication courses have made me aware of a whole new developing segment of technology and the need to manage it. The business and finance classes have provided me with a better understanding of the economy around me. Similarly, each of the remaining courses has provided me with a refining education that will add to my value in the workplace. Finally, my decision to attend DeVry played a key factor in enabling me to visualize completing my education and applying the acquired knowledge to future employment. Only when I firmly decided to attend DeVry was I hit with the momentousness of my decision. For the first time in all of my educational experiences, I could actually visualize completing school and receiving a college degree. DeVry successfully converted me to the pursuit of a higher level of education. Through the various courses I have already taken, I have now become a stronger advocate of education. Experience may be very important to an employer but education is the foundation upon which I can firmly build that experience.

On the whole, my decision to attend and complete my education at DeVry has resulted in many changes in my life, both present and future. Just as a caterpillar needs to develop a cocoon to someday become a beautiful butterfly, it appears I, too, have felt the effects of the need to develop and change to reach my potential.

This Is Not a Tall Person's World

Student

I feel that our world is made for tall people and not short people like me. No one ever makes a comment about being too tall; it is always the short people like me that comments are made to. I do not make it through the day without a comment being made about my height. I can do just as many things as tall people can do. Being short hinders playing some sports, creates problems with everyday activities, and causes many remarks to be made.

Being short makes some sports hard to do. The teams for basketball have tall people on them. I never got to be one of the starting five, because my coach felt I was not tall enough to play basketball. I could shoot and score just as well as the starters, but because of my height, I could not start. I had to wait until one of the starters made a mistake before I could get a chance to play. I do not see many short people playing football. When football is mentioned tall guys come to mind. The short guys would get knocked down easier than the tall guys would. Volleyball is another sport that I have had trouble with because of my height. I can serve, bump, and set the ball fine, but the spiking part of the game is a different story. The net is too tall for me to get above it to have a good spike or block. My coach wanted someone that could spike and block, so I had to work extra hard to convince her to let me start. My other good abilities outweighed the weakness of spiking and blocking.

Being short creates some problems with my everyday activities. If I want something out of the top cabinet in our kitchen, I have to get a chair or climb up on the cabinet to reach it. This takes extra time for me that a person with ordinary height would never encounter. Some of the mirrors on the restroom walls are too high that I can not see myself without having to jump. When I go to the store, I can not reach some things off the top shelf. I can not take a chair with me or climb up on the shelf like I do at home. I have to ask a clerk from the store to get it for me. Some seats in places are made too tall; when I sit in them my feet dangle. My feet do not reach the floor like a person's with normal height would. Some of the peepholes on motel rooms and apartment doors are up too high for me to see out of. By the time I get a chair to see outside, the person waiting is wondering if anyone is going to answer the door. When I am driving my car, I have to have the seat up close to see over the dashboard. When there are crowds of people around, I can never see what is actually going on because I can not see over the people in front of me. I always have to move up front if I want to see what is happening. When I am with my friends, I am usually the only one who has to show some type of identification to verify my age. When I walk with my dad, I feel like I am in a walking marathon trying to keep up with him. He is six feet tall, and one of his strides make up two of mine. These are just some of the problems that I encounter thanks to my height.

I have been called a variety of names. At my last job it was not "Hello Jennifer," but "Hello Munchkin." Shorty is probably the most ordinary name used. Tidbit and short-stuff are some other names that I hear. People will ask me if I get the children's discount, even though they know my age. Some of my friends will make the remark that I should look at the children's menu or ask me if I need a highchair to eat in a restaurant. When people tell me to grow up, they think that this might disturb me, but I have heard this remark too many times to let it bother me. Just because I am short does not mean that I am still a child.

I can do just about anything that people with ordinary height can do. I may have a few more problems, but it is not my fault that I did not grow a few more inches.

Why I Believe Everyone Should Do Military Service

Student

Military service—everyone cringes when those two words are mentioned. Why? That's the first question that I ask when I see that cringe. Sure, not everyone is made for service, but if everyone were required to do at least one term of service, they would come out of the service a much stronger, better person all around. The country would also have a stronger ability to respond to a world crisis in a much faster way; this is why I believe everyone should do military service. Among other reasons are for the discipline, personal experiences, and the benefits to other people, to work and to society.

The discipline a person learns from military service is possibly one of the best things that could be taught to anyone, especially if that person happens to be a "rotten apple." Military service will teach self discipline, and also in upper ranks teach people how to discipline others. First, with self-discipline, many people will learn the importance of timeliness and cleanliness. An example of this would be while I was in boot camp. Our company had to keep the barracks (living quarters) for nearly 100 people very clean. We never knew when we would get inspected. If we left the barracks in disorder, we would get "hit" for that discrepancy, and our company commander would come down on us like a little white tornado, throwing things around, shouting, and basically giving us a very hard time. The self-discipline we learned taught us to keep everything we possessed very neat and tidy. The advantage with this is that we didn't have to worry about pests such as cockroaches. If learned properly, this will carry over into your normal life, giving you a sense of well being, and also a much healthier standard of living.

The other type of discipline learned from military service is how to discipline others in a meaningful way. By this I mean not degrading the offender but

196

showing that person where they went wrong and then giving them a project or something that had to be checked every day to ensure it has been done correctly. One example of this type of discipline is if someone qualified to work on some equipment messes up and takes the equipment off line without proper authorization, that person may have to go through the whole process of re-qualifying for that equipment before he/she can work on it again without supervision. The offending person may also find themselves restricted to base or ship while others can come and go as they please. It's almost like putting someone in the corner and not allowing them to leave that corner until given permission.

To follow along with discipline is the personal experiences one will have while in the military. Among these things are travel and educational experiences. The opportunity for anyone to travel to foreign countries for a minimal cost to oneself is definitely a plus in my books. While in the service I had the opportunity to travel to Greece, Turkey, and Scotland. Each of these countries opened my eyes a little more to the realization that there is more to life than just staying in one place or country my whole life. Also while being stationed in Greece and Scotland, I learned a lot about each country's style of life, culture, and some of their language, which can never hurt anyone. If, for instance, someone enters the military service with a very bad attitude towards other countries, the travel and duty stations in other countries will often bring about a change in that person's attitude. It also promotes friendly relations among different countries, which in current times is something that is of utmost importance.

The educational side of the military is an ongoing thing. Each day brings about something different to learn. I don't think I ever stopped learning while I was in the navy. If it wasn't something to do with my job, it dealt with the host country, or even on a personal basis, such things as management and budgeting personal finances. The military also has continuing educational options like the G. I. Bill where a service person can have a certain amount of money kept out of their paycheck every two weeks and the government will match that amount by over 900%. This may sound like a high percentage but when I was in the military I had $1200 kept out of my pay for 12 months and I was supposed to get back $10,800 for college tuition; the amount has increased over the years. In my opinion, life is an ongoing learning experience, and military service just brings that learning to the front of a person's perspective; there was never a day that I didn't learn something new in the military and also so far in civilian life.

Each of the topics discussed above brings me to my final topic of the benefits of military service to people in general, to work, and also to society. With the discipline and personal experiences of military service, I have been able to relate to people of differing backgrounds and nationalities, often making very strong friendships with these people. Military service can also help in the work environment because of the discipline one learns from the service. This discipline helps you to cope with the stresses of today's highly competitive work environment, completing projects on time, etc. Often a company will see a person with military service and choose that person over another simply because of that service. The company knows that the ex-military person will have the organizational skills, determination, and experience to get the job done in a high stress situation. This, in the end, benefits not only the single person but also society as a whole, because without all these attributes given and taught by military service, I believe that society would eventually end up in total chaos. That chaos is something that has to be avoided at all costs because any society in chaos will not exist for very long. Just about all if not all of our heads of state have done some type of military service, and they know how important that service is to our country as a whole and as an individual.

What Makes a Good Internet Page?

Student

"I don't ever want to see you again!" "You're boring!" "You suck!" These phrases could all easily lead to the assumption that you could be turning people off. In the fast paced and highly competitive world we live in, the last thing people intentionally look for is a "turn off." Traffic jams, detours, slow construction zones, toll booths, and speed limits are all "turn offs." We face them every day in our transits to and from, and very similarly on the internet. People can't avoid these "turn off's" on the road, but they can and do on the internet. The reality of life on and off the internet is that you just don't often hear the friendly terms "Here take one of these . . . they're free," "Let me help you," or "Look what I have for you." On a really good internet page you might find all three. A good internet page is like a dream salesman. . . . It has services that suit the needs of your search, a professional approach, and free stuff just for you.

Properly composed pages take you where you really want to be. A proper page can get you the information you need quickly and easily. "I don't ever want to see you again" might be something said about your site if you have a slow loading or confusing site. Users tend to shy away from sites that can not hook and deliver in a quick manner. A nicely composed page is user friendly and displays all the relevant material that suits the interest's of the surfers search in a timely manner. The "Best Buy Online" site is a quick loading and informative site that covers almost every aspect of their retail business in a simple and convenient layout.

A professional approach consists of care, education, and experience. To create a page that keeps users happy, you must constantly update it with information about your business. A good psychological trick is to show recent updates that prove to your viewers that you are always working for them. By staying current with the latest tricks of the trade for site construction, you will keep your viewers satisfied with the look and feel of your site. Constant updates and user feedback can arm you with the knowledge and experience needed to keep your site running with the best. A compilation of these skills should steer your site clear of the "You suck!" credibility implanted in unsatisfied viewers' minds. The "Netscape Netcenter" and the "YAHOO.com" sites are updated with news and information on a daily basis and have an unending supply of services that are interesting, useful, and up to date. These sites are vivid examples of how to represent your cause in an all out race for first place in the modem day "Avoid the detour dash."

"Look what I have for you!" A neat trick in popular site construction is the bait and catch method. Simply lure unsuspecting customers/viewers in with a free download or two. There are tons of free goodies circulating the web at all times. Just offer some catchy downloads and maybe even trade links with a quality site that supports your mission, and you are headed for the front of the pack. "MP3.com" and "Download.com" are two sites that feed users with a constant array of free programs of every imaginable kind. Keep enough exciting handouts around for your guests and you will stay far away from the dreaded "You're boring" section of internet pages.

In closing, try to remember: keep it up to date, keep it useful, and keep it interesting. You can open up new worlds for yourself and your business on the internet with a well published site. However, you can just as easily ruin hopes of gaining any newcomers to your clientele with a poor representation of yourself on the internet. A successful site will not turn your viewers off and will definitely not remind them of the traffic jams, toll booths, and speed limits they are so used to. You wouldn't hire a salesperson that can't compete successfully on the sales floor . . . so don't hire one that can't compete on the internet.

"BEST BUY ONLINE" 8/11/98

"Netscape Netcenter" 8/11/98

"YAHOO" 8/11/98

"MP3.com" 8/11/98

"Download.com" 8/11/98

CHAPTER 9

Definition

Definitions allow readers to understand complex terms and abstract concepts. Without shared definitions, we would be unable to communicate with each other. The ability to understand definitions and use them effectively orally and in writing helps us to maintain a level of communication that is both accurate and user friendly to many people.

Why Learn to Write a Definition Essay?

When you define, you explain a word, an occurrence, an item, a concept, or a belief that otherwise would be foreign to your readers. By defining clearly, you provide a focus for your readers so that they can relate to the term. Clear definitions connect you as a writer with your reader thereby fostering communication and making your essay easier and more enjoyable to read.

In business, you define in order to share technological terms with your audience. Definition in business is particularly important in documents such as user manuals.

Types of Definitions

A definition could be quite short, a brief dictionary-length summary of a term, including its language origins, parts of speech, etc.

You can also use longer, extended definitions that could form an entire essay. Words or ideas which require such long definitions are often abstract, complex or controversial. They might have many levels of meaning, far beyond the denotative (literal), moving into the connotative (deeper levels of meaning).

You can define things a number of ways. You can define a term by giving analogies for it or by giving synonyms for the word you're defining. You can define attributively, that is, by listing all the attributes or characteristics a particular thing has. Perhaps the clearest way to define something is by offering a formal definition. A formal definition follows a particular formula: term = genus + differentia, that is, the thing being defined (term) is placed within the general class of things to which it belongs (its genus), and then enough differences between it and other members of that class (differentia) are given to make the thing distinct within the class.

How to Write a Definition Essay

1. After choosing a subject, prewrite so that you understand what you are defining and how you will approach the definition.

2. Determine your audience's level of knowledge so that you have direction about the extent of your definition.

3. Place your term in a general category, and then contrast the word with other words in that group. For example, take the term "technical writing." It is a type of writing; however, it's different from expository writing, expressive writing, creative writing, and journalism. You could then say the main purpose of technical writing is writing for the business world. This would include documents such as letters, memos, reports, brochures, user manuals, and email. These are all very different documents from essays.

4. You could also trace a word's origins. For example, take the term "baby boomer." This term originated in newspapers and magazines from the 1940's and 1950's to characterize babies born in postwar America.

5. Expand your definition by using description, narration, example, process analysis, division/classification, comparison/contrast.

Usefulness of Definition in Other Essays

You will often find it helpful in other essays to remember to define terms or concepts which otherwise would prevent your audience from understanding what you're writing about. Many writing situations require that you first define what you're writing about before continuing with your process analysis, causal analysis, description, etc.

Topic Ideas for Definition Essays

An act of courage

Happiness/unhappiness

Faith

Successful parenting

A boring job

An easy-to-navigate web site

A loyal friend

A hard worker
Unconditional love
Beauty
The perfect gift
The perfect date
The most difficult exam
A learning experience

Peer Evaluation for Definition Essay

1. Does the writer introduce the term in an interesting way?
2. Is the term clearly stated?
3. Do you understand the term's category?
4. Does the writer provide contrasts to the term?
5. Does the writer use a variety of examples to illustrate the term?
6. Could you use the term in your own writing to enhance a topic?
7. Does the writer use other forms of expression such as description, narration, division/classification, comparison/contrast, etc. to develop the term?
8. Does the writer have a logical pattern of organization for the entire essay?
9. Does the writer divide the essay into logical paragraphs of development so that you can understand the term?
10. Did the writer avoid grammar, punctuation and spelling errors?
11. Does the writer vary sentence patterns?

Barrier Signals

Desmond Morris

People feel safer behind some kind of physical barrier. If a social situation is in any way threatening, then there is an immediate urge to set up such a barricade. For a tiny child faced with a stranger, the problem is usually solved by hiding behind its mother's body and peeping out at the intruder to see what he or she will do next. If the mother's body is not available, then a chair or some other piece of solid furniture will do. If the stranger insists on coming closer, then the peeping face must be hidden too. If the insensitive intruder continues to approach despite these obvious signals of fear, then there is nothing for it but to scream or flee.

This pattern is gradually reduced as the child matures. In teenage girls it may still be detected in the giggling cover-up of the face, with hands or papers, when acutely or jokingly embarrassed. But by the time we are adult, the childhood hiding which dwindled to adolescent shyness, is expected to disappear altogether, as we bravely stride out to meet our guests, hosts, companions, relatives, colleagues, customers, clients, or friends. Each social occasion involves us, once again, in encounters similar to the ones which made us hide as scared infants and, as then, each encounter is slightly threatening. In other words, the fears are still there, but their expression is blocked. Our adult roles demand control and suppression of any primitive urge to withdraw and hide ourselves away. The more formal the occasion and the more dominant or unfamiliar our social companions, the more worrying the moment of encounter becomes. Watching people under these conditions, it is possible to observe the many small ways in which they continue to "hide behind their mother's skirts." The actions are still there, but they are transformed into less obvious movements and postures. It is these that are the Barrier Signals of adult life.

The most popular form of Barrier Signal is the Body-cross. In this, the hands or arms are brought into contact with one another in front of the body, forming a temporary "bar" across the trunk, rather like a bumper or fender on the front of a motor-car. This is not done as a physical act of fending off the other person, as when raising a forearm horizontally across the front of the body to push through a struggling crowd. It is done, usually at quite a distance, as a nervous guest approaches a dominant host. The action is performed unconsciously and, if tackled on the subject immediately afterwards, the guest will not be able to remember having made the gesture. It is always camouflaged in some way, because if it were performed as a primitive fending-off or covering-up action, it would obviously be too transparent. The disguise it wears varies from person to person. Here are some examples:

The special guest on a gala occasion is alighting from his official limousine. Before he can meet and shake hands with the reception committee, he has to walk alone across the open space in front of the main entrance to the building where the function is being held. A large crowd has come to watch his arrival and the press cameras are flashing. Even for the most experienced of celebrities this is a slightly nervous moment, and the mild fear that is felt expresses itself just as he is halfway across the "greeting-space." As he walks forward, his right hand reaches across his body and makes a last-minute adjustment to his left cuff-link. It pauses there momentarily as he takes a few more steps, and then, at last, he is close enough to reach out his hand for the first of the many handshakes.

On a similar occasion, the special guest is a female. At just the point where her male counterpart would have fiddled with his cuff, she reaches across her body with her right hand and slightly shifts the position of her handbag, which is hanging from her left forearm.

There are other variations on this theme. A male may finger a button or the strap of a wristwatch instead of his cuff. A female may smooth out an imaginary crease in a sleeve, or re-position a scarf or coat held over her left arm. But in all cases there is one essential feature: at the peak moment of nervousness there is a Body-cross, in which one arm makes contact with the other across the front of the body, constructing a fleeting barrier between the guest and the reception committee.

Sometimes the barrier is incomplete. One arm swings across but does not actually make contact with the other. Instead it deals with some trivial clothing-adjustment task on the opposite side of the body. With even heavier camouflage, the hand comes up and across, but goes no further than the far side of the head or face, with a mild stroking or touching action.

Less disguised forms of the Body-cross are seen with less experienced individuals. The man entering the restaurant, as he walks across an open space, rubs his hands together, as if washing them. Or he advances with them clasped firmly in front of him.

Such are the Barrier Signals of the greeting situation, where one person is advancing on another. Interestingly, field observations reveal that it is most unlikely that both the greeter *and* the greeted will perform such actions. Regardless of status, it is nearly always the new arrival who makes the body-cross movement, because it is he who is invading the home territory of the greeters. They are on their own ground or, even if they are not, they were there first and have at least temporary territorial "rights" over the place. This gives them an indisputable dominance at the moment of the greeting. Only if they are extremely subordinate to the new arrival, and perhaps in serious trouble with him, will there be a likelihood of them taking the "body-cross role." And if they do, this will mean that the new arrival on the scene will omit it as he enters.

These observations tell us something about the secret language of Barrier Signals, and indicate that, although the sending and receiving of the signals are both unconsciously done, the message gets across, nonetheless. The message says: "I am nervous but I will not retreat"; and this makes it into an act of subordination which automatically makes the other person feel slightly more dominant and more comfortable.

The situation is different after greetings are over and people are standing about talking to one another. Now, if one man edges too close to another, perhaps to hear better in all the noise of chattering voices, the boxed-in companion may feel the same sort of threatening sensation that the arriving celebrity felt as he walked towards the reception committee. What is needed now, however, is something more long-lasting than a mere cuff-fumble. It is simply not possible to go fiddling with a button for as long as this companion is going to thrust himself forward. So a more composed posture is needed. The favorite Body-cross employed in this situation is the arm-fold, in which the left and right arms intertwine themselves across the front of the chest. This posture, a perfect, frontal Barrier Signal, can be held for a very long time without appearing strange. Unconsciously it transmits a "come-no-farther" message and is used a great deal at crowded gatherings. It has also been used by poster artists as a deliberate "They-shall-not pass!" gesture, and is rather formally employed by bodyguards when standing outside a protected doorway.

The same device of arm-folding can be used in a sitting relationship where the companion is approaching too close, and it can be amplified by a crossing of the legs *away* from the companion. Another variant is to press the tightly clasped hands down on to the crotch and squeeze them there between the legs, as if protecting the genitals. The message of this particular form of barrier is clear enough, even though neither side becomes consciously aware of it. But perhaps the major Barrier Signal for the seated person is that ubiquitous device, the desk. Many a businessman would feel naked without one and hides behind it gratefully every day, wearing it like a vast, wooden chastity-belt. Sitting beyond it he feels fully protected from the visitor exposed on the far side. It is the supreme barrier, both physical and psychological, giving him an immediate and lasting comfort while he remains in its solid embrace.

The Holocaust

Bruno Bettelheim

To begin with, it was not the hapless victims of the Nazis who named their incomprehensible and totally unmasterable fate the "holocaust." It was the Americans who applied this artificial and highly technical term to the Nazi extermination of the European Jews. But while the event when named as mass murder most foul evokes the most immediate, most powerful revulsion, when it is designated by a rare technical term, we must first in our minds translate it back into emotionally meaningful language. Using technical or specially created terms instead of words from our common vocabulary is one of the best-known and most widely used distancing devices, separating the intellectual from the emotional experience. Talking about "the holocaust" permits us to manage it intellectually where the raw facts, when given their ordinary names, would overwhelm us emotionally because it was catastrophe beyond comprehension, beyond the limits of our imagination, unless we force ourselves against our desire to extend it to encompass these terrible events.

This linguistic circumlocution began while it all was only in the planning stage. Even the Nazis—usually given to grossness in language and action—shied away from facing openly what they were up to and called this vile mass murder "the final solution of the Jewish problem." After all, solving a problem can be made to appear like an honorable enterprise, as long as we are not forced to recognize that the solution we are about to embark on consists of the completely unprovoked, vicious murder of millions of helpless men, women, and children. The Nuremberg judges of these Nazi criminals followed their example of circumlocution by coining a neologism out of one Greek and one Latin root: genocide. These artificially created technical terms fail to connect with our strongest feelings. The horror of murder is part of our most common human heritage. From earliest infancy on, it arouses violent abhorrence in us. Therefore in whatever form it appears we should give such an act its true designation and not hide it behind polite, erudite terms created out of classical words.

To call this vile mass murder "the holocaust" is not to give it a special name emphasizing its uniqueness which would permit, over time, the word becoming invested with feelings germane to the event it refers to. The correct definition of *holocaust* is "burnt offering." As such, it is part of the language of the psalmist, a meaningful word to all who have some acquaintance with the Bible, full of the richest emotional connotations. By using the term "holocaust," entirely false associations are established through conscious and unconscious connotations between the most vicious of mass murders and ancient rituals of a deeply religious nature.

Using a word with such strong unconscious religious connotations when speaking of the murder of millions of Jews robs the victims of this abominable mass murder of the only thing left to them: their uniqueness. Calling the most callous, most brutal, most horrid, most heinous mass murder a burnt offering is a sacrilege, a profanation of God and man.

Martyrdom is part of our religious heritage. A martyr, burned at the stake, is a burnt offering to his god. And it is true that after the Jews were asphyxiated, the victims' corpses were burned. But I believe we fool ourselves if we think we are honoring the victims of systematic murder by using this term, which has the highest moral connotations. By doing so, we connect for our own psychological reasons what happened in the extermination camps with historical events we deeply regret, but also greatly admire. We do so because this makes it easier for us to cope; only in doing so we cope with our distorted image of what happened, not with the events the way they did happen.

By calling the victims of the Nazis martyrs, we falsify their fate. The true meaning of *martyr* is: "One who voluntarily undergoes the penalty of death for refusing to renounce his faith" *(Oxford English Dictionary)*. The Nazis made sure that nobody could mistakenly think that their victims were murdered for their religious beliefs. Renouncing their faith would have saved none of them. Those who had converted to Christianity were gassed, as were those who were atheists, and those who were deeply religious Jews. They did not die for any conviction, and certainly not out of choice.

Millions of Jews were systematically slaughtered, as were untold other "undesirables," not for any convictions of theirs, but only because they stood in the way of the realization of an illusion. They neither died for their convictions, nor were they slaughtered because of their convictions, but only in consequence of the Nazis' delusional belief about what was required to protect the purity of their assumed superior racial endowment, and what they thought necessary to guarantee them the living space they believed they needed and were entitled to. Thus while these millions were slaughtered for an idea, they did not die for one.

Millions—men, women, and children—were processed after they had been utterly brutalized, their humanity destroyed, their clothes torn from their bodies. Naked, they were sorted into those who were destined to be murdered immediately, and those others who had a short-term usefulness as slave labor. But after a brief interval they, too, were to be herded into the same gas chambers into which the others were immediately piled, there to be asphyxiated so that, in their last moments, they could not prevent themselves from fighting each other in vain for a last breath of air.

To call these most wretched victims of a murderous delusion, of destructive drives run rampant, martyrs or a burnt offering is a distortion invented for our comfort, small as it may be. It pretends that this most vicious of mass murders had some deeper meaning; that in some fashion the victims either offered themselves or at least became sacrifices to a higher cause. It robs them of the last recognition which could be theirs, denies them the last dignity we could accord them: to face and accept what their death was all about, not embellishing it for the small psychological relief this may give us.

We could feel so much better if the victims had acted out of choice. For our emotional relief, therefore, we dwell on the tiny minority who did exercise some choice: the resistance fighters of the Warsaw ghetto, example, and others like them. We are ready to overlook the fact that these people fought back only at a time when everything was lost, when the overwhelming majority of those who had been forced into the ghettos had already been exterminated without resisting. Certainly those few who finally fought for their survival and their convictions, risking and losing their lives in doing so, deserve our admiration; their deeds give us a moral lift. But the more we dwell on these few, the more unfair are we to the memory of the millions who were slaughtered—who gave in, did not fight back—because we deny them the only thing which up to the very end remained uniquely their own: their fate.

Pornoviolence

Tom Wolfe

"Keeps His Mom-in-law in Chains, meet *Kills Son and Feeds Corpse to Pigs."*

"Pleased to meet you."

"Teenager Twists Off Corpse's Head . . . to Get Gold Teeth, meet *Strangles Girl Friend, Then Chops Her to Pieces."*

"How you doing?"

"Nurse's Aide Sees Fingers Chopped Off in Meat Grinder, meet *I Left My Babies in the Deep Freeze."*

"It's a pleasure."

It's a pleasure! No doubt about that! In all these years of journalism I have covered more conventions than I care to remember. Podiatrists, theosophists, Professional Budget Finance dentists, oyster farmers, mathematicians, truckers, dry cleaners, stamp collectors, Esperantists, nudists, and newspaper editors—I have seen them all, together, in vast assemblies, sloughing through the wall-to-wall of a thousand hotel lobbies (the nudists excepted) in their shimmering gray-metal suits and pajama-stripe shirts with white Plasti-Coat name cards on their chests, and I have sat through their speeches and seminars (the nudists included) and attentively endured ear baths such as you wouldn't believe. And yet none has ever been quite like the convention of the stringers for the *National Enquirer.*

The *Enquirer* is a weekly newspaper that is probably known by sight to millions more than know it by name. No one who ever came face-to-face with the *Enquirer* on a newsstand in its wildest days is likely to have forgotten the sight: a tabloid with great inky shocks of type all over the front page saying something on the order of *Gouges Out Wife's Eyes to Make Her Ugly, Dad Hurls Hot Grease in Daughter's Face, Wife Commits Suicide After 2 Years of Poisoning Fails to Kill Husband.*

The stories themselves were supplied largely by stringers, i.e., correspondents, from all over the country, the world, for that matter, mostly copy editors and reporters on local newspapers. Every so often they would come upon a story, usually via the police beat, that was so grotesque the local sheet would discard it or run it in a highly glossed form rather than offend or perplex its readers. The stringers would preserve them for the *Enquirer,* which always rewarded them well and respectfully.

One year the *Enquirer* convened and feted them at a hotel in Manhattan. This convention was a success in every way. The only awkward moment was at the outset when the stringers all pulled in. None of them knew each other. Their hosts got around the problem by introducing them by the stories they had supplied. The introductions went like this:

"Harry, I want you to meet Frank here. Frank did that story, you remember that story, *Midget Murderer Throws Girl Off Cliff After She Refuses to Dance with Him.*"

"Pleased to meet you. That was some story."

"And Harry did the one about *I Spent Three Days Trapped at Bottom of Forty-Foot-Deep Mine Shaft and Was Saved by a Swarm of Flies.*"

"Likewise, I'm sure."

And *Midget Murderer Throws Girl Off Cliff* shakes hands with *I Spent Three Days Trapped at Bottom of Forty-Foot-Deep Mine Shaft,* and *Buries Her Baby Alive* shakes hands with *Boy, Twelve, Strangles Two-Year-Old Girl,* and *Kills Son and Feeds Corpse to Pigs* shakes hands with *He Strangles Old Woman and Smears Corpse with Syrup, Ketchup, and Oatmeal . . .* and *. . .*

. . . There was a great deal of esprit about the whole thing. These men were, in fact, the avant-garde of a new genre that since then has become institutionalized throughout the nation without anyone knowing its proper name. I speak of the new pornography, the pornography of violence.

Pornography comes from the Greek word *porne,* meaning "harlot," and pornography is literally the depiction of the acts of harlots. In the new pornography, the theme is not sex. The new pornography depicts practitioners acting out another, murkier drive: people staving teeth in, ripping guts open, blowing brains out, and getting even with all those bastards . . .

The success of the *Enquirer* prompted many imitators to enter the field, *Midnight,* the *Star Chronicle,* the *National Insider, Inside News,* the *National Close-up,* the *National Tattler,* the *National Examiner.* A truly competitive free press evolved, and soon a reader could go to the newspaper of his choice for *Kill the Retarded! (Won't You Join My Movement?)* and *Unfaithful Wife? Burn Her Bed!, Harem Master's Mistress Chops Him with Machete, Babe Bites Off Boy's Tongue,* and *Cuts Buddy's Face to Pieces for Stealing His Business and Fiancée.*

And yet the last time I surveyed the Violence press, I noticed a curious thing. These pioneering journals seem to have pulled back. They seem to be regressing to what is by now the Redi-Mix staple of literate Americans, mere sex. *Ecstasy and Me (by Hedy Lamarr),*[1] says the *National Enquirer. I Run a Sex Art Gallery,* says the *National Insider.* What has happened, I think, is something that has happened

---

[1] *Ecstasy,* an early, European-made Hedy Lamarr film, was notorious for its scenes *of* soft-core lovemaking. Later, paired with Charles ("Come with me to the Casbah") Boyer, Lamarr rose to Hollywood stardom in *Algiers* (1938).

to avant-gardes in many fields, from William Morris and the Craftsmen to the Bauhaus group.[2] Namely, their discoveries have been preempted by the Establishment and so thoroughly dissolved into the mainstream they no longer look original.

Robert Harrison, the former publisher of *Confidential*, and later publisher of the aforementioned *Inside News,* was perhaps the first person to see it coming. I was interviewing Harrison early in January 1964 for a story in *Esquire* about six weeks after the assassination of President Kennedy, and we were in a cab in the West Fifties in Manhattan, at a stoplight, by a newsstand, and Harrison suddenly pointed at the newsstand and said, "Look at that. They're doing the same thing the *Enquirer* does."

There on the stand was a row of slick-paper, magazine-size publications, known in the trade as one-shots, with titles like *Four Days That Shook the World, Death of a President, An American Tragedy,* or just *John Fitzgerald Kennedy (1921—1963).* "You want to know why people buy those things?" said Harrison. "People buy those things to see a man get his head blown off."

And, of course, he was right. Only now the publishers were in many cases the pillars of the American press. Invariably, these "special coverages" of the assassination bore introductions piously commemorating the fallen President, exhorting the American people to strength and unity in a time of crisis, urging greater vigilance and safeguards for the new President, and even raising the nice metaphysical question of collective guilt in "an age of violence."

In the years since then, of course, there has been an incessant replay, with every recoverable clinical detail, of those less than five seconds in which a man got his head blown off. And throughout this deluge of words, pictures, and film frames, I have been intrigued with one thing: The point of view, the vantage point, is almost never that of the victim, riding in the Presidential Lincoln Continental. What you get is . . . the view from Oswald's rifle. You can step right up here and look point-blank right through the very hairline cross in Lee Harvey Oswald's Optics Ordinance in weaponry four-power Japanese telescope sight and watch, frame by frame by frame by frame, as that man there's head comes apart. Just a little History there before your very eyes.

The television networks have schooled us in the view from Oswald's rifle and made it seem a normal pastime. The TV viewpoint is nearly always that of the man who is going to strike. The last time I watched *Gunsmoke,* which was not known as a very violent Western in TV terms, the action went like this: The Wellington agents and the stagecoach driver pull guns on the badlands gang leader's daughter and Kitty, the heart-of-gold saloonkeeper, and kidnap them. Then the badlands gang shoots two Wellington agents. Then they tie up five more and talk about shooting them. Then they desist because they might not be able to get a hotel room in the next town if the word got around. Then one badlands gang gunslinger attempts to rape Kitty while the gang leader's younger daughter looks on. Then

---

[2] Morris (1834–96), an English artist, poet, printer, and socialist, founded a company of craftspeople to bring tasteful design to furniture (the Morris chair) and other implements of everyday life. The Bauhaus, an influential art school in Germany (1919–33), taught crafts and brought new ideas of design to architecture and to goods produced in factories.

Kitty resists, so he slugs her one in the jaw. Then the gang leader slugs him. Then the gang leader slugs Kitty. Then Kitty throws hot stew in a gang member's face and hits him over the back of the head with a revolver. Then he knocks her down with a rock. Then the gang sticks up a bank. Here comes the marshal, Matt Dillon. He shoots a gang member and breaks it up. Then the gang leader shoots the guy who was guarding his daughter and the woman. Then the marshal shoots the gang leader. The final exploding bullet signals The End.

It is not the accumulated slayings and bone crushings that make this pornoviolence, however. What makes it pornoviolence is that in almost every case the camera angle, therefore the viewer, is with the gun, the fist, the rock. The pornography of violence has no point of view in the old sense that novels do. You do not live the action through the hero's eyes. You live with the aggressor, whoever he may be. One moment you are the hero. The next you are the villain. No matter whose side you may be on consciously, you are in fact with the muscle, and it is you who disintegrate all comers, villains, lawmen, women, anybody. On the rare occasions in which the gun is emptied into the camera—i.e., into your face—the effect is so startling that the pornography of violence all but loses its fantasy charm. There are not nearly so many masochists as sadists among those little devils whispering into one's ears.

In fact, sex—"sadomasochism"—is only a part of the pornography of violence. Violence is much more wrapped up, simply, with status. Violence is the simple, ultimate solution for problems of status competition, just as gambling is the simple, ultimate solution for economic competition. The old pornography was the fantasy of easy sexual delights in a world where sex was kept unavailable. The new pornography is the fantasy of easy triumph in a world where status competition has become so complicated and frustrating.

Already the old pornography is losing its kick because of overexposure. In the late thirties, Nathanael West published his last and best-regarded novel, *The Day of the Locust,* and it was a terrible flop commercially, and his publisher said if he ever published another book about Hollywood it would "have to be *My Thirty-nine Ways of Making Love by Hedy Lamarr.*" He thought he was saying something that was funny because it was beyond the realm of possibility. Less than thirty years later, however, Hedy Lamarr's *Ecstasy and Me* was published. Whether she mentions thirty-nine ways, I'm not sure, but she gets off to a flying start: "The men in my life have ranged from a classic case history of impotence, to a whip-brandishing sadist who enjoyed sex only after he tied my arms behind me with the sash of his robe. There was another man who took his pleasure with a girl in my own bed, while he thought I was asleep in it."

Yet she was too late. The book very nearly sank without a trace. The sin itself is wearing out. Pornography cannot exist without certified taboo to violate. And today Lust, like the rest of the Seven Deadly Sins—Pride, Sloth, Envy, Greed, Anger, and Gluttony—is becoming a rather minor vice. The Seven Deadly Sins, after all, are only sins against the self. Theologically, the idea of Lust—well, the idea is that if you seduce some poor girl from Akron, it is not a sin because you are mining her, but because you are wasting your time and your energies and damaging your own spirit. This goes back to the old work ethic, when the idea was to keep every able-bodied man's shoulder to the wheel. In an age of riches for all, the ethic becomes more nearly: Let him do anything he pleases, as long as he doesn't get in my way. And if he does get in my way, or even if he doesn't . . . well . . . we have *new* fantasies for that. *Put hair on the walls.*

"Hair on the walls" is the invisible subtitle of Truman Capote's book *In Cold Blood.* The book is neither a who-done-it nor a will-they-be-caught, since the answers to both questions are known from the outset. It does ask why-did-they-do-it, but the answer is soon as clear as it is going to be. Instead, the book's suspense is based largely on a totally new idea in detective stories: the promise of gory details, and the withholding of them until the end. Early in the game one of the two murderers, Dick, starts promising to put "plenty of hair on them-those walls" with a shotgun. So read on, gentle readers, and on and on; you are led up to the moment before the crime on page 60—yet the specifics, what happened, the gory details, are kept out of sight, in grisly dangle, until page 244.

But Dick and Perry, Capote's killers, are only a couple of Low Rent bums. With James Bond the new pornography reached a dead center, the bureaucratic middle class. The appeal of Bond has been explained as the appeal of the lone man who can solve enormously complicated, even world problems through his own bravery and initiative. But Bond is not a lone man at all, of course. He is not the Lone Ranger. He is much easier to identify than that. He is a salaried functionary in a bureaucracy. He is a sport, but a believable one; not a millionaire, but a bureaucrat on an expense account. He is not even a high-level bureaucrat. He is an operative. This point is carefully and repeatedly made by having his superiors dress him down for violations of standard operating procedure. Bond, like the Lone Ranger, solves problems with guns and fists. When it is over, however, the Lone Ranger leaves a silver bullet. Bond, like the rest of us, fills out a report in triplicate.

Marshall McLuhan[3] says we are in a period in which it will become harder and harder to stimulate lust through words and pictures—i.e., the old pornography. In the latest round of pornographic movies the producers have found it necessary to introduce violence, bondage, torture, and aggressive physical destruction to an extraordinary degree. The same sort of bloody escalation may very well happen in the pure pornography of violence. Even such able craftsmen as Truman Capote, Ian Fleming, NBC, and CBS may not suffice. Fortunately, there are historical models to rescue us from this frustration. In the latter days of the Roman Empire, the Emperor Commodus became jealous of the celebrity of the great gladiators. He took to the arena himself, with his sword, and began dispatching suitably screened cripples and hobbled fighters. Audience participation became so popular that soon various *illuminati* of the Commodus set, various boys and girls of the year, were out there, suited up, gaily cutting a sequence of dwarfs and feebles down to short ribs. Ah, swinging generations, what new delights await?

---

[3] Canadian English professor, author of *Understanding Media* (1964), *The Medium Is the Message* (1967), and other books, McLuhan (1911-80) analyzed the effects on world society of television and other electronic media.

The Bureaucrat

Citicorp N. A.

Bureaucracy is a state of mind. True, every bureaucrat needs an organization, a milieu—to choose another useful word from the French—but it is the bureaucrat who makes the milieu, not the other way around.

Most of us associate bureaucracy and all its attendant evils with large organizations, especially governments, and we are not surprised to see it getting worse. As the earth's population grows and computers multiply along with the people, burgeoning bureaucracy appears a natural consequence. What Thomas Carlyle, a hundred years ago, could dismiss contemptuously as "the Continental nuisance called 'Bureaucracy'" is now to become the fate of all humanity because there are so many of us.

Before resigning ourselves to the inevitable, however, we might pause to consider that one of the most pervasive bureaucracies the world has ever known was oppressing the population of the Nile Valley 5,000 years ago, when there were fewer people in the entire world than now live in North America. Add to this the thought that the same number of people can be organized into *(a)* an army, *(b)* a crowd or *(c)* a mob, and it is clear that something more must be involved than time and numbers.

What distinguishes each of the aforementioned groups is not how many people it contains, nor where they happen to congregate, but their purpose for being there. And so it is with the bureaucrat.

The true bureaucrat is any individual who has lost sight of the underlying purpose of the job at hand, whether in government, industry—or a bank. The purpose of a library, for example, is to facilitate the reading of books. Yet to a certain type of librarian, perfection consists of a well-stocked library with a place for every book—and every book in its place. The reader who insists on taking books home, leaving empty spaces on shelves, is this librarian's natural enemy.

It is a cast of mind invulnerable even to the vicissitudes of war. We see it in James Jones's novel *From Here to Eternity* where American soldiers under surprise attack by Japanese planes at the outbreak of World War II rush to the arsenal for weapons, only to find the door barred by a comrade-in-arms loudly proclaiming that he cannot pass out live ammunition without a written request signed by a commissioned officer.

One of these custodians forgot the purpose of a library, the other the purpose of an army. Both illustrate how, in institutionalized endeavors, means have a way of displacing the ends they are originally designed to serve. In fact, it is one of the bureaucrat's distinguishing features that, for him or for her, the means become the ends.

The struggle to prevent this subtle subversion is—or should be—a continual challenge to every policy maker in any organization, public or private. Bureaucrats love any policy and can be counted on to enforce it faithfully, as in, "I'm sorry, but that's the policy here." Unfortunately, they don't understand what a policy is.

A policy is a standard solution to a constantly recurring problem, not an inviolable law. As a weapon in the hands of literal-minded people, however, a "firm policy'" can be as deadly as a repeating rifle. When matters finally become intolerable, the harassed administrator will usually "change the policy." Of course, this never helps because the problem was not the policy in the first place, but the manner of its application.

Every college student seeking entry into a course for which he lacks the exact prerequisite, every shopper trying to return a gift without receipt of purchase, every bank customer seeking to correct an error in an account is in danger of discovering that the rules imagined by Joseph Heller are in service wherever rote is more revered than reason.

The application of binary logic to human affairs through electronic computers has done nothing to retard the spread of *Catch 22* into the wider world. And thus the thought occurs that modern bureaucracy does, after all, present some problems new to history. Nothing lends itself so readily to "a standard solution to a constantly recurring problem" as a computer.

In the best of all possible worlds we might look forward to the day when computers handle all standard solutions, freeing human brains to concentrate on the singular and the exceptional. In the real world, it does not always work out that way—as anyone knows who has ever become trapped in a two-way correspondence with a computer and appealed in vain for human intervention.

A favorite student protest sign of the sixties read, "I am a Human Being. Do not fold, spindle or mutilate." What they objected to is real, only the fault is not in our computers, but in ourselves. It lies in our human propensity to let means become ends, and all too often to resemble Santayana's description of a fanatic; one who, having forgotten his purpose, redoubles his efforts.

We can denounce the bureaucrats and condemn their works, but they will not go away. They have been with us since the dawn of history, and if they seem to be getting worse, it is because we are getting worse. For, in the words of the comic strip *Pogo*: "We has met the enemy, and they is us."

Bureaucracy is a state of mind, and the best way to fight it—whether you work for government, industry, a private foundation or a bank—is not to be a bureaucrat. Or at least try not to.

The Sweet Smell of Success Isn't All That Sweet

Laurence Shames

John Milton was a failure. In writing "Paradise Lost," his stated aim was to "justify the ways of God to men." Inevitably, he fell short of accomplishing that and only wrote a monumental poem. Beethoven, whose music was conceived to transcend Fate, was a failure, as was Socrates, whose ambition was to make people happy by making them reasonable and just. The inescapable conclusion seems to be that the surest, noblest way to fail is to set one's own standards titanically high.

The flip-side of that proposition also seems true, and it provides the safe but dreary logic by which most of us live: The surest way to succeed is to keep one's strivings low—at least to direct them along already charted paths. Don't set yourself the probably thankless task of making the legal system better; just shoot at becoming a partner in the firm. Don't agonize over questions about where your talents and proclivities might most fulfillingly lead you; just do a heads-up job of determining where the educational or business opportunities seem most secure.

After all, if "success" itself—rather than the substance of the achievements that make for success—is the criterion by which we measure ourselves and from which we derive our self-esteem, why make things more difficult by reaching for the stars?

What is this contemporary version of success really all about?

According to certain beer commercials, it consists in moving up to a premium brand that costs a dime or so more per bottle. Credit-card companies would have you believe success inheres in owning their particular piece of plastic.

If these examples sound petty, they are. But take those petty privileges, weave them into a fabric that passes for a value system and what you've got is a national mood that has vast motivating power that can shape at least the near future of the entire country.

Under the flag of success, modern-style, liberal arts colleges are withering while business schools are burgeoning—and yet even business schools are having an increasingly hard time finding faculty members, because teaching isn't considered "successful" enough. Amid a broad consensus that there is a glut of lawyers and an epidemic of strangling litigation, record numbers of young people continue to flock to law school because, for the individual practitioner, a law degree is still considered a safe ticket.

The most sobering thought of all is that today's M.B.A.s and lawyers are tomorrow's M.B.A.s and lawyers: Having invested so much time and money in their training, only a tiny percentage of them will ever opt out of their early chosen fields. Decisions made in accordance with today's hothouse notions of ambition are locking people into careers that will define and also limit their activities and yearnings for virtually the rest of their lives.

Many by external standards, will be "successes." They will own homes, eat in better restaurants, dress well and, in some instances, perform socially useful work. Yet there is a deadening and dangerous flaw in their philosophy: It has little room, little sympathy and less respect for the noble failure, for the person who ventures past the limits, who aims gloriously high and falls unashamedly short.

That sort of ambition doesn't have much place in a world where success is proved by worldly reward rather than by accomplishment itself. That sort of ambition is increasingly thought of as the domain of irredeemable eccentrics, of people who haven't quite caught on—and there is great social pressure not to be one of them.

The result is that fewer people are drawn to the cutting edge of noncommercial scientific research. Fewer are taking on the sublime, unwinnable challenges of the arts. Fewer are asking questions that matter—the ones that can't be answered. Fewer are putting themselves on the line, making as much of their minds and talents as they might.

The irony is that today's success-chasers seem obsessed with the idea of *not settling*. They take advanced degrees in business because they won't settle for just a so-so job. They compete for slots at law firms and investment houses because they won't settle for any but the fastest track. They seem to regard it as axiomatic that "success" and "settling" are opposites.

Yet in doggedly pursuing the rather brittle species of success now in fashion, they are restricting themselves to a chokingly narrow swath of turf along the entire range of human possibilities. Does it ever occur to them that, frequently, success is what people settle for when they can't think of something noble enough to be worth failing at?

Television Addiction

Marie Winn

Cookies or Heroin?

The word "addiction" is often used loosely and wryly in conversation. People will refer to themselves as "mystery book addicts" or "cookie addicts." E. B. White wrote of his annual surge of interest in gardening: "We are hooked and are making an attempt to kick the habit." Yet nobody really believes that reading mysteries or ordering seeds by catalogue is serious enough to be compared with addictions to heroin or alcohol. The word "addiction" is here used jokingly to denote a tendency to overindulge in some pleasurable activity.

People often refer to being "hooked on TV." Does this, too, fall into the light-hearted category of cookie eating and other pleasures that people pursue with unusual intensity, or is there a kind of television viewing that falls into the more serious category of destructive addiction?

When we think about addiction to drugs or alcohol we frequently focus on negative aspects, ignoring the pleasures that accompany drinking or drug-taking. And yet the essence of any serious addiction is a pursuit of pleasure, a search for a "high" that normal life does not supply. It is only the inability to function without the addictive substance that is dismaying, the dependence of the organism upon a certain experience and an increasing inability to function normally without it. Thus people will take two or three drinks at the end of the day not merely for the pleasure drinking provides, but also because they "don't feel normal" without them.

Real addicts do not merely pursue a pleasurable experience one time in order to function normally. They need to *repeat* it again and again. Something about that particular experience makes life without it less than complete. Other potentially pleasurable experiences are no longer possible, for under the spell of the addictive experience, their lives are peculiarly distorted. The addict craves an experience and yet is never really satisfied. The organism may be temporarily sated, but soon it begins to crave again.

Finally, a serious addiction is distinguished from a harmless pursuit of pleasure by its distinctly destructive elements. Heroin addicts, for instance, lead a damaged life: their increasing need for heroin in increasing doses prevents them from working, from maintaining relationships, from developing in human ways. Similarly alcoholics' lives are narrowed and dehumanized by their dependence on alcohol.

Let us consider television viewing in the light of the conditions that define serious addictions.

Not unlike drugs or alcohol, the television experience allows the participant to blot out the real world and enter into a pleasurable and passive mental state. The worries and anxieties of reality are as effectively deferred by becoming absorbed in a television program as by going on a trip induced by drugs or alcohol. And just as alcoholics are only vaguely aware of their addiction, feeling that they control their drinking more than they really do ("I can cut it out any time I want—I just like to have three or four drinks before dinner"), people similarly overestimate their control over television watching. Even as they put off other activities to spend hour after hour watching television, they feel they could easily resume living in a different, less passive style. But somehow or other, while the television set is present in their homes, the click doesn't sound. With television pleasures available, those other experiences seem less attractive, more difficult somehow.

A heavy viewer (a college English instructor) observes:

"I find television almost irresistible. When the set is on, I cannot ignore it. I can't turn it off. I feel sapped, will-less, enervated. As I reach out to turn off the set, the strength goes out of my arms. So I sit there for hours and hours."

Self-confessed television addicts often feel they "ought" to do other things—but the fact that they don't read and don't plant their garden or sew or crochet or play games or have conversations means that those activities are no longer as desirable as television viewing. In a way the lives of heavy viewers are as imbalanced by their television "habit" as a drug addict's or an alcoholic's. They are living in a holding pattern, as it were, passing up the activities that lead to growth or development or a sense of accomplishment. This is one reason people talk about their television viewing so ruefully, so apologetically. They are aware that it is an unproductive experience, that almost any other endeavor is more worthwhile by any human measure.

Finally it is the adverse effect of television viewing on the lives of so many people that defines it as a serious addiction. The television habit distorts the sense of time. It renders other experiences vague and curiously unreal while taking on a greater reality for itself. It weakens relationships by reducing and sometimes eliminating normal opportunities for talking, for communicating.

And yet television does not satisfy, else why would the viewer continue to watch hour after hour, day after day? "The measure of health," writes Lawrence Kubie, "is flexibility . . . and especially the freedom to cease when sated." But heavy television viewers can never be sated with their television experience—these do not provide the true nourishment that satiation requires—and thus they find that they cannot stop watching.

A former heavy watcher (filmmaker) describes such a syndrome:

"I remember when we first got the set I'd watch for hours and hours, whenever I could, and I remember that feeling of tiredness and anxiety that always followed those orgies, a sense of time terribly wasted. It was like eating cotton candy; television promised so much richness, I couldn't wait for it, and, then it just evaporated into air. I remember feeling terribly drained after watching for a long time."

Similarly a nursery school teacher remembers her own childhood television experience:

"I remember bingeing on television when I was a child and having that vapid feeling after watching hours of TV. I'd look forward to watching whenever I could, but it just didn't give back a real feeling of pleasure. It was like no orgasm, no catharsis, very frustrating. Television just wasn't giving me the promised satisfaction, and yet I kept on watching. It filled some sort of need, or had to do with an inability to get something started."

The testimonies of ex-television addicts often have the evangelistic overtones of stories heard at Alcoholics Anonymous meetings.

A handbag repair shop owner says:

"I'd get on the subway home from work with the newspaper and immediately turn to the TV page to plan out my evening's watching. I'd come home, wash, change my clothes, and tell my wife to start the machine so it would be warmed up. (We had an old-fashioned set that took a few seconds before an image appeared.) And then we'd watch TV for the rest of the evening. We'd eat our dinner in the living room while watching, and we'd only talk every once in a while, during the ads, if at all. I'd watch anything, good, bad, or indifferent.

"All the while we were watching I'd feel terribly angry at myself for wasting all that time watching junk. I could never go to sleep until at least the eleven o'clock news, and then sometimes I'd still stay up for the late-night talk show. I had a feeling that I *had* to watch the news programs, that I *had* to know what was happening, even though most of the time nothing much was happening and I could easily find out what was by reading the paper the next morning. Usually my wife would fall asleep on the couch while I was watching. I'd get angry at her for doing that. Actually, I was angry at myself. I had a collection of three years of back issues of different magazines that I planned to read sometime, but I never got around to reading them. I never got around to sorting or labeling my collection of slides I had made when traveling. I only had time for television. We'd take the telephone off the hook while watching so we wouldn't be interrupted! We like classical music, but we never listened to any, never!

"Then one day the set broke. I said to my wife, 'Let's not fix it. Let's just see what happens.' Well, that was the smartest thing we ever did. We haven't had a TV in the house since then.

"Now I look back and I can hardly believe we could have lived like that. I feel that my mind was completely mummified for all those years. I was glued to that machine and couldn't get loose, somehow. It really frightens me to think of it. Yes, I'm frightened of TV now. I don't think I could control it if we had a set in the house again. I think it would take over no matter what I did."

A further sign of addiction is that "an exclusive craving for something is accompanied by a loss of discrimination towards the object which satisfies the craving. . . . The alcoholic is not interested in the taste of liquor that is available; likewise the compulsive eater is not particular about what he eats when there is food around" write the authors of a book about the nature of addiction. And just so, for many viewers the process of *watching* television is far more important than the actual contents of the programs being watched. The knowledge that the act of watching is more important than *what* is being watched lies behind the practice of "road blocking," invented by television advertisers and adopted by political candidates who purchase the same half-hour on all three channels in order to force-feed their message to the public. As one prominent candidate put it, "People will watch television no matter what is on, and if you allow them no other choice they will watch your show."

The comparison between television addiction and drug addictions is often made by addicts themselves. A lawyer says:

"I watch TV the way an alcoholic drinks. If I come home and sit in front of the TV, I'll watch any program at all, even if there's nothing on that especially appeals to me. Then the next thing I know it's eleven o'clock and I'm watching the Johnny Carson show, and I'll realize I've spent the whole evening watching TV. What's more, I can't stand Johnny Carson! But I'll still sit there watching him. I'm addicted to TV, when it's there, and I'm not happy about the addiction. I'll sit there getting madder and madder at myself for watching, but still I'll sit there. I can't turn it off."

Nor is the television addict always blind to the dysfunctional aspects of his addiction. A housewife says:

"Sometimes a friend will come over while I'm watching TV. I'll say, 'Wait a second. Just let me finish watching this,' and then I'll feel bad about that, letting the machine take precedence over people. And I'll do that for the stupidest programs, just because I have to watch, somehow."

In spite of the potentially destructive nature of television addiction, it is rarely taken seriously in American society. Critics mockingly refer to television as a "cultural barbiturate" and joke about "mainlining the tube." Indeed, a spectacle called a "Media Burn," which took place in San Francisco in 1975 and which involved the piling of 44 old television sets on top of each other in the parking lot of the old Cow Palace, soaking them with kerosene, and applying a torch, perfectly illustrates the feeling of good fun that surrounds the issue of television addiction. According to the programs distributed before the event, everybody was supposed to experience "a cathartic explosion" and "be free at last from the addiction to television."

The issue of television addiction takes on a more serious air when the addicts are our own children. A mother reports:

"My ten-year-old is as hooked on TV as an alcoholic is hooked on drink. He tries to strike desperate bargains: 'If you let me watch just ten more minutes, I won't watch at all tomorrow,' he says. It's pathetic. It scares me."

Another mother tells about her six-year-old son:

"We were in Israel last summer where the TV stations sign off for the night at about ten. Well, my son would turn on the set and watch the Arabic stations that were still on, even though he couldn't understand a word, just because he had to watch *something*."

Other signs of serious addiction come out in parents' descriptions of their children's viewing behavior:

"We used to have very bad reception before we got on Cable TV. I'd come into the room and see my eight-year-old watching this terrible, blurry picture and I'd say, 'Heavens, how can you see? Let me try to fix it,' and he'd get frantic and scream, 'Don't touch it!' It really worried me, that he wanted to watch so badly that he was even willing to watch a completely blurred image."

Another mother tells of her eight-year-old son's behavior when deprived of television:

"There was a time when both TV sets were out for about two weeks, and Jerry reached a point where I felt that if he didn't watch something, he was really going to start climbing the walls. He was fidgety and nervous. He'd crawl all over the furniture. He just didn't know what to do with himself, and it seemed to get worse every day. I said to my husband, 'He's having withdrawal symptoms,' and I really think that's what it was. Finally I asked one of my friends if he could go and watch the Saturday cartoons at their house."

The Right Stuff

Tom Wolfe

A young man might go into military flight training believing that he was entering some sort of technical school in which he was simply going to acquire a certain set of skills. Instead, he found himself all at once enclosed in a fraternity. And in this fraternity, even though it was military, men were not rated by their outward rank as ensigns, lieutenants, commanders, or whatever. No, herein the world was divided into those who had it and those who did not. This quality, this *it*, was never named, however, nor was it talked about in any way.

As to just what this ineffable quality was . . . well, it obviously involved bravery. But it was not bravery in the simple sense of being willing to risk your life. The idea seemed to be that any fool could do that, if that was all that was required, just as any fool could throw away his life in the process. No, the idea here (in the all-enclosing fraternity) seemed to be that a man should have the ability to go up in a hurtling piece of machinery and put his hide on the line and then have the moxie, the reflexes, the experience, the coolness, to pull it back in the last yawning moment—and then to go up again *the next day*, and the next day, and every next day, even if the series should prove infinite—and, ultimately, in its best expression, do so in a cause that means something to thousands, to a people, nation, to humanity, to God. Nor was there *a test* to show whether or not a pilot had this righteous quality. There was, instead, a seemingly infinite series of tests. A career in flying was like climbing one of those ancient Babylonian pyramids made up of a dizzy progression of steps and ledges, a ziggurat, a pyramid extraordinarily high and steep; and the idea was to prove at every foot of the way up that pyramid that you were one of the elected and anointed ones who had *the right stuff* and could move higher and higher and even—ultimately, God willing, one day—that you might be able to join that special few at the very top, that elite who had the capacity to bring tears to men's eyes, the very Brotherhood of the Right Stuff itself.

None of this was to be mentioned, and yet it was acted out in a way that a young man could not fail to understand. When a new flight (i.e., a class) of trainees

224

arrived at Pensacola, they were brought into an auditorium for a little lecture. An officer would tell them: "Take a look at the man on either side of you." Quite a few actually swiveled their heads this way and that, in the interest of appearing diligent. Then the officer would say: "One of the three of you is not going to make it!"—meaning, not get his wings. That was the opening theme, the *motif* of primary training. We already know that one-third of you do not have the right stuff—it only remains to find out who.

Furthermore, that was the way it turned out. At every level in one's progress up that staggeringly high pyramid, the world was once more divided into those men who had the right stuff to continue the climb and those who had to be *left behind* in the most obvious way. Some were eliminated in the course of the opening classroom work, as either not smart enough or not hard-working enough, and were left behind. Then came the basic flight instruction, in single-engine, propeller-driven trainers, and a few more—even though the military tried to make this stage easy— were washed out and left behind. Then came more demanding levels, one after the other, formation flying, instrument flying, jet training, all-weather flying, gunnery, and at each level more were washed out and left behind. By this point easily a third of the original candidates had been, indeed, eliminated . . . from the ranks of those who might prove to have the right stuff.

In the Navy, in addition to the stages that Air Force trainees went through, the neophyte always had waiting for him, out in the ocean, a certain grim gray slab; namely, the deck of an aircraft carrier; and with it perhaps the most difficult routine in military flying, carrier landings. He was shown films about it, he heard lectures about it, and he knew that carrier landings were hazardous. He first practiced touching down on the shape of a flight deck painted on an airfield. He was instructed to touch down and gun right off. This was safe enough—the shape didn't move, at least—but it could do terrible things to, let us say, the gyroscope of the soul. *That shape!—it's so damned small!* And more candidates were washed out and left behind. Then came the day, without warning, when those who remained were sent out over the ocean for the first of many days of reckoning with the slab. The first day was always a clear day with little wind and a calm sea. The carrier was so steady that it seemed, from up there in the air, to be resting on pilings, and the candidate usually made his first carrier landing successfully, with relief and even *élan.* Many young candidates looked like terrific aviators up to that very point—and it was not until they were actually standing on the carrier deck that they first began to wonder if they had the proper stuff, after all. In the training film the flight deck was a grand piece of gray geometry, perilous, to be sure, but an amazing abstract shape as one looks down upon it on the screen. And yet once the newcomer's two feet were on it . . . *Geometry*—my God, man, this is a . . . skillet! It *heaved*, it moved up and down underneath his feet. It pitched up, it pitched down, it rolled to port (this great beast *rolled!*), and it rolled to starboard, as the ship moved into the wind and, therefore, into the waves, and the wind kept sweeping across, sixty feet up in the air out in the open sea, and there were no railings whatsoever. This was a *skillet!*—a flying pan!— a short-order grill!—not gray but black smeared with skid marks from one end to the other and glistening with pools of hydraulic fluid and the occasional jet-fuel slick, all of it still hot, sticky, greasy, runny, virulent from God knows what traumas— still ablaze!—consumed in detonations, explosions, flames, combustion, roars,

shrieks, whines, blasts, horrible shudders, fracturing impacts, as little men in screaming red and yellow and purple and green shirts with black Mickey Mouse helmets
over their ears skittered about on the surface as if for their very lives (you've said it
now!), hooking fighter planes onto the catapult shuttles so that they can explode their
afterburners and be slung off the deck in a red-mad fury with a *kaboom!* that pounds
through the entire deck—a procedure that seems absolutely controlled, orderly, sublime, however, compared to what he is about to watch as aircraft return to the ship
for what is known in the engineering stoicisms of the military as "recovery and
arrest." To say that an F-4 was coming back onto this heaving barbecue from out
of the sky at a speed of 135 knots . . . that might have been the truth in the training lecture, but it did not begin to get across the idea of what the newcomer saw from
the deck itself, because it created the notion that perhaps the plane was gliding in.
On the deck one knew differently! As the aircraft came closer and the carrier heaved
on into the waves and the plane's speed did not diminish and the deck did not grow
steady—indeed, it pitched up and down five or ten feet per greasy heave—one experienced a neural alarm that no lecture could have prepared him for: This is not an
airplane coming toward me, it is a brick with some poor sonofabitch riding it (*someone much like myself!*), and it is not *gliding*, it is *falling*, a thirty-thousand-pound
brick, headed not for a stripe on the deck but for *me*—and with a horrible *smash!*
it hits the skillet, and with a blur of momentum as big as a freight train's it hurtles
toward the far end of the deck—another blinding storm!—another roar as the pilot
pushes the throttle up to full military power and another smear of rubber screams
out over the skillet—and this is nominal!—quite okay!—for a wire stretched across
the deck has grabbed the hook on the end of the plane as it hit the deck tail down,
and the smash was the rest of the fifteen-ton brute slamming onto the deck, as it
tripped up, so that it is now straining against the wire at full throttle, in case it
hadn't held and the plane had "boltered" off the end of the deck and had to struggle up into the air again. And already the Mickey Mouse helmets are running toward
the fiery monster. . . .

And the candidate, looking on, begins to *feel* that great heaving sun-blazing
deathboard of a deck wallowing in his own vestibule system—and suddenly he
finds himself backed up against his own limits. He ends up going to the flight surgeon with so-called conversion symptoms. Overnight he develops blurred vision or
numbness in his hands and feet or sinusitis so severe that he cannot tolerate changes
in altitude. On one level the symptom is real. He really cannot see too well or use
his fingers or stand the pain. But somewhere in his subconscious he knows it is a
plea and a beg-off; he shows not the slightest concern (the flight surgeon notes) that
the condition might be permanent and affect him in whatever life awaits him outside the arena of the right stuff.

Those who remained, those who qualified for carrier duty—and even more so
those who later on qualified for *night* carrier duty—began to feel a bit like Gideon's
warriors. *So many have been left behind!* The young warriors were now treated to
a deathly sweet and quite unmentionable sight. They could gaze at length upon the
crushed and wilted pariahs who had washed out. They could inspect those who did
not have that righteous stuff.

The military did not have very merciful instincts. Rather than packing up these
poor souls and sending them home, the Navy, like the Air Force and the Marines,

would try to make use of them in some other role, such as flight controller. So the washout has to keep taking classes with the rest of his group, even though he can no longer touch an airplane. He sits there in the classes staring at sheets of paper with cataracts of sheer human mortification over his eyes while the rest steal looks at him . . . this man reduced to an ant, this untouchable, this poor sonofabitch. And in what test had he been found wanting? Why, it seemed to be nothing less than *manhood* itself. Naturally, this was never mentioned, either. Yet there it was. *Manliness, manhood, manly courage* . . . there was something ancient, primordial, irresistible about the challenge of this stuff, no matter what a sophisticated and rational age one might think he lived in.

What Is a Lamer?

Student

What is a lamer? A lamer is a person who thinks that the online world belongs to him or her. The lamer doesn't take well to threats, and genuinely has less knowledge than the average user, although the lamer will often seem full of knowledge and godlike to other users. A lamer is a person who is a frequent member of the online community, especially chat rooms, who thinks he or she knows everything, when really knowing less than the average user.

First, a lamer is very ignorant. The lamer throws around phrases that he or she has picked up in chat rooms though not having a clue as how to use these phrases, for example, something outrageous like "My mainframe is my soundcard." First of all, a mainframe doesn't have a soundcard. Second, the average Joe Blow doesn't have a mainframe. Finally, if a mainframe did have a soundcard, it would be an accessory, not part of the system. The irony of it all is that the words "soundcard" and "mainframe" are not common words, and your average online user may think the lamer is pretty smart because he or she knows words that the average user doesn't.

Second, a lamer is obnoxiously egotistical. The lamer has an ego the size of the universe, so big it can't be defined. A lamer will not only go around blabbing fallacies around the online forum, but also says them in such a way as to make him or her look cool, for instance, typing the word "elite" as "31337" to look so cool. The substituting of letters for numbers is called "elite speak." Talking in "elite speak" really just takes a lot more time and makes the message of the lamer less substantial than it already is. The lamer also will brag about what warez (pirated software) he or she has. In truth, all the lamer does to get the software he or she wants is tell an unknowing person that he or she has certain software and then rip them off by taking their software and not trading, as agreed. But the biggest problem concerning a lamer's ego is not knowing when to stop. The lamer will keep rambling on and on, bragging about things that he or she doesn't have a clue about, and—boom—the lamer is kicked out of the channel or chat room that he or she is typing in and not allowed back. The members of the channel then rejoice and talk about how lame the lamer was.

Third, a lamer is sadly unskillful; in fact, the lamer has very few computer skills at all. The lamer, unfortunately, does have the skills to get online, but the learning process seems to stop there. The lamer will brag on and on about how much skill he or she has, but knows nothing about what he or she is talking about. The lamer simply has picked up something along the way and types it. The lamer has no idea what it means, just that it sounds smart. The lamer also will say that he or she has hacked web sites, etc., but what the lamer really has done is modified his or her own web site and act like it was hacked. Hacking your own web site is probably one of the lamest things a person can do.

Fourth, a lamer is undoubtedly lazy and does not want to learn anything. If you ever run into a lamer, he or she will ask you for information instead of taking the initiative to find it on his or her own. Lamers will also ask you questions revealing their own stupidity and then try to prove that they aren't lamers by putting out a little, tiny bit of effort to show you up. Then they will simply accuse you of being wrong and go on like nothing happened.

A lamer, most of all, is insecure, having one of the biggest insecurity problems any one person can. If the lamer is made fun of or called a "lamer," the lamer will resort to saying "shut up" and using some non-intelligent, substance-lacking, slang expletives. He or she will continue saying how elite and better than you he or she is. The lamer, after being made fun of long enough, probably goes home and cries to his or her mommy because of this insecurity problem.

Overall, a lamer is just that—"lame." Being a lamer should be illegal on the planet Earth, but the Internet, with free speech and free reign, means that the lamer has just as much a right to be online as you or I. This having been said, you have the ethical right to put the lamer in his or her place because, again, the Internet grants you free speech and free reign.

Failure

Student

What is my definition of failure? *I believe failure is when you set goals for yourself and do nothing to achieve them.* It is like you say you are going to do something and never do it because something comes up. There is always an excuse for not pushing yourself to do what you need to do to be successful. Other people believe that not reaching a goal that you have set for yourself is failure. I don't believe that is true. If they really try to reach a goal but just can't accomplish the task, they are still a success because they at least tried to see what would happen and how close they could get to their goal. Just setting goals and honestly trying to reach them is the key to not becoming a failure.

Success

Student

Success is defined in many different ways by many different people. To me success is achieving something that I strived for a long time. In my life I have only one instance of success. I started training for that moment when I was eleven. It took six months of training and practicing every year. Six years later, I was ready to give up and quit, but I decided to keep trying and not give up until I succeeded. My freshman year in college I made the varsity football team, and I thought that maybe finally this was my chance. We were three and zero, and we were playing a team that had not won all year. They had us down 23 to zero with only five minutes left in the game, and we ended up coming back for the win. We won all of our games that year and became national champions of our division. This was my lifelong dream, and it had finally came true. This was something that I had worked my whole life to try and be a part of, and this is why I feel that I have succeeded in my life.

CHAPTER 10

Argument and Persuasion

In almost all your essays, you are trying to persuade the reader about something. This art of using language persuasively is called rhetoric. Whether you're trying to persuade your reader to adopt your opinions and ideas or just asking your reader to generally accept what you write as something worth reading, you are using rhetorical techniques. In business, this element of persuasion is at the core of all your documents—memos, letters, reports, user manuals, web sites, email, resumes, etc.

An essay of argument and persuasion is one of the most worthwhile types of essays for a college student to learn how to write. This style of writing will help you to develop both your writing skills and, by paying attention to the logic of your ideas, your thinking skills as well.

An *argument* is an appeal predominantly to your reader's reason and intellect. *Persuasion,* in contrast, is a more general term meaning to appeal to one or more of the following: reason, emotion, or a sense of ethics.

What Is the Process of Persuasion?

An appeal to reason relies on logic and intellect and is usually used most effectively when you are expecting your readers to disagree with you. This type of appeal can help to change your reader's mind.

Emotional appeals, however, attempt to arouse your reader's feelings, instincts, senses, and biases. These appeals are used most successfully when your reader agrees with you. This type of appeal validates or reinforces your topic.

An appeal to ethics involves using a sincere, honest tone that will make you seem reliable, experienced, qualified, intelligent, and in command of your subject matter. This appeal works by establishing your credibility.

How to Organize an Argumentative Essay

To organize and construct a logical argument, you can use two patterns of organization:

- Inductive reasoning—relies on several examples to lead up to a generalization.
- Deductive reasoning—begins with a broad, general statement and then uses particular examples to support this statement.

Problems to Avoid When You Write an Argumentative Essay

1. Giving too few examples. Writers often give too few examples and fail to support their assertions. Remember that readers can't know what you know unless you tell them. In an essay of argument, you want to persuade a reader to accept your point of view. Without sufficient explanation and examples, you won't accomplish this goal. When you build your argument on true statements and abundant, accurate evidence, your essay will be more effective.

2. Failing to control emotional responses. When you are trying to persuade by appealing to your readers' emotions, you need to control their emotional responses. Your failure to do so will prevent the readers from having the desired response. You can control their emotional response by choosing your words very carefully and by using examples which precisely illustrate your point.

3. Failing to control your tone. If you are making an ethical appeal that establishes you as a reliable, well-informed person, you need to control the tone of your essay. You control tone through word choice and sentence construction. The number and type of examples used to illustrate the topic will also contribute to the tone.

Criteria to Follow When Writing an Argumentative Essay

1. Choose a worthwhile topic. To write an essay of argument and persuasion, you need to consider something that is both meaningful to the audience and something that may be somewhat controversial. If you and potentially the audience have no concern with the topic or are already fully in agreement on the topic, why write about it?

2. Begin the essay with an assertion (a thesis statement) stating what you believe about a certain issue. This thesis statement is usually phrased as a debatable statement. You might use a thesis statement such as the following: "If Texas changed its laws, fewer people would automatically go to jail for first drug offenses, and the crime rate would drop immediately, saving the taxpayers millions of dollars."

3. Justify the significance of your thesis. You could accomplish this by saying something like the following: "Such a decline in the crime rate would affect all citizens in Texas and make Texas a safer state."

4. In the body of the essay, support your thesis statement in a variety of ways. You can use the appropriate number of paragraphs to achieve the desired length of the essay. In these body paragraphs, develop your argument and its supports by using facts, figures, examples, opinions by recognized authorities (cite sources where necessary), case histories, narrative/anecdotes, comparison/contrast, causal analysis writing, quotes from sources (cite sources), paraphrases from sources (citations necessary).

5. Examine both sides of an argument so that your reader knows that you aren't slanting the argument in your favor.

6. Organize your essay from least to most important so that your reader is led through your thought processes and can logically follow the development of your argument.

7. Be sure to address any potential opposition to your argument by recognizing the other point of view and answering possible objections.

8. Use a combination of logical, emotional, and ethical appeals in the body of the essay.

9. Lead to a logical conclusion based on the examples, support, and different types of appeals.

10. Restate the main topic in the conclusion. Offer some constructive recommendations about the topic that you have been discussing. This will draw in the readers so they feel they are part of the conclusion. The conclusion should clearly close your argument and, in one final attempt, move your audience to accept or to act on your viewpoint.

11. Provide a works cited page if you have relied on any source material to support your argument.

Topic Ideas

Argue for or against any of the following about which you feel strongly. For a good intellectual exercise, pick one of the topics that you feel strongly about and argue the opposite side of the argument.

The welfare system

Mandatory military service for all men and women

Optional service to the country for all men and women

Mandatory year of work after high school for all men and women before they can enter college

Restructuring of college grading

Reworking of college curricula to omit any general education classes

Capital punishment

The flat income tax

Tax credits for college students who purchase a computer

Abolition of smoking in all public spaces and buildings

Drug legalization

A particular problem or shortcoming at your school

Peer Evaluation for Argumentative Essays

1. Has the writer picked a worthwhile topic? Is it controversial? Is it meaningful?

2. Does the writer examine both sides of the argument in a logical, fair manner?

3. Is the essay aimed at a specific target audience that will be concerned with the topic?

4. Is the argument effectively divided into major points?

5. Does the writer effectively support the main points with logical arguments and sound, adequate, and appropriate evidence?

6. If authorities are used, do they seem qualified and valid?

7. Does the writer eliminate all logical fallacies from the argument?

8. Has the writer anticipated objections to the argument and addressed them?

9. If the writer used an emotional appeal, does it center on those emotions most likely to sway the target audience?

10. Does the writer convince you?

11. Does the writer persuade you to act?

12. Do you believe that the writer is honestly concerned about the topic and your response to it?

13. Does the writer convince you to care about the argument?

14. Has the writer used a mature, varied, unbiased vocabulary?

15. Has the writer varied the sentence patterns?

Get a Knife, Get a Dog, but Get Rid of Guns

Molly Ivins

Guns. Everywhere guns.

Let me start this discussion by pointing out that I am not antigun. I'm pro-knife. Consider the merits of the knife.

In the first place, you have to catch up with someone in order to stab him. A general substitution of knives for guns would promote physical fitness. We'd turn into a whole nation of great runners. Plus, knives don't ricochet. And people are seldom killed while cleaning their knives.

As a civil libertarian, I of course support the Second Amendment. And I believe it means exactly what it says:

A well-regulated militia being necessary to the security of a free state, the right of the people to keep and bear arms shall not be infringed. Fourteen-year-old boys are not part of a well-regulated militia. Members of wacky religious cults are not part of a well-regulated militia. Permitting unregulated citizens to have guns is destroying the security of this free state.

I am intrigued by the arguments of those who claim to follow the judicial doctrine of original intent. How do they know it was the dearest wish of Thomas Jefferson's heart that teenage drug dealers should cruise the cities of this nation perforating their fellow citizens with assault rifles? Channeling?

There is more hooey spread about the Second Amendment. It says quite clearly that guns are for those who form part of a well-regulated militia, that is, the armed forces, including the National Guard. The reasons for keeping them away from everyone else get clearer by the day.

The comparison most often used is that of the automobile, another lethal object that is regularly used to wreak great carnage. Obviously, this society is full of people who haven't enough common sense to use an automobile properly. But we haven't outlawed cars yet.

We do, however, license them and their owners, restrict their use to presumably sane and sober adults, and keep track of who sells them to whom. At a minimum, we should do the same with guns.

In truth, there is no rational argument for guns in this society. This is no longer a frontier nation in which people hunt their own food. It is a crowded, overwhelmingly urban country in which letting people have access to guns is a continuing disaster. Those who want guns—whether for target shooting, hunting, or potting rattlesnakes (get a hoe)—should be subject to the same restrictions placed on gun owners in England, a nation in which liberty has survived nicely without an armed populace.

The argument that "guns don't kill people" is patent nonsense. Anyone who has ever worked in a cop shop knows how many family arguments end in murder because there was a gun in the house. Did the gun kill someone? No. But if there had been no gun, no one would have died. At least not without a good foot race first. Guns do kill. Unlike cars, that is all they do.

Michael Crichton makes an interesting argument about technology in his thriller *Jurassic Park*. He points out that power without discipline is making this society into a wreckage. By the time someone who studies the martial arts becomes a master—literally able to kill with bare hands—that person has also undergone years of training and discipline. But any fool can pick up a gun and kill with it.

"A well-regulated militia" surely implies both long training and long discipline. That is the least, the very least, that should be required of those who are permitted to have guns, because a gun is literally the power to kill. For years I used to enjoy taunting my gun-nut friends about their psychosexual hang-ups—always in a spirit of good cheer, you understand. But letting the noisy minority in the NRA force us to allow this carnage to continue is just plain insane.

I do think gun nuts have a power hang-up. I don't know what is missing in their psyches that they need to feel they have the power to kill. But no sane society would allow this to continue.

Ban the damn things. Ban them all.

You want protection? Get a dog.

Putting in a Good Word for Guilt

Ellen Goodman

Feeling guilty is nothing to feel guilty about. Yes, guilt can be the excess baggage that keeps us paralyzed unless we dump it. But it can also be the engine that fuels us. Yes, it can be a self-punishing activity, but it can also be the conscience that keeps us civilized.

Not too long ago I wrote a story about that amusing couple, Guilt and the Working Mother. I'll tell you more about that later. Through the mail someone sent me a gift coffee mug carrying the message "I gave up guilt for Lent."

My first reaction was to giggle. But then it occurred to me that this particular Lent has been too lengthy. For the past decade or more, the pop psychologists who use book jackets rather than couches all were busy telling us that I am okay, you are okay and whatever we do is okay.

In most of their books, guilt was given a bad name—or rather, an assortment of bad names. It was a (1) Puritan (2) Jewish (3) Catholic hangover from our (1) parents (2) culture (3) religion. To be truly liberated was to be free of guilt about being rich, powerful, number one, bad to your mother, thoughtless, late, a smoker or about cheating on your spouse.

There was a popular notion, in fact, that self-love began by slaying one's guilt. People all around us spent a great portion of the last decade trying to tune out guilt instead of decoding its message and learning what it was trying to tell us.

With that sort of success, guilt was ripe for revival. Somewhere along the I'm-okay-you're-okay way, many of us realized that, in fact, I am not always okay and neither are you. Furthermore, we did not want to join the legions who conquered their guilt en route to new depths of narcissistic rottenness.

At the deepest, most devastating level, guilt is the criminal in us that longs to be caught. It is the horrible, pit-of-the-stomach sense of having done wrong. It is, as Lady Macbeth obsessively knew, the spot that no one else may see . . . and we can't see around.

To be without guilt is to be without a conscience. Guilt-free people don't feel bad when they cause pain to others, and so they go on guilt-freely causing more pain. The last thing we need more of is less conscience.

Freud once said, "As regards conscience, God has done an uneven and careless piece of work, for a large majority of men have brought along with them only a modest amount of it, or scarcely enough to be worth mentioning."

Now, I am not suggesting that we all sign up for a new guilt trip. But there has to be some line between the accusation that we all should feel guilty for, say, poverty or racism and the assertion that the oppressed have "chosen" their lot in life.

There has to be something between Puritanism and hedonism. There has to be something between the parents who guilt-trip their children across every stage of life and those who offer no guidance, no—gulp—moral or ethical point of view.

At quite regular intervals, for example, my daughter looks up at me in the midst of a discussion (she would call it a lecture) and says: "You're making me feel guilty." For a long time this made me, in turn, feel guilty. But now I realize that I am doing precisely what I am supposed to be doing: instilling in her a sense of right and wrong so that she will feel uncomfortable if she behaves in hurtful ways.

This is, of course, a very tricky business. Guilt is ultimately the way we judge ourselves. It is the part of us that says, "I deserve to be punished." But we all know people who feel guilty just for being alive. We know people who are paralyzed by irrational guilt. And we certainly don't want to be among them, or to shepherd our children into their flock.

But it seems to me that the trick isn't to become flaccidly nonjudgmental, but to figure out whether we are being fair judges of ourselves. Karl Menninger once wrote that one aim of psychiatric treatment isn't to get rid of guilt but "to get people's guilt feelings attached to the 'right' things."

In his book *Feelings*, Willard Gaylin quotes a Reverend Tillotson's definition of guilt as "nothing else but trouble arising in our mind from our consciousness of having done contrary to what we are verily persuaded [sic] was our Duty."

We may, however, have wildly different senses of duty. I had lunch with two friends a month ago when they both started talking about feeling guilty for neglecting their mothers. One, it turned out, worried that she didn't call "home" every day; the other hadn't even chatted with her mother since Christmas.

We are also particularly vulnerable to feelings of duty in a time of change. Today an older and ingrained sense of what we should do may conflict with a new one. In the gaps that open between what we once were taught and what we now believe grows a rich crop of guilt.

Mothers now often tell me that they feel guilty if they are working and guilty if they aren't. One set of older expectations, to be a perfect milk-and-cookies supermom, conflicts with another, to be an independent woman or an economic helpmate.

But duty has its uses. It sets us down at the typewriter, hustles us to the job on a morning when everything has gone wrong, pushes us toward the crying baby at 3 A.M.

If guilt is a struggle between our acceptance of should and should nots, it is a powerful and intensely human one. Gaylin writes, "Guilt represents the noblest and most painful of struggles. It is between us and ourselves." It is better to struggle with ourselves than give up on ourselves.

This worst emotion, in a sense, helps bring out the best in us. The desire to avoid feeling guilty makes us avoid the worst sort of behavior. The early guilt of a child who has hurt a younger sister or brother, even when no one else knows, is a message. The adult who has inflicted pain on an innocent, who has cheated, lied, stolen, to get ahead of another—each of us has a list—wakes up in the middle of the night and remembers it.

In that sense guilt is the great civilizer, the internal commandment that helps us choose to be kind to each other rather than to join in a stampede of me-firsts. "If guilt is coming back," said Harvard Professor David Riesman, who wrote *The Lonely Crowd*, "one reason is that a tremendous surge of young people over-powered the adults in the sixties. You might say the barbarians took Rome. Now there are more adults around who are trying to restore some stability."

Guilt is the adult in each of us, the parent, the one who upholds the standards. It is the internal guide against which we argue in vain that "everybody else is doing it."

We even wrestle with ethical dilemmas and conflicts of conscience so that we can live with ourselves more comfortably. I know two people who were faced with a crisis about their infidelities. One woman resolved the triangle she was in by ending her marriage. The other ended her affair. In both cases, it was the pain that had motivated them to change.

It is not easy to attach our guilt to the right things. It is never easy to separate right from wrong, rational guilt from neurotic guilt. We may resolve one by changing our view of it and another by changing our behavior.

In my own life as a working mother, I have done both half a dozen times. When my daughter was small and I was working, I worried that I was not following the pattern of the good mother, my mother. Only through time and perspective and reality did I change that view; I realized that my daughter clearly did not feel neglected and I clearly was not uncaring. Good child care, love, luck and support helped me to resolve my early guilt feelings.

Then again, last winter I found myself out of town more than I was comfortable with. This time I changed my schedule instead of my mind.

For all of us, in the dozens of daily decisions we make, guilt is one of the many proper motivations. I am not saying our lives are ruled by guilt. Hardly. But guilt is inherent in the underlying question: "If I do that, can I live with myself?"

People who don't ask themselves that question, people who never get no for an answer, may seem lucky. They can, we think, be self-centered without self-punishment, hedonistic without qualms. They can worry about me-first and forget about the others.

It is easy to be jealous of those who go through life without a moment of wrenching guilt. But envying the guiltless is like envying a house pet. Striving to follow their lead is like accepting a catatonic as your role model. They are not the free but the antisocial. In a world in which guilt is one of the few emotions experienced only by human beings, they are, even, inhuman.

Guilt is one of the most human of dilemmas. It is the claim of others on the self, the recognition both of our flaws and of our desire to be the people we want to be.

I Have a Dream

Martin Luther King, Jr.

I am happy to join with you today in what will go down in history as the greatest demonstration for freedom in the history of our nation.

Five score years ago, a great American, in whose symbolic shadow we stand today, signed the Emancipation Proclamation. This momentous decree came as a great beacon light of hope to millions of Negro slaves who had been seared in the flames of withering injustice. It came as a joyous daybreak to end the long night of their captivity.

But one hundred years later, the Negro still is not free; one hundred years later, the life of the Negro is still sadly crippled by the manacles of segregation and the chains of discrimination; one hundred years later, the Negro lives on a lonely island of poverty in the midst of a vast ocean of material prosperity; one hundred years later, the Negro is still languishing in the corners of American society and finds himself in exile in his own land.

So we've come here today to dramatize a shameful condition. In a sense we've come to our nation's capital to cash a check. When the architects of our republic wrote the magnificent words of the Constitution and the Declaration of Independence, they were signing a promissory note to which every American was to fall heir. This note was the promise that all men, yes, black men as well as white men, would be guaranteed the unalienable rights of life, liberty, and the pursuit of happiness.

It is obvious today that America has defaulted on this promissory note in so far as her citizens of color are concerned. Instead of honoring this sacred obligation, America has given the Negro people a bad check; a check which has come back marked "insufficient funds." But we refuse to believe that the bank of justice is bankrupt. We refuse to believe that there are insufficient funds in the great vaults of opportunity of this nation. And so we've come to cash this check, a check that will give us upon demand the riches of freedom and the security of justice.

We have also come to this hallowed spot to remind America of the fierce urgency of now. This is no time to engage in the luxury of cooling off or to take the tranquilizing drug of gradualism. Now is the time to make real the promises of democracy; now is the time to rise from the dark and desolate valley of segregation to the sunlit path of racial justice; now is the time to lift our nation from the quicksand's of racial injustice to the solid rock of brotherhood; now is the time to make justice a reality for all of God's children. It would be fatal for the nation to overlook the urgency of the moment. This sweltering summer of the Negro's legitimate discontent will not pass until there is an invigorating autumn of freedom and equality.

Nineteen sixty-three is not an end, but a beginning. And those who hope that the Negro needed to blow off steam and will now be content will have a rude awakening if the nation returns to business as usual. There will be neither rest nor tranquility in America until the Negro is granted his citizenship rights. The whirlwinds of revolt will continue to shake the foundations of our nation until the bright day of justice emerges.

But there is something that I must say to my people, who stand on the worn threshold which leads into the palace of justice. In the process of gaining our rightful place, we must not be guilty of wrongful deeds. Let us not seek to satisfy our thirst for freedom by drinking from the cup of bitterness and hatred. We must forever conduct our struggle on the high plain of dignity and discipline. We must not allow our creative protests to degenerate into physical violence. Again and again we must rise to the majestic heights of meeting physical force with soul force. The marvelous new militancy, which has engulfed the Negro community, must not lead us to a distrust of all white people. For many of our white brothers, as evidenced by their presence here today, have come to realize that their destiny is tied up with our destiny. And they have come to realize that their freedom is inextricably bound to our freedom. We cannot walk alone. And as we walk, we must make the pledge that we shall always march ahead. We cannot turn back.

There are those who are asking the devotees of Civil Rights, "When will you be satisfied?" We can never be satisfied as long as the Negro is the victim of the unspeakable horrors of police brutality: we can never be satisfied as long as our bodies, heavy with the fatigue of travel, cannot gain lodging in the motels of the highways and the hotels of the cities; we cannot be satisfied as long as the Negro's basic mobility is from a smaller ghetto to a larger one; we can never be satisfied as long as our children are stripped of their selfhood and robbed of their dignity by signs stating "For White Only"; we cannot be satisfied as long as the Negro in Mississippi cannot vote and a Negro in New York believes he has nothing for which to vote. No! No, we are not satisfied, and we will not be satisfied until justice rolls down like waters and righteousness like a mighty stream.

I am not unmindful that some of you have come here out of great trials and tribulations. Some of you have come fresh from narrow jail cells. Some of you have come from areas where your quest for freedom left you battered by the storms of persecution and staggered by the winds of police brutality. You have been the veterans of creative suffering. Continue to work with the faith that unearned suffering is redemptive. Go back to Mississippi. Go back to Alabama. Go back to South Carolina. Go back to Georgia. Go back to Louisiana. Go back to the slums and ghettos of our Northern cities, knowing that somehow this situation can and will be changed. Let us not wallow in the valley of despair.

I say to you today, my friends, that even though we face the difficulties of today and tomorrow, I still have a dream. It is a dream deeply rooted in the American dream. I have a dream that one day this nation will rise up and live out the true meaning of its creed, "We hold these truths to be self-evident, that all men are created equal." I have a dream that one day on the red hills of Georgia, sons of former slaves and the sons of former slave owners will be able to sit down together at the table of brotherhood. I have a dream that one day even the state of Mississippi, a state sweltering with the heat of injustice, sweltering with the heat of oppression, will be transformed into an oasis of freedom and justice. I have a dream that my four little children will one day live in a nation where they will not be judged by the color of their skin, but by the content of their character.

I HAVE A DREAM TODAY!

I have a dream that one day down in Alabama—with its vicious racists, with its Governor having his lips dripping with the words of interposition and nullification—one day right there in Alabama, little black boys and black girls will be able to join hands with little white boys and white girls as sisters and brothers.

I HAVE A DREAM TODAY!

I have a dream that one day every valley shall be exalted, every hill and mountain shall be made low. The rough places will be plain and the crooked places will be made straight, "and the glory of the Lord shall be revealed, and all flesh shall see it together."

This is our hope. This is the faith that I go back to the South with. With this faith we will be able to hew out of the mountain of despair, a stone of hope. With this faith we will be able to transform the jangling discords of our nation into a beautiful symphony of brotherhood. With this faith we will be able to work together, to pray together, to struggle together, to go to jail together, to stand up for freedom together, knowing that we will be free one day. And this will be the day. This will be the day when all of God's children will be able to sing with new meaning, "My country 'tis of thee, sweet land of liberty, of thee I sing. Land where my fathers died, land of the pilgrim's pride, from every mountain side, let freedom ring." And if America is to be a great nation, this must become true.

So let freedom ring from the prodigious hilltops of New Hampshire; let freedom ring from the mighty mountains of New York; let freedom ring from the heightening Alleghenies of Pennsylvania; let freedom ring from the snow-capped Rockies of Colorado; let freedom ring from the curvaceous slopes of California. But not only that. Let freedom ring from Stone Mountain of Georgia; let freedom ring from Lookout Mountain of Tennessee: let freedom ring from every hill and mole hill of Mississippi. "From every mountainside, let freedom ring."

And when this happens, and when we allow freedom to ring, when we let it ring from every village and every hamlet, from every state and every city, we will be able to speed up that day when all of God's children, black men and white men, Jews and Gentiles, Protestants and Catholics, will be able to join hands and sing in the words of the old Negro spiritual: "Free at last. Free at last. Thank God Almighty, we are free at last."

Gettysburg Address

Abraham Lincoln

Speech at the Dedication of the National Cemetery of Gettysburg

November 19, 1863

Four score and seven years ago our fathers brought forth on this continent a new nation, conceived in liberty and dedicated to the proposition that all men are created equal. Now we are engaged in a great civil war, testing whether that nation or any nation so conceived and so dedicated can long endure. We are met on a great battlefield of that war. We have come to dedicate a portion of that field as a final resting-place for those who here gave their lives that that nation might live. It is altogether fitting and proper that we should do this. But in a larger sense, we cannot dedicate, we cannot consecrate, we cannot hallow this ground. The brave men, living and dead who struggled here have consecrated it far above our poor power to add or detract. The world will little note nor long remember what we say here, but it can never forget what they did here. It is for us the living rather to be dedicated here to the unfinished work which they who fought here have thus far so nobly advanced. It is rather for us to be here dedicated to the great task remaining before us, that from these honored dead we take increased devotion to that cause for which they gave the last full measure of devotion; that we here highly resolve that these dead shall not have died in vain, that this nation under God shall have a new birth of freedom, and that government of the people, by the people, for the people shall not perish from the earth.

Drug Testing Violates Workers' Rights

The New Republic

The President's Commission on Organized Crime spent 32 months and nearly five million dollars preparing its report on drug abuse and trafficking. There's something for everyone in the panel's 1,000-page study, but here's the gist of its recommendation: since law-enforcement techniques have failed to curtail the supply of illegal narcotics, we should try to diminish the demand. In pursuit of that goal, the commission argues, the president should direct all federal agencies to implement "suitable drug testing programs." State and local governments and the private sector should follow suit, and federal contracts should be denied to firms that don't test for drugs. In other words, practically everyone should have his or her urine tested. Laboratory owners and manufacturers of small plastic cups should be delighted with the scheme.

Several members of the panel have dissented publicly, saying that the controversial suggestion was added without their knowledge. U.S. Court of Appeals Judge Irving R. Kaufman, who chairs the commission, and supports the idea, has refused to answer their objections. But the report has been greeted with signs of approbation as well. Attorney General Edwin Meese III caused some confusion in the press when he stopped short of endorsing the plan (saying it might be too expensive), yet argued that drug testing doesn't violate anyone's constitutional rights. Representative Clay Shaw of Florida embraced the idea unreservedly. He volunteered himself and his staff for urine tests as soon as they can be arranged.

Too Close for Comfort

In fact, we are already much closer to universal urine testing than most people realize. One-quarter of all Fortune 500 companies, including IBM and General Motors, now administer urinalysis tests to applicants or current employees. Another

20 percent are planning to institute programs. . . . According to a *USA Today* survey cited in the Kaufman Commission report, two-thirds of those firms won't hire anyone who fails a test. Of those testing current employees, 25 percent fire those who fail, while 64 percent require treatment, strongly recommend it, or take disciplinary action. Since a urine sample is usually taken as part of a medical examination, applicants and employees often don't know that they are being checked for drug use.

The tests are probably justified for air traffic controllers and Drug Enforcement Administration agents who now undergo them regularly. There's even a case to be made for testing professional athletes, part of whose job is to serve as role models to children. But need the same standards be applied to the entire work force? The *Los Angeles Times*, the *Chicago Tribune,* and the *New York Times,* for example, screen all new employees for drug use. Although the *New York Times* doesn't tell applicants that their urine will be tested for narcotics, a spokesman says the company's policy is to not hire anyone whose medical examination indicates use of illegal drugs, including marijuana. Once you are hired, there are no further tests.

And urinalysis is only one of the more intrusive new ways to search people for drugs. Many bus drivers and amusement park ride operators are required to produce saliva samples, which are tested for the presence of marijuana. . . . It is now possible to test hair samples for drugs. Some companies have searched lockers and cars, frisked workers on their way into the factory, and set up hidden video cameras. G.M. hired undercover agents to pose as assembly-line workers in order to catch drug dealers. Capital Cities/ABC and the *Kansas City Times* and *Star* called off the drug-sniffing dogs after reporters ridiculed their plans for canine searches in the newsroom.

There is already a body of case law on the Fourth Amendment questions raised by the various drug tests. If a warrant is required to search someone's home, you need a probable cause to impound some of his urine. The Kaufman report notes that the Supreme Court ruled in favor of the Federal Railroad Administration's right to employ a range of tests for drugs and alcohol. But the commission ignores the fact that the railroad regulations delineate the need for "reasonable suspicion" that employees are under the influence on the job—not that they've used drugs away from work in previous weeks.

Invasion of Privacy

Beyond the constitutional questions, most would agree that asking people to produce a urine specimen if they want to apply for a job, or to keep the one they've got, is an unwarranted invasion of their privacy. To assure an honest sample, a supervisor must witness its production. The Coast Guard has someone follow each of its 38,000 employees into the bathroom. "We don't want them to bring in baby's urine," one Coast Guard officer told the *Washington Post*.

Why are these officers and supervisors, who administer the tests, always assumed to be clean? Programs for widespread testing almost always reflect class bias. Regulations are usually written for equipment operators or assembly-line workers without reference to supervisors or management. Isn't it just as important that they be drug-free? If we test train conductors, shouldn't we also analyze the urine of the railroad bosses? As the Kaufman Commission report indicates, heroin has been climbing up the socioeconomic ladder as cocaine has been descending. Yet lawyers, stock brokers, and senators are rarely included in drug-testing programs, perhaps because they are better able to fight the imposition of such indignities.

Besides running roughshod over personal privacy, the tests are impractical and imprecise. Urinalysis can't tell you whether someone is high on the job—only whether she has traces of narcotics in her system. Cocaine, heroin, and PCP—the drugs employers claim to be most worried about—vanish from the bloodstream in less than 48 hours. If the tests are scheduled, as most are, an employee can avoid detection by staying clean for a couple of days.

But THC, the active chemical in marijuana, remains in the blood months after it is ingested. That's why the vast majority of those who fail drug tests register positive for pot. What do we do with them? Nearly 40 million citizens smoke marijuana at least once a year. Half that number use the drug regularly. Should all of them be fired? If passing a drug test ought to be a condition of all kinds of employment, should a large segment of the population be unemployable? Eleven states have eliminated criminal penalties for possession of marijuana, and Alaskans can grow it legally in their backyards. Rather than weeding 20 million weed-smokers from the work force, employers ought to discipline, treat, or fire those who perform poorly at work, whether or not they use drugs. Axing workers who test positive but demonstrate no other problems doesn't make sense.

Unconstitutional

Even if drug tests were free and 100 percent accurate, they would still be unconstitutional. There is going to be a lot of legal rhubarb over this, and I don't know what a Rehnquist-led Supreme Court is finally going to decide. But I take the same attitude toward the Constitution as Reformation Protestants took toward the Bible: Anyone can read it and witness the truth thereof. Amendment Four is perfectly straightforward:

The right of the people to be secure in their persons, houses, papers and effects against unreasonable searches and seizures shall not be violated, and no warrants shall issue but upon probable cause, supported by an oath or affirmation and particularly describing the place to be searched and the persons or things to be seized.

It's hard to see how scatter-shot drug testing could be legal under the Fourth Amendment, no matter how particularly the Government describes the way you take a leak. (P.J. O'Rourke, Playboy, February 1987.)

Like those who advocate widespread use of polygraph tests, the Kaufman panel puts boundless faith in far-from-perfect scientific techniques. Although the tests have been widely used for only a few years, they've ruined lives and fingered thousands of innocent people. The Pentagon, which administers six million urinalysis tests a year, provides plenty of examples. Urinalysis tests said time and again that a Navy doctor named Dale Mitchell was using morphine. When he failed a polygraph test, he began sending out job applications. Then someone at the Navy lab figured out that Mitchell was testing positive for poppy seed bagels. In 1982 and 1983 a group of 9,100 employees the Army said were using illegal drugs weren't so lucky. They had already gotten their dishonorable discharges when the Pentagon tried to track them down to apologize for convicting them on faulty evidence including mixed-up samples.

Most drug-testing laboratories acknowledge a margin of error of two or three percent. Even by that conservative estimate, four million innocents would lose their jobs if we tested the entire work force. But the conclusions of a secret study of the labs by the National Centers for Disease Control are far less optimistic. According to an article in the *Journal of the American Medical Association,* the worst laboratories indicated false positive results as much as 66 percent of the time. Only one lab was credited with acceptable performance in testing for cocaine. The CDC study didn't include any marijuana samples, which pose similar, if not more severe, lab problems. Herbal tea and prescription drugs can trigger false positive results, as can being in a room with people smoking marijuana. Those terminated unfairly may waste years and fortunes proving their innocence, if they are able to do so at all.

Little Plastic Cups

Despite the abundant hype, the use of legal and illegal drugs has decreased markedly over the past several years. Fewer people are taking heroin, PCP, marijuana, alcohol, and tobacco than they were ten years ago. LSD and Quaaludes have all but vanished. Cocaine use has increased slightly, but may well decline when its dangers become better known—which is what happened with heroin and PCP.

The failure of our policy of interdiction has combined with the hysteria to send the law-enforcement establishment on a search for sweeping solutions. [Attorney General Edwin] Meese suggested stepping up efforts to prosecute consumers of illegal drugs. What sort of indiscriminate check will catch the corporate imagination next? Strip searches for weapons? Polygraphs for potential office thieves? Blood tests for AIDS? All hold forth a similar promise of purity in the workplace, which is why they appeal so strongly to those who run businesses and governments. But such forms of social control, which force people to prove their innocence of crimes they haven't even been charged with, are abhorrent. What starts with little plastic cups ends in the urinalysis state.

In Praise of the F Word

Mary Sherry

Tens of thousands of 18-year-olds will graduate this year and be handed meaningless diplomas. These diplomas won't look any different from those awarded their luckier classmates. Their validity will be questioned only when their employers discover that these graduates are semiliterate.

Eventually a fortunate few will find their way into educational-repair shops—adult-literacy programs, such as the one where I teach basic grammar and writing. There, high school graduates and high school dropouts pursuing graduate-equivalency certificates will learn the skills they should have learned in school. They will also discover they have been cheated by our educational system.

As I teach, I learn a lot about our schools. Early in each session I ask my students to write about an unpleasant experience they had in school. No writers' block here! "I wish someone would have made me stop doing drugs and made me study." "I liked to party and no one seemed to care." "I was a good kid and didn't cause any trouble, so they just passed me along even though I didn't read well and couldn't write." And so on.

I am your basic do-gooder, and prior to teaching this class I blamed the poor academic skills our kids have today on drugs, divorce, and other impediments to concentration necessary for doing well in school. But, as I rediscover each time I walk into the classroom, before a teacher can expect students to concentrate, he has to get their attention, no matter what distractions may be at hand. There are many ways to do this, and they have much to do with teaching style. However, if style alone won't do it, there is another way to show who holds the winning hand in the classroom. That is to reveal the trump card of failure.

I will never forget a teacher who played that card to get the attention of one of my children. Our youngest, a world-class charmer, did little to develop his intellectual talents but always got by. Until Mrs. Stifter.

Our son was a high school senior when he had her for English. "He sits in the back of the room talking to his friends," she told me. "Why don't you move him

250

to the front row?" I urged, believing the embarrassment would get him to settle down. Mrs. Stifter looked at me steely-eyed over her glasses. "I don't move seniors," she said. "I flunk them." I was flustered. Our son's academic life flashed before my eyes. No teacher had ever threatened him with that before. I regained my composure and managed to say that I thought she was right. By the time I got home, I was feeling pretty good about this. It was a radical approach for these times, but, well, why not? "She's going to flunk you," I told my son. I did not discuss it any further. Suddenly English became a priority in his life. He finished out the semester with an A.

I know one example doesn't make a case, but at night I see a parade of students who are angry and resentful for having been passed along until they could no longer even pretend to keep up. Of average intelligence or better; they eventually quit school, concluding they were too dumb to finish. "I should have been held back," is a comment I hear frequently. Even sadder are those students who are high school graduates who say to me after a few weeks of class, "I don't know how I ever got a high school diploma."

Passing students who have not mastered the work cheats them and the employers who expect graduates to have basic skills. We excuse this dishonest behavior by saying kids can't learn if they come from terrible environments. No one seems to stop to think that—no matter what environments they come from—most kids don't put school first on their list unless they perceive something is at stake. They'd rather be sailing.

Many students I see at night could give expert testimony on unemployment, chemical dependency, abusive relationships. In spite of these difficulties, they have decided to make education a priority. They are motivated by the desire for a better job or the need to hang on to the one they've got. They have a healthy fear of failure.

People of all ages can rise above their problems, but they need to have a reason to do so. Young people generally don't have the maturity to value education in the same way my adult students value it. But fear of failure, whether economic or academic, can motivate both.

Flunking as a regular policy has just as much merit today as it did two generations ago. We must review the threat of flunking and see it as it really is—a positive teaching tool. It is an expression of confidence by both teachers and parents that the students have the ability to learn the material presented to them. However, making it work again would take a dedicated, caring conspiracy between teachers and parents. It would mean facing the tough reality that passing kids who haven't learned the material—while it might save them grief for the short term—dooms them to long-term illiteracy. It would mean that teachers would have to follow through on their threats, and parents would have to stand behind them, knowing their children's best interests are indeed at stake. This means no more doing Scott's assignments for him because he might fail. No more passing Jodi because she's such a nice kid.

This is a policy that worked in the past and can work today. A wise teacher, with the support of his parents, gave our son the opportunity to succeed—or fail. It's time we return this choice to all students.

Welcome to Cyberbia

Heidi Pollock

Computer networking offers the soundest basis for world peace that has yet been presented. Peace must be created on the bulwark of understanding. International computer networks will knit together the peoples of the world in bonds of mutual respect; its possibilities are vast, indeed.

—*Scientific American,* June 1994

Computer bulletin board services offer up the glories of e-mail, the thought provocation of newsgroups, the sharing of ideas implicit in public posting, and the interaction of real-time chats. The fabulous, wonderful, limitless world of communication is just waiting for you to log on. Sure. Yeah. Right. What this whole delirious, interconnected, global community of a world needs is a little reality check.

Let's face facts. The U.S. government by and large foots the bill for the Internet, through maintaining the structural (hardware) backbone, including, among other things, funding to major universities. As surely as the Department of Defense started this whole thing, AT&T or Ted Turner[1] is going to end up running it, so I don't think it's too unrealistic to take a look at the Net as it exists in its commercial form in order to expose some of the realities lurking behind the regurgitated media rhetoric and the religious fanaticism of Net junkies.

Let's pretend that you have as much time and as much money to spend online as you damn well want. What do you actually do online?

Well, you download some cool shareware, you post technical questions in the computer user group forums, you check your stocks, you read the news and

---

[1] Ted Turner owned a conglomerate of media companies that is now part of Time Warner, where he is an executive.

maybe some reviews. And, of course, since computer networks are supposed to make it easy to reach out and touch strangers who share a particular obsession or concern, you are also participating in the online forums, discussion groups, and conferences.

Let's review the structure of forums. For the purposes of this essay, we will examine the largest of the major user-friendly commercial services—America Online (AOL). There is no precise statistic available (at least none that the company will reveal—you have to do the research by HAND!!!) on exactly how many subject-specific discussion areas (folders) exist on America Online. Any online service is going to have zillions of posts—contributions from users—pertaining to computer usage (the computer games area of America Online, for example, breaks into 500 separate topics with over 100,000 individual posts), so let's look at a less popular area: the "Lifestyles and Interests" department.

For starters, as I write this, there are 57 initial categories within the Lifestyles and Interests area. One of these categories is Ham Radio. Ham Radio? How can there possibly be 5,909 separate, individual posts about Ham Radio? There are 5,865 postings in the Biking (and that's just bicycles, not motorcycles) category. Genealogy—22,525 posts. The Gay and Lesbian category is slightly more substantial—36,333 posts. There are five separate categories for political and issue discussion. The big catchall topic area, the Exchange, has over 100,000 posts. Servicewide, there are over a million posts.

You may want to join the online revolution, but obviously you can't wade through everything that's being discussed—you need to decide which topics interest you, which folders to browse. Within the Exchange alone (one of 57 subdivisions within one of another 50 higher divisions) there are 1,492 separate topic-specific folders—each containing a rough average of 50 posts, but many containing closer to 400. (Note: America Online automatically empties folders when their post totals reach 400, so total post numbers do not reflect the overall historical totals for a given topic. Sometimes the posting is so frequent that the "shelf life" of a given post is no more than four weeks.)

So, there you are, J. Individual, ready to start interacting with folks, sharing stories and communicating. You have narrowed yourself into a single folder, three tiers down in the America Online hierarchy, and now you must choose between nearly 1,500 folders. Of course, once you choose a few of these folders, you will then have to read all the posts in order to catch up, be current, and not merely repeat a previous post.

A polite post is no more than two paragraphs long (a screenful of text, which obviously has a number of intellectually negative implications). Let's say you choose 10 folders (out of 1,500). Each folder contains an average of 50 posts. Five hundred posts, at, say, one paragraph each, and you're now looking at the equivalent of a 200-page book.

Enough with the stats. Let me back up a minute and present you with some very disturbing, but rational, assumptions. J. Individual wants to join the online revolution, to connect and communicate. But J. is not going to read all one million posts on AOL. (After all, J. has a second online service.) Exercising choice is J. Individual's God-given right as an American, and, by gosh, J. Individual is going to make some decisions. So J. is going to ignore all the support groups—after all,

J. is a normal, well-adjusted person, and all of J.'s friends are normal, well-adjusted people; what does J. need to know about alcoholism or incest victims? J. Individual is white. So J. Individual is going to ignore all the multicultural folders. J. couldn't give a hoot about gender issues and does not want to discuss religion or philosophy. Ultimately, J. Individual does not engage in topics that do not interest J. Individual. So who is J. meeting? Why, people who are *just like* J.

J. Individual has now joined the electronic community. Surfed the Net. Found some friends. *Tuned in, turned on, and geeked out.* Traveled the Information Highway and, just a few miles down that great democratic expressway, J. Individual has settled into an electronic suburb.

Are any of us so very different? It's my time and my money and I am not going to waste any of it reading posts by disgruntled Robert-Bly drum-beating men's-movement boys who think that they should have some say over, for instance, whether or not I choose to carry a child to term simply because a condom broke. I know where I stand. I'm an adult. I know what's up and I am not going to waste my money arguing with a bunch of Neanderthals.

Oh yeah; I am so connected, so enlightened, so open to the opposing viewpoint. I'm out there, meeting all kinds of people from different economic backgrounds (who have about $20 a month to burn), from all religions (yeah, right, like anyone actually discusses religion anymore from a user standpoint), from all kinds of different ethnic backgrounds and with all kinds of sexual orientations (as if any of this ever comes up outside of the appropriate topic folder).

People are drawn to topics and folders that interest them and therefore people will only meet people who are interested in the same topics in the same folders. Rarely does anyone venture into a random folder just to see what others (the Other?) are talking about.

Basically, with the sheer number of topics and individual posts, the great Information Highway is not a place where you will enter an "amazing web of new people, places, and ideas." One does not encounter people from "all walks of life" because there are too many people and too many folders. Diversity might be out there (and personally I don't think it is), but the simple fact is that the average person will not encounter it because with one brain, one job, one partner, one family, and one life, no one has the time!

Just in case these arguments based on time aren't completely convincing, let me bring up a historical reference. Please take another look at the opening quote of this essay, from *Scientific American*. It was featured in their "50 Years Ago Today" column. Where you read "computer networking," the quote originally contained the word *television*. Amusing, isn't it?

Live Free and Starve

Chitra Divakaruni

Some days back, the House passed a bill that stated that the United States would no longer permit the import of goods from factories where forced or indentured child labor was used. My liberal friends applauded the bill. It was a triumphant advance in the field of human rights. Now children in Third World countries wouldn't have to spend their days chained to their posts in factories manufacturing goods for other people to enjoy while their childhoods slipped by them. They could be free and happy, like American children.

I am not so sure.

It is true that child labor is a terrible thing, especially for those children who are sold to employers by their parents at the age of five or six and have no way to protect themselves from abuse. In many cases it will be decades—perhaps a lifetime, due to the fines heaped upon them whenever they make mistakes—before they can buy back their freedom. Meanwhile these children, mostly employed by rugmakers, spend their days in dark, ill-ventilated rooms doing work that damages their eyes and lungs. They aren't even allowed to stand up and stretch. Each time they go to the bathroom, they suffer a pay cut.

But is this bill, which, if it passes the Senate and is signed by President Clinton, will lead to the unemployment of almost a million children, the answer? If the children themselves were asked whether they would rather work under such harsh conditions or enjoy a leisure that comes without the benefit of food or clothing or shelter, I wonder what their response would be.

It is easy for us in America to make the error of evaluating situations in the rest of the world as though they were happening in this country and propose solutions that make excellent sense—in the context of our society. Even we immigrants, who should know better, have wiped from our minds the memory of what it is to live under the kind of desperate conditions that force a parent to sell his or her child.

Looking down from the heights of Maslow's pyramid,[1] it seems inconceivable to us that someone could actually prefer bread to freedom.

When I was growing up in Calcutta, there was a boy who used to work in our house. His name was Nimai, and when he came to us, he must have been about ten or so, just a little older than my brother and I. He'd been brought to our home by his uncle, who lived in our ancestral village and was a field laborer for my grandfather. The uncle explained to my mother that Nimai's parents were too poor to feed their several children, and while his older brothers were already working in the fields and earning their keep, Nimai was too frail to do so. My mother was reluctant to take on a sickly child who might prove more of a burden than a help, but finally she agreed, and Nimai lived and worked in our home for six or seven years. My mother was a good employer—Nimai ate the same food that we children did and was given new clothes during Indian New Year, just as we were. In the time between his chores—dusting and sweeping and pumping water from the tube-well and running to the market—my mother encouraged him to learn to read and write. Still, I would not disagree with anyone who says that it was hardly a desirable existence for a child.

But what would life have been like for Nimai if an anti-child-labor law had prohibited my mother from hiring him? Every year, when we went to visit our grandfather in the village, we were struck by the many children we saw by the mud roads, their ribs sticking out through the rags they wore. They trailed after us, begging for a few paise.[2] When the hunger was too much to bear, they stole into the neighbors' fields and ate whatever they could find—raw potatoes, cauliflower, green sugar cane and corn torn from the stalk—even though they knew they'd be beaten for it. Whenever Nimai passed these children, he always walked a little taller. And when he handed the bulk of his earnings over to his father, there was a certain pride in his eye. Exploitation, you might be thinking. But he thought he was a responsible member of his family.

A bill like the one we've just passed is of no use unless it goes hand in hand with programs that will offer a new life to these newly released children. But where are the schools in which they are to be educated? Where is the money to buy them food and clothing and medication, so that they don't return home to become the extra weight that capsizes the already shaky raft of their family's finances? Their own governments, mired in countless other problems, seem incapable of bringing these services to them. Are we in America who, with one blithe stroke of our congressional pen, rendered these children jobless, willing to shoulder that burden? And when many of these children turn to the streets, to survival through thievery and violence and begging and prostitution—as surely in the absence of other options they must—are we willing to shoulder that responsibility?

----

[1] The psychologist Abraham Maslow (1908–70) proposed a "hierarchy of needs" in the shape of a five-level pyramid with survival needs at the bottom and "self-actualization" and "self-transcendence" at the top. According to Maslow, one must satisfy the needs at each level before moving up to the next.

[2] *Paise* are the smallest unit of Indian currency, worth a fraction of an American penny.

America's "Garbage Crisis": A Toxic Myth

Patricia Poore

Let us recall, for a moment, the *Mobro*—the infamous garbage barge that, in 1987, laden with an increasingly ripe pile of waste, wandered from port to port in search of a home. The *Mobro*, which was carrying plain old municipal solid waste—household garbage—occasioned head-lines about the nation's looming "garbage crisis": we were throwing away too much, our landfills were running out of space, and soon the seas would be full of *Mobros,* all looking for a place to dump our trash. And yet here we are, seven years later, and our landfills are not overflowing; our waterways are not crowded with wandering barges. What happened to the garbage crisis?

The environmental movement continues to focus its attention on garbage and recycling, as if household garbage were the single most important issue we face and recycling the only solution. Of course, garbage does have an environmental impact; so does almost everything, from prairie-grass fires to the breath you just took. But, contrary to the rhetoric of some environmentalists, garbage is not a serious environmental hazard. True hazards are ones that threaten human lives and health. There are plenty of these, including toxic waste (which is quite distinct from household garbage), groundwater pollution, and urban smog. Compared with these real crises, the problems of municipal garbage disposal pale. There are times and places when household garbage *can* cause environmental problems—like when toxic runoff leaches into drinking water—but these are increasingly rare. Newer landfills are double-lined, piped, vented, leachate-tested, and eventually capped. These new standards have made current American waste management safer by far than ever before.

Some critics argue that we shouldn't downplay the threat of garbage because of its symbolic value to the environmentalist agenda. Environmental organizations are well aware of the emotional power of garbage: nothing can trigger a boun-teous direct-mail response or inspire a powerful grass-roots campaign like the threat of a new landfill or incineration plant. But when symbols like the *Mobro* barge are used to divert attention and money from more pressing environmental and social problems, the symbol itself becomes a threat.

If there is a garbage crisis, it is that we are treating garbage as an environmental threat and not as what it is: a manageable—though admittedly complex—civic issue. Although many old urban landfills are reaching their capacity, the reality is that there is—and always will be—plenty of room in this country for safe landfill. We've chosen to look at garbage not as a management issue, however, but as a moral cri-sis. The result is recycling is now seen as an irreproachable virtue, beyond the scrutiny of cost-benefit analysis. But in the real world, the money municipalities spend on recycling is money that can't be spent on schools, libraries, health clinics, and police. In the real world, the sort of gigantic recycling programs that many cities and towns have embarked upon may not be the best use of scarce govern-ment funds.

These programs were often sold to local taxpayers as money-saving ventures. In fact, the costs associated with consumer education, separate pickup (often in newly purchased trucks), hand- and machine-sorting, transfer stations, trucking, cleaning, and reprocessing are considerably higher than initial estimates, far higher than receipts from buyers of recyclables, and, in many areas, higher than disposal costs.

Putting aside financial concerns, let's consider other justifications for the recy-cling-above-all-else movement. Do we need recycling to extend the life of land-fills? No. Landfill sites, in fact, are not scarce, and incineration remains a reasonable and safe option. The most ambitious collection programs still leave well over half of municipal waste to be disposed of, so recycling cannot completely replace dis-posal facilities, even if we needed it to.

Do we need recycling to save resources? No, not in the real world. The reason recycling is unprofitable is that most of the materials being recycled are either renewable (paper from tree farms) or cheap and plentiful (glass from silica). Alu-minum is profitable to recycle—and private concerns were already recycling it before the legislated mandates.

Recycling is beginning to lose its halo as its costs become apparent and its effect on the volume of waste is found to be smaller than anticipated. Quotas and fines may force people to separate their trash, but they can't create industrial markets for the waste we recycle. Recycling can work, very effectively on a region-by-region and commodity-by-commodity basis. But recycling as a government-mandated garbage-management option has largely failed.

Although the special attention we pay to garbage, to the exclusion of more serious environmental threats, may be irrational, it does make a certain emotional sense. We as individuals are intimate with our trash, which makes it a more tan-gible issue than, say, groundwater contamination. Nobody particularly likes garbage; nobody likes taking it out or paying to have it hauled away. We feel we should be able to control it. Furthermore, controlling it—whether by banning plas-tics or sorting materials neatly at curbside—alleviates consumer guilt. "There," we say tossing our bundled newspapers on the curb, "I've done my part for the environment."

But for all the psychological benefit that approach may confer, it is distracting us from much more pressing national problems. Trash-handling issues should be debated and decided regionally, and those decisions have to be based, at least in part, on economics. That can't happen when one option—recycling—is elevated by environmentalist rhetoric into a national moral imperative. We have real environmental problems to worry about: We have to protect the water supply. We must improve the quality of the air we breathe. We need a better plan for energy management. And we have to monitor toxic waste more effectively. In that context, it is foolish and extremely wasteful to expend so much effort wringing our hands (and spending our money) on garbage.

A Modest Proposal

For Preventing The Children of Poor People in Ireland From Being A Burden to Their Parents or Country, and For Making Them Beneficial to The Public

Jonathan Swift

It is a melancholy object to those who walk through this great town or travel in the country, when they see the streets, the road, and cabin doors, crowded with beggars of the female sex, followed by three, four, or six children, all in rags and importuning every passenger for an alms. These mothers, instead of being able to work for their honest livelihood, are forced to employ all their time in strolling to beg sustenance for their helpless infants: who as they grow up either turn thieves for want of work, or leave their dear native country to fight for the Pretender in Spain, or sell themselves to the Barbadoes.

I think it is agreed by all parties that this prodigious number of children in the arms, or on the backs, or at the beds of their mothers, and frequently of their fathers, is in the present deplorable state of the kingdom a very great additional grievance; and, therefore, whoever could find out a fair, cheap, and easy method of making these children sound, useful members of the commonwealth, would deserve so well of the public as to have his statue set up for a preserver of the nation.

But my intention is very far from being confined to provide only for the children of professed beggars; it is of a much greater extent, and shall take in the whole number of infants at a certain age who are born of parents in effect as little able to support them as those who demand our charity in the streets.

As to my own part, having turned my thoughts for many years upon this important subject, and maturely weighed the several schemes of other projectors, I have always found them grossly mistaken in the computation. It is true, a child just dropped from its dam may be supported by her milk for a solar year, with little other nourishment; at most not above the value of 2s., which the mother may certainly get, or the value in scraps, by her lawful occupation of begging; and it is exactly at one year old that I propose to provide for them in such a manner as instead of being a charge upon their parents or the parish, or wanting food and raiment for the rest of their lives, they shall on the contrary contribute to the feeding, and partly to the clothing, of many thousands.

There is likewise another great advantage in my scheme, that it will prevent those voluntary abortions, and that horrid practice of women murdering their bastard children, alas! too frequent among us! sacrificing the poor innocent babes I doubt more to avoid the expense than the shame, which would move tears and pity in the most savage and inhuman breast.

The number of souls in this kingdom being usually reckoned one million and a half, of these I calculate there may be about two hundred thousand couple whose wives are breeders; from which number I subtract thirty thousand couples who are able to maintain their own children, although I apprehend there cannot be so many, under the present distresses of the kingdom; but this being granted, there will remain an hundred and seventy thousand breeders. I again subtract fifty thousand for those women who miscarry, or whose children die by accident or disease within the year. There only remains one hundred and twenty thousand children of poor parents annually born. The question therefore is, how this number shall be reared and provided for, which, as I have already said, under the present situation of affairs, is utterly impossible by all the methods hitherto proposed. For we can neither employ them in handicraft or agriculture; we neither build houses (I mean in the country) nor cultivate land: they can very seldom pick up a livelihood by stealing, till they arrive at six years old, except where they are of towardly parts, although I confess they learn the rudiments much earlier, during which time, they can however be properly looked upon only as probationers, as I have been informed by a principal gentleman in the county of Cavan, who protested to me that he never knew above one or two instances under the age of six, even in a part of the kingdom so renowned for the quickest proficiency in that art.

I am assured by our merchants, that a boy or a girl before twelve years old is no salable commodity; and even when they come to this age they will not yield above three pounds, or three pounds and half-a-crown at most on the exchange which cannot turn to account either to the parents or kingdom, the charge of nutriment and rags having been at least four times that value.

I shall now therefore humbly propose my own thoughts, which I hope will not be liable to the least objection.

I have been assured by a very knowing American of my acquaintance in London, that a young healthy child well nursed is at a year old a most delicious, nourishing, and wholesome food, whether stewed, roasted, baked, or boiled; and I make no doubt that it will equally serve in a fricassee or a ragout.

I do therefore humbly offer it to public consideration that of the hundred and twenty thousand children already computed, twenty thousand may be reserved for breed, whereof only one-fourth part to be males; which is more than we allow to sheep, black cattle or swine; and my reason is, that these children are seldom the fruits of marriage, a circumstance not much regarded by our savages, therefore one male will be sufficient to serve four females. That the remaining hundred thousand may, at a year old, be offered in the sale to the persons of quality and fortune through the kingdom; always advising the mother to let them suck plentifully in the last month, so as to render them plump and fat for a good table. A child will make two dishes at an entertainment for friends; and when the family dines alone, the fore or hind quarter will make a reasonable dish, and seasoned with a little pepper or salt will be very good boiled on the fourth day, especially in winter.

I have reckoned upon a medium that a child just born will weigh 12 pounds, and in a solar year, if tolerably nursed, increaseth to 28 pounds.

I grant this food will be somewhat dear, and therefore very proper for landlords, who, as they have already devoured most of the parents, seem to have the best title to the children.

Infant's flesh will be in season throughout the year, but more plentiful in March, and a little before and after; for we are told by a grave author, an eminent French physician, that fish being a prolific diet, there are more children born in Roman Catholic countries about nine months after Lent than at any other season; therefore, reckoning a year after Lent, the markets will be more glutted than usual, because the number of popish infants is at least three to one in this kingdom: and therefore it will have one other collateral advantage, by lessening the number of papists among us.

I have already computed the charge of nursing a beggar's child (in which list I reckon all cottagers, laborers, and four-fifths of the farmers) to be about two shillings per annum, rags included; and I believe no gentleman would repine to give ten shillings for the carcass of a good fat child, which, as I have said, will make four dishes of excellent nutritive meat, when he hath only some particular friend or his own family to dine with him. Thus the squire will learn to be a good landlord, and grow popular among his tenants; the mother will have eight shillings net profit, and be fit for work till she produces another child.

Those who are more thrifty (as I must confess the times require) may flay the carcass; the skin of which artificially dressed will make admirable gloves for ladies, and summer boots for fine gentlemen.

As to our city of Dublin, shambles may be appointed for this purpose in the most convenient parts of it, and butchers we may be assured will not be wanting; although I rather recommend buying the children alive, and dressing them hot from the knife, as we do roasting pigs.

A very worthy person, a true lover of his country, and whose virtues I highly esteem, was lately pleased in discoursing on this matter to offer a refinement upon my scheme. He said that many gentlemen of this kingdom, having of late destroyed their deer, he conceived that the want of venison might be well supplied by the bodies of young lads and maidens, not exceeding fourteen years of age nor under twelve; so great a number of both sexes in every country being now ready to starve for want of work and service; and these to be disposed of by their parents, if alive, or otherwise by their nearest relations. But with due deference to so excellent a friend and so deserving a patriot, I cannot be altogether in his sentiments; for as to the males, my American acquaintance assured me, from frequent experience, that their flesh was generally tough and lean, like that of our schoolboys by continual exercise, and their taste disagreeable; and to fatten them would not answer the charge. Then as to the females it would, I think, with humble submission be a loss to the public, because they soon would become breeders themselves; and besides, it is not improbable that some scrupulous people might be apt to censure such a practice (although indeed very unjustly), as a little bordering upon cruelty; which I confess, hath always been with me the strongest objection against any project, however so well intended

But in order to justify my friend, he confessed that this expedient was put into his head by the famous Psalmanazer, a native of the island Formosa, who came from thence to London above twenty years ago, and in conversation told my friend, that in his country when any young person happened to be put to death, the executioner sold the carcass to persons of quality as a prime dainty; and that in his time the body of a plump girl of fifteen, who was crucified for an attempt to poison the emperor, was sold to his imperial majesty's prime minister of state, and other great mandarins of the court, in joints from the gibbet, at four hundred crowns. Neither indeed can I deny, that if the same use were made of several plump young girls in this town, who without one single groat to their fortunes cannot stir abroad without a chair, and appear at playhouse and assemblies in foreign fineries which they never will pay for, the kingdom would not be the worse.

Some persons of a desponding spirit are in great concern about that vast number of poor people, who are aged, diseased, or maimed, and I have been desired to employ my thoughts what course may be taken to ease the nation of so grievous an encumbrance. But I am not in the least pain upon that matter, because it is very well known that they are every day dying and rotting by cold and famine, and filth and vermin, as fast as can be reasonably expected. And as to the young laborers, they are now in as hopeful a condition; they cannot get work, and consequently pine away for want of nourishment, to a degree that if at any time they are accidentally hired to common labor, they have not strength to perform it; and thus the country and themselves are happily delivered from the evils to come.

I have too long digressed, and therefore shall return to my subject. I think the advantages by the proposal which I have made are obvious and many, as well as of the highest importance.

For first, as I have already observed, it would greatly lessen the number of papists, with whom we are yearly overrun, being the principal breeders of the nation as well as our most dangerous enemies; and who stay at home on purpose with a design to deliver the kingdom to the Pretender, hoping to take their advantage by the absence of so many good protestants, who have chosen rather to leave their country than stay at home and pay tithes against their conscience to an episcopal curate.

Secondly, The poorer tenants will have something valuable of their own, which by law may be made liable to distress and help to pay their landlord's rent, their corn and cattle being already seized, and money a thing unknown.

Thirdly, Whereas the maintenance of an hundred thousand children, from two years old and upward, cannot be computed at less than ten shillings a-piece per annum, the nation's stock will be thereby increased fifty thousand pounds per annum, beside the profit of a new dish introduced to the tables of all gentlemen of fortune in the kingdom who have any refinement in taste. And the money will circulate among ourselves, the goods being entirely of our own growth and manufacture.

Fourthly, The constant breeders, beside the gain of eight shillings sterling per annum by the sale of their children, will be rid of the charge of maintaining them after the first year.

Fifthly, This food would likewise bring great custom to taverns; where the vintners will certainly be so prudent as to procure the best receipts for dressing it to perfection, and consequently have their houses frequented by all the fine gentlemen, who justly value themselves upon their knowledge in good eating: and a skilful cook, who understands how to oblige his guests, will contrive to make it as expensive as they please.

Sixthly, This would be a great inducement to marriage, which all wise nations have either encouraged by rewards or enforced by laws and penalties. It would increase the care and tenderness of mothers toward their children, when they were sure of a settlement for life to the poor babes, provided in some sort by the public, to their annual profit instead of expense. We should see an honest emulation among the married women, which of them could bring the fattest child to the market. Men would become as fond of their wives during the time of their pregnancy as they are now of their mares in foal, their cows in calf, their sows when they are ready to farrow, nor offer to beat or kick them (as is too frequent a practice) for fear of a miscarriage.

Many other advantages might be enumerated. For instance, the addition of some thousand carcasses in our exportation of barreled beef; the propagation of swine's flesh, and improvement in the art of making good bacon, so much wanted among us by the great destruction of pigs, too frequent at our tables; which are no way comparable in taste or magnificence to a well-grown, fat, yearling child, which roasted whole will make a considerable figure at a lord mayor's feast or any other public entertainment. But this and many others I omit, being studious of brevity.

After all, I am not so violently bent upon my own opinion as to reject any offer proposed by wise men, which shall be found equally innocent, cheap, easy, and effectual. But before something of that kind shall be advanced in contradiction to my scheme, and offering a better, I desire the author or authors will be pleased maturely to consider two points. First, as things now stand, how they will be able to find food and raiment for an hundred thousand useless mouths and backs. And secondly, there being a round million of creatures in human figure throughout this kingdom, whose whole subsistence put into a common stock would leave them in debt two millions of pounds sterling, adding those who are beggars by profession to the bulk of farmers, cottagers, and laborers, with their wives and children who are beggars in effect: I desire those politicians who dislike my overture, and may perhaps be so bold as to attempt an answer, that they will first ask the parents of these mortals, whether they would not at this day think it a great happiness to have been sold for food, at a year old in the manner I prescribe and thereby have avoided such a perpetual scene of misfortunes as they have since gone through by the oppression of landlords, the impossibility of paying rent without money or trade, the want of common sustenance, with neither house nor clothes to cover them from the inclemencies of the weather, and the most inevitable prospect of entailing the like or greater miseries upon their breed for ever.

I profess, in the sincerity of my heart, that I have not the least personal interest in endeavoring to promote this necessary work, having no other motive than the public good of my country, by advancing our trade, providing for infants, relieving the poor, and giving some pleasure to the rich. I have no children by which I can propose to get a single penny the youngest being nine years old, and my wife past child-bearing.

The End

The Psychology of the Future

Alvin Toffler

All education springs from some image of the future. If the image of the future held by a society is grossly inaccurate, its education system will betray its youth.

Imagine an Indian tribe which for centuries has sailed its dugouts on the river at its doorstep. During all this time the economy and culture of the tribe have depended upon fishing, preparing and cooking the products of the river, growing food in soil fertilized by the river, building boats and appropriate tools. So long as the rate of technological change in such a community stays slow, so long as no wars, invasions, epidemics or other natural disasters upset the even rhythm of life, it is simple for the tribe to formulate a workable image of its own future, since tomorrow merely repeats yesterday.

It is from this image that education flows. Schools may not even exist in the tribe; yet there is a curriculum's cluster of skills, values and rituals to be learned. Boys are taught to scrape bark and hollow out trees, just as their ancestors did before them. The teacher in such a system knows what he is doing, secure in the knowledge that tradition—the past—will work in the future.

What happens to such a tribe, however, when it pursues its traditional methods unaware that five hundred miles upstream men are constructing a gigantic dam that will dry up their branch of the river? Suddenly the tribe's image of the future, the set of assumptions on which its members base their present behavior, becomes dangerously misleading. Tomorrow will not replicate today. The tribal investment in preparing its children to live in a riverine culture becomes a pointless and potentially tragic waste. A false image of the future destroys the relevance of the education effort.

This is our situation today—only it is we, ironically, not some distant strangers—who are building the dam that will annihilate the culture of the present. Never before has any culture subjected itself to so intense and prolonged a bombardment of technological, social, and info-psychological change. This change is accelerating and we witness everywhere in the high-technology societies evidence that the old industrial-era structures can no longer carry out their functions.

Yet our political leaders for the most part propagate (and believe) the myth that industrial society is destined to perpetuate itself indefinitely. Like the elders of the tribe living on the riverbank, they blindly assume that the main features of the present social system will extend indefinitely into the future. And most educators, including most of those who regard themselves as agents of change, unthinkingly accept this myth.

They fail to recognize that the acceleration of change—in technology, in family structure, marriage and divorce patterns, mobility rates, division of labor, in urbanization, ethnic and subcultural conflict and international relations—means, by definition, the swift arrival of a future that is radically different from the present. They have never tried to imagine what a super-industrial civilization might look like, and what this might mean for their students. And so, most schools, colleges and universities base their teaching on the usually tacit notion that tomorrow's world will be basically familiar; the present writ large. Nothing, I believe, could be more profoundly deceptive.

I would contend, in fact, that no educational institution today can set sensible goals or do an effective job until its members—from chancellor or principal down to the newest faculty recruit, not to mention its students—subject their own assumptions about tomorrow to critical analysis. For their shared or collective image of the future dominates the decisions made in the institution.

The primitive father teaching his son how to carve a canoe had in mind an image of the future his son would inhabit. Since he assumed that the future would replicate the present, just as the present replicated the past, his image of the future was just as rich, detailed, comprehensive and structured as his image of the present. It *was* his image of the present. Yet when change struck, his imagery proved not merely obsolete but antiadaptive because it left out the possibility of radical change.

Like our distant ancestor, educators, too, need an image of tomorrow's society. But this image must include the possibility—indeed, the high likelihood—of radical change. This image need not be "correct" or "final"; it cannot be. There are no certainties, and any picture of a foreseeable society that depicts it as static or stable is probably delusory. Thus, to design educational systems for tomorrow (or even for today) we need not images of a future frozen in amber, as it were, but something far more complicated: sets of images of successive and alternative futures, each one tentative and different from the next.

What applies to the educator and the institution applies even more strongly to the learner. Just as all social groups and institutions have, in effect, collectively shared images of the future, each individual also has, in his or her cranium, a set of assumptions, an architecture of premises, about events to come. The child, almost from birth, begins to build up a set of expectations from its daily experience. Later these expectations become more complexly organized, and they begin to encompass more and more distant reaches of future time. Each person's private image of the future shapes his or her decision-making m crucial ways.

Students today receive a vast amount of undigested information and misinformation from newspapers, records, TV, movies, radio and other sources. As a result, they are aware of the rapidity with which the world is changing. But if many young people are prepared to contemplate the idea of radical change in the real world, this does not mean that they have the slightest idea about the implications of high-speed change for their own lives.

Some time ago I performed an unusual and confusedly nonscientific experiment with thirty three high-school students, mainly fifteen- and sixteen-year-olds. I asked each of them to help formulate a collective image of the future by writing down on a slip of paper seven events he or she thought likely to occur in the future, and to then date these events. I avoided saying anything that would restrict the kind of events or their *distance* into the future. The class threw itself enthusiastically into the exercise, and in a few minutes I had collected from them 193 forecast events, each of them duly dated. The results indicated that these urban, middle-class, rather sophisticated teenagers had accumulated many notions about the world of tomorrow.

From their forecasts there emerged, for example, a terrifying future for the United States in which, presumably, they would live out at least a part of their lives. The class scenario begins peacefully enough with predictions that the Vietnam War would end and United States relations with China would improve, both in 1972. (The exercise was run a year earlier, in 1971.) But soon events become more turbulent. New York City breaks away to become a state in 1973, and 1974 is a bad year characterized by race riots in June and a United States pullout from the United Nations. While both marijuana and prostitution are legalized, internal political events must be bleak because 1975 sees a political revolution in the United States.

In 1976 the value of the dollar declines, other nations ostracize the United States, and gas masks are distributed, presumably because of pollution. By 1977 the space program has ended and United States citizens are under constant surveillance in streets and homes. Senator Kennedy emerges somehow as President in 1978 (a special election?), but a major financial crisis occurs, and the following year, 1979, we break off relations with Europe. We learn to cure cancer, but by then pollution has become irreversible and we are highly dependent upon the oceans for food. All this, however, is merely a prelude to a cataclysmic year, 1980. That year can be described in a burst of screaming headlines:

AMERICAN REVOLUTION OVERTHROWS PRESENT GOVERNMENT
CULTURAL AND POLITICAL REVOLUTION BREAKS OUT IN U.S.
MAJOR RIVERS AND STREAMS DIE
NATURAL DISASTER WIPES OUT MANY PEOPLE
FAMILY SIZE LIMITED
MARS LANDING
COLONY PLANTED ON MARS
NUCLEAR WAR BREAKS OUT!

America's time of troubles is far from over. In 1981, Richard Nixon is assassinated, and while race relations take a turn for the better, and the renewed space program results in new missions to the planets, by 1983 we have a military dictatorship ruling the nation. Now the Soviet Union joins with the United States in a war against China (this is, after all, 1984 by now). Scientific progress continues and the rate of change accelerates further—indeed, embryos now take only six hours, instead of nine months, to gestate. But science is of no help when California, hit, one assumes, by an earthquake, slips into the Pacific Ocean in 1986. We are beginning to colonize the moon, while population on earth reaches a crisis point, and the dollar is now worth only 25 percent of its 1971 value.

As the 1990s open, the Russo-Chinese War is still on, but things begin to improve. Peace among the great powers becomes more likely. Nuclear energy, especially in the form of fusion reactors, is widely in use, and a three-day work week is initiated. Our ecological problems are still extremely pressing, but solutions are at least in sight. In fact, 1995 looks like a good year. The government changes, the space effort expands once more, we finally develop a "more organized system" of education, and, apparently, young people are making their political weight felt, for we elect a new President who is only twenty years old. (Scoffers might note that William Pitt became prime minister of Britain at twenty four.) We are now also experiencing zero population growth.

I will not go on to describe their forecasts after 2000 A.D., but there is enough here presumably to suggest that at least this group of teenagers do not look forward to a stable world, or one progressing smoothly along well-worn grooves. They look forward to high turbulence for at least the next two decades.

The Impersonal Future

Perhaps the most striking fact about these forecasts has to do with the role of the student, his or her self-image as seen in relationship to the outside world. Indeed, in asking the students for their images of the future, I was less interested in the future, as such, or in their attitudes toward it, than I was in their attitudes toward *change*.

I was, therefore, fascinated and troubled to discover that for this class, while the future was clearly exciting as subject matter, it was distinctly impersonal. Thus, of the 193 responses, fully 177 referred to events that would occur "out there" somewhere in the world or the universe. Only sixteen events made any reference to "I"— the student making the forecast. Of the thirty-three students in the class who submitted usable responses, only six saw themselves as part of the picture.

One student, along with such forecasts as antigravity cars (1984) and destruction of the earth (2050–2100), scheduled his or her own life as follows:

Graduation	1976
Working	1977
Marriage	?
Success	1984
Death	2030–2040

Another forecast marriage in 1980 and concluded "I will be a great lawyer" by 1988. He, too (a boy, I would guess from his prediction that the football Giants would win the 1974 Super Bowl), slated himself to die in 2040. One respondent foresaw his or her own death by 1996—i.e., at about age forty.

Having tried a similar experiment with another much smaller group earlier, I was not surprised by the lopsided emphasis on the impersonal or nonpersonal in thinking about the future. In general, at least for the teenagers I have experimented with, the future is something that happens to somebody else.

I must emphasize that the teenagers making these forecasts were incontestably bright, lively, and probably more sophisticated than their counterparts in smaller cities. Yet no matter how turbulent a world they pictured, no matter how many new technologies might appear or what political revolutions might take place, the way of life foreseen for themselves as individuals seldom differed from the way of life possible in the present and actually lived by many today. It is as though they believed that everything happening outside one's life simply by-passes the individual. The respondents, in short, made no provision for change in themselves, no provision for adaptation to a world exploding with change.

I pursue this not because I think these experiments are anything more than suggestive; I would expect different groups to formulate quite different images of tomorrow and to reflect different degrees of connectedness with the racing pulse of change. Rather, I raise it because I believe that the schools and universities, with their heavy emphasis on the past, not only implicitly convey a false message about the future—the idea that it will resemble the present—but also that they create millions of candidates for future shock by encouraging the divorce between the individual's self-image and his or her expectations with regard to social change. More deeply, they encourage the student to think of his or her "self" not as subject to change, growth or adaptation, but as something static.

Action and Imagery

Education is not just something that happens in the head. It involves our muscles, our senses, our hormonal defenses, our total biochemistry. Nor does it occur solely *within* the individual. Education springs from the interplay between the individual and a changing environment. The movement to heighten future-consciousness in education, therefore, must be seen as one step toward a deep restructuring of the links between schools, colleges, universities and the communities that surround them.

When we introduce change and, therefore, higher levels of novelty into the environment, we create a totally new relationship between the limited reality of the classroom and the larger reality of life. Abstractions are symbolic reflections of aspects of reality. As the rate of change alters technological, social and moral realities, we are compelled to do more than revise our abstractions: we are also forced to test them more frequently against the realities they are supposed to represent or explain.

But the university and the lower schools, as organized today, are designed to construct or transmit abstractions, not to test them. This is why we need to accelerate the trend in many colleges and universities to offer credit for action-learning done off-campus through participation in real work, in business, in community political organizing, in pollution-control projects, or other activities. Many of these efforts today are badly organized, ill-thought-through, and regarded by the university as basically insignificant—concessions to the restlessness of students who no longer want to remain cooped up in the classroom. I would argue that such efforts not only must be continued, but must be radically expanded, must be linked more imaginatively to the formal learning process, must be extended downward to younger and younger students in the secondary schools and even, through adaptation of the idea, to primary-school children. Indeed, for older students, this action-learning ought to become the dominant form of learning, with classroom learning seen as a support rather than as the central element in education.

In the United States we herd 8,000,000 university students and some 51,000,000 younger children into educational institutions, assuring them all the while that it is for their own future benefit. It is all done with the best of intentions. It keeps them out of the labor force and, for a while, off the streets.

This policy, however, is based on a perilously faulty image of the future. By maintaining the false distinction between work and learning, and between school and community, we not only divorce theory from practice and deprive ourselves of enormous energies that might be channeled into socially useful action, we also infantalize the young and rob them of the motivation to learn.

On the other hand, by linking learning to action—whether that takes the form of constructing buildings on campus, or measuring traffic flow at an intersection and designing an overpass, or campaigning for environmental legislation, or interning at city hall, or helping to police a high-crime area, or serving as sanitation and health aides, or building a stage set, or doing research for a trade union, or working out a marketing problem for a corporation—we change the source of motivation.

The motive to learn is no longer the fear of a teacher's power to grade or the displeasure of the parent, but the desire to do something useful, productive and respected—to change the community, to make a dent, if even a small one, on reality. This desire to leave a dent, to make an impact, today fuels a wide range of antisocial activity from spray-painting graffiti on a public wall or vandalizing a school building to committing murder. It is not unrelated to the fact that most crime is the work of the young.

Today, unfortunately, most action-learning programs scarcely begin to take advantage of their full potentials. For example, most are seen as forms of independent study. For many students, they might be far more effective as group ventures. The organization of groups of students (self-organization would be better) into problem-solving or work teams makes it possible to design additional learning—learning about organization and group dynamics—into the situation. By consciously including people of varied ages in such teams, it becomes possible to provide "generational bridges"—a way of breaking down some of the trained incapacity of different age groups to talk to one another.

Through focusing on some sharply defined external objective or desired change, the group develops a degree of shared intimacy and attacks the prevailing sense of loneliness and isolation felt by so many students even on small campuses. Most important, however, the motivation for learning changes. The group itself generates internal social reinforcements for learning, and the nature of the problem being attacked defines the nature of the learning required, so that the definition of relevance is created by the real situation rather than by the say-so of a teacher.

In the meantime, decision-making, so crucial to coping with change, becomes, itself, a subject of the learning process. Most students in most schools and universities seldom participate in group decision-making. While they may be asked to make decisions about themselves—such as which courses to take (and even this is restricted at the lower levels)—they are seldom called upon to make personal decisions *that affect the work or performance of others.* The decisions they are characteristically called upon to make have little or no impact on anyone's life but their own. In this sense, they "don't count." They are isolates. Attempting to solve real-life problems, action-learning done in the context of a goalsharing group, trains the participants in decisional skills and begins to develop an understanding that their decisions do count—that personal decisions can have important consequences.

It is precisely at this point that action-learning converges with future-consciousness. For, when we speak of an image of the future, we are speaking of the ram)fied consequences of present-day decisions, whether public or personal. Action-learning, particularly when carried out by groups, is a useful tool for demonstrating the necessity for a future-orientation—the need to study alternatives, to develop long-range plans, to think in terms of contingencies—and especially to think through the *consequences,* including second- and third-order consequences, of action.

In short, the combination of action-learning with academic work, and both of these with a future orientation, creates a powerfully motivating and powerfully personal learning situation. It helps close the gap between change occurring "out there" and change occurring within the individual, so that learners no longer regard the world as divorced from themselves, and themselves as immune to (and perhaps incapable of) change. In a turbulent, high-change environment, it is only through the development of a "psychology of the future" that education can come to terms with learning.

Wearing Motorcycle Helmets . . . or Not

Student

I am sure everyone will agree motorcycle helmets will save your life if you are ever in an accident. Just the thought of seeing someone wearing an expensive piece of technologically advanced hardware on their cranium makes even the most foolish person believe in the capabilities of these pieces of "Tupperware." Do motorcycle helmets really help contribute to safety? Motorcycle helmets give a false sense of security. They restrict the senses, are uncomfortable to wear, and the government should not make them mandatory for everyone to wear.

Motorcycle helmets restrict your senses by impairing your ability to see, hear, and feel what is going on around you. Being a veteran motorcycle rider myself, I would argue with anyone that feels they do not have their senses severely limited by donning these "brain buckets." For example, helmets limit your field of vision. The helmet either rides too high on the head, limiting your vision from your chin down. Or it rides too low, limiting your vision above your direct line of sight. Any limitation of vision on a motorcycle can spell disaster. Helmets also limit your ability to hear what is going on around you in your environment. I have lived in California, a state with a mandatory helmet law, most of my life. When I moved to Kansas where there is no helmet law, I decided to try a cruise on my favorite bike without a helmet. After all, I had never ridden without a helmet before, and I wanted to see what all the controversy was about. I was amazed at the difference! I could not believe how much better I could hear and how I could really *feel* my surroundings. Many of you have never ridden a motorcycle; therefore, you may not understand how you can *feel* your environment. It is much different than driving a car. In a car most of us zone out listening to music, talking on the phone, or looking at our reflection in the mirror. On a bike you are part of your surroundings; you must have a keen sense to navigate the urban jungle safely. A motorcycle helmet dulls these vital senses.

Motorcycle helmets are also very uncomfortable to wear. Last Saturday, I went on the "Bikers for Babies for the March of Dimes"; we went on a drive around the Plaza and Westport before going on a 60-mile scenic ride. By the time I was twenty minutes into the ride, I was tugging and pulling at my helmet because it was so uncomfortable. The whole ride I had my right ear bent over and it was pinching off the flow of circulation. I was miserable! And this was a $450 helmet. Even helmets costing several hundred dollars are bulky and cumbersome. This causes a person to constantly adjust and fidget with these obtrusive beasts. Can you imagine someone cruising down the road tugging and pulling and shouting obscenities at their helmet because some buckle is digging into their melon? This causes them to take their eye and attention off of the road for just a split second. A split second is all it takes to plow into the side of a bridge abutment or the back of some old fogie putting at 15 MPH in the fast lane. In this instance, a motorcycle helmet would actually contribute to an accident. Helmets don't just cause accidents but they cause neck injuries. In the July issue of *Newsweek Magazine,* John George reported that motorcycle helmets might have contributed to more than 32,169 serious neck related injuries last year. In this report, Dr. John Ebly states, "When a motorcyclist wears a helmet and is involved in an accident, he is greatly increasing his chances of severe neck and spinal cord injuries."

The Federal government bullies most states into enforcing a mandatory helmet law under the guise of "safety." If the state does not comply with the government's demand to enforce wearing a motorcycle helmet, the Federal government will withhold Federal money to the state. The government feels it knows what is best for its docile, passive citizens, so it mandates helmets must be worn at all times. Since when does the government know what is best for us? I suppose the radiation testing the government was performing in the 1940's on unknowing citizens was in their best interest, too. Motorcycle helmets have been proven not to save lives, in fact, they may cause more injuries than they protect against. We know they impair the wearers' ability to operate a motor vehicle safely. Why does the government enforce their use? The government doesn't mandate the use of helmets for bicyclists. So where will it stop? Will the government start requiring mandatory military service, or ban the ownership of handguns?

Helmets are a costly and unsafe way for the government to interfere with the motorcycling community. The government should not force the public to wear helmets because they restrict the senses, are uncomfortable to wear, and they have no business requiring us to wear something that can contribute to neck injuries and traffic accidents. I support the freedom to choose whether or not I wear a helmet. I do this based on my own judgment. After all, who is better to make a decision about something that affects us than ourselves?

Requiring Senior Citizens to Retake the Driver's Test

Student

Picture this: You're driving down a four-lane road, your car is in the right lane and you're next to a car in the left lane. The car is so close to the center that you think they want to get into your lane, but you soon realize that is just how they are driving. You start to get upset at how dangerously this person is driving, and then suddenly they veer into your lane, cutting you off and almost causing an accident. Finally, once you pass them you realize that it is a senior citizen and just excuse the entire event and blame it on old age. Well, it is time that we stop excusing these deadly driving skills and do something about it. Senior Citizens should be required to retake the driver's test once they turn 65 years old. Safety is the biggest concern for this action. The statistics and the medical facts prove that this law should be implemented.

One day after work I was running late for a doctor's appointment and my grandmother was supposed to pick me up. She arrived about fifteen minutes late, and when I asked her why, she said traffic was bad. I couldn't understand why since it was two o' clock in the afternoon and traffic seemed great. Once she started driving, I could feel the nervousness boiling in my body. We were on the highway, in the left lane going 35mph! I assumed she noticed the sign for our exit, but she didn't; when I told her, she immediately veered into the right lane and came inches from causing a potentially serious accident. The car behind us started to honk their horn at her and she said "those teenage drivers are causing so many accidents." I knew then that it wasn't the "bad traffic" that made her late; it was *her* awful driving. I didn't have the heart to tell her that she wasn't fit to drive anymore. So many fatal accidents are caused by people over 65, whose families didn't have the heart to tell them they couldn't drive anymore. If it were required for her to have taken the driver's test again, then the law would have done so for me.

According to the National Highway Traffic Safety Administration, there are 17.1 million senior drivers in the U.S. Based on current rates, the number of elderly traffic deaths in the year 2030 will be 35% higher than the total number of alcohol related traffic deaths in 1995. To be fair, this doesn't mean that senior citizens are altogether unsafe though. Senior citizens have the lowest proportion of intoxicated drivers, and 2/3 of senior citizens always buckle up. Yet, the Senate Transportation Committee says that very young drivers (16-18) and people over the age of 65 cause the most accidents. These are just a few of the statistics that show how people over 65 are causing a lot of serious and sometimes deadly accidents. There are also some medical reasons to this proposal too.

Many senior citizens know that they should not be driving; yet they continue to do so for fear of losing their freedom. And part of this is that a lot of them outlive their ability to drive safely. It is a fact that the aging process impairs perception, safe driving abilities, and above all your judgment. I know that this doesn't apply to everyone over the age of 65, but it's a fact that the body ages more rapidly at this period of time. They need more light to see well, their reaction time is slower, and their ability to perceive color may diminish.

The American Association of Retired Persons (AARP) is completely against people having to retake the driver's test, which to me says that they are against public safety. They believe that this is an issue over ageism, but do you notice how they put up a fight when a senior citizen actually has to do jail time for manslaughter? That is what I call ageism. So why are they putting up such a fight? If they have full faith in the fact that all senior citizens are safe drivers, then they shouldn't have to dispute this. Or maybe they're disputing because they know that all the statistics and medical information are true. Requiring people over the age of 65 is not only safer for themselves, but everyone else out on the road too.

I love my grandmother very much and would hate to see her not be able to drive herself to church every Sunday; but I would also hate to see her or someone else seriously injured in an accident that could have been prevented. Like many people her age, she knows that she is unfit to drive; she is just too stubborn to admit it. This law isn't saying that people over 65 can't drive; it is just making them take a test to prove they can. If you have to do it when you're younger, then you should have to do it when you're older. The only people I see being opposed to this are the ones who fear they won't pass.

Homeless, Not Jobless

Student

He sits on the street corner like a dirty, unwanted, limp, rag doll that has been tossed aside on the side of the road. He is holding a sign that says, "Will work for food." He is homeless, jobless, and completely clueless as to where his next meal will come from. Maybe someone will stop and give him some money, or maybe he will have to resort to digging through trashcans, again, to find a little leftover food to eat. This is the stereotypical homeless person, a crazy, old man who is too strung out on alcohol to get a job and help himself out of his destitution. "Why doesn't he just get a job?" is the comment heard as people pass him on the street. Many people think that people are homeless because they are lazy and do not want to work. Even though some homeless people do fit this description, a large portion of the homeless community does not. Contrary to popular belief, most people are not homeless because of an unwillingness to work.

People are homeless for many reasons, one of which is declining wages. Even though the stereotypical homeless person is thought to be unemployed, many homeless people have full-time jobs. A survey of 30 American cities by the U.S. Conference of Mayors found that 22% of the urban population was employed (NCH "Who" 3). Unfortunately, their jobs do not pay enough to support the cost of food, housing and other basic needs. In fact, for a minimum-wage worker to be able to afford a two-bedroom apartment at 30 percent of his income, he would have to work 87 hours each week (NCH "Why" 2). Finding a daycare facility that could accommodate that schedule would be like winning the lottery, the odds are not favorable. One problem leads to another, and eventually these families end up on the streets.

Another reason people find themselves homeless is the lack of low-rent housing. Most of the downtown cities in America have many old, rundown, abandoned buildings. These buildings used to be affordable apartments for low-wage workers and their families. Now, they are torn down or converted into upscale apartments that are unaffordable for minimum wage Americans. This is causing a major shortage of low-rent units in the U.S. A 1999 study by the U.S. Department of Housing and Urban Development "found that the number of housing units that rent for less than $300 . . . declined from 6.8 million in 1996 to 5.5 million in 1998" (NCH "Why" 4). Today, the demand for low-rent housing is much greater than the supply. This forces many people to live in shelters, waiting for months, sometimes years, to find an affordable place to live.

People become homeless for a number of reasons. Two of the largest reasons, today, are the decline in wages and the lack of affordable housing. Even though there are still your stereotypical winos on the streets, large portions of the homeless are hardworking people who are just trying to make it in today's society. A society where the rich seem to be getting richer, and the poor seem to be getting poorer. Unfortunately, until more low-rent housing units are in place, and the minimum wage is raised to a level that can support the basic needs of life, Americans are going to continue to become homeless.

Works Cited

National Coalition for the Homeless. "Who is Homeless?' *Fact Sheet #3*. Feb. 1999: 1–5 <http::://nch.an.net.who.html> 19 May 2000.

National Coalition for the Homeless. "Why Are People Homeless?" *Fact Sheet #1*. June 1999: 1–9 <http://nch.an.net.causes.html> 19 May 2000.

CHAPTER 11

The Research Paper

A research paper is an analytical essay in which you use outside sources as supporting information for your comments and analyses. Your source material can be obtained from internet sources, from books, from journals, from magazines, from newspapers, etc. When you quote or paraphrase from the source material, you must provide a source citation so that you are not plagiarizing other people's words or ideas.

Learning how to integrate source material into your own writing is an important part of your college education. Equally important is your ability to use a standardized documentation style to indicate the sources of your quotations, paraphrases and summaries. Most college instructors, not just English instructors, will expect you to be able to write and correctly document a research paper.

Writing a Research Paper

Preparing a research paper allows you to draw on all you have learned about writing an expository essay. You have to perform sophisticated combining of your analytical and critical thinking skills. To write a research paper, you should remember that it can combine all types of exposition: analysis, classification/division, definition, comparison/contrast, argument/persuasion.

Resources for Writing a Research Paper

Your best resource is a grammar handbook which contains information in detail about the research paper. Most comprehensive grammar handbooks, such as the Troyka handbook, offer excellent information about the research paper and instructions for documenting an essay in several different styles, such as MLA, APA, etc.

Criteria for Writing a Research Paper

1. Choose a meaningful, interesting topic, one which has not been overused and might prove boring for your reader. For example, topics such as legalizing marijuana, abortion, equal rights for women, etc. are somewhat overused as topics by students. Try to choose a topic which is at once more topical and, therefore, more informative and entertaining.

2. Research your topic using a variety of sources including the internet and the library. You can also use questionnaires or interviews for timely source material.

3. Making copies of your sources (except for entire books!) will allow you to read and reread your material so that you can become familiar with the contents. The more familiar you are with source material, the more confident you will be that you can assimilate the material and use it appropriately in the research paper.

4. Choose the two or three major points about your topic that you also find mentioned in the source material. The source material should support your arguments, so having the comments in the source material gives you direction.

5. Write a thesis statement that contains your topic and the major points that you want to develop in your essay.

6. Use the major points stated in the thesis as the basis for the body paragraphs. You can write topic sentences that relate to the thesis thereby creating overall unity and coherence.

7. Use as many body paragraphs as you need for each main point. Just remember to use transitional words and phrases to connect two or three different paragraphs which are developing one main idea.

8. Rely on quotations and paraphrases to support your ideas. Only using quotations will make your research paper look like a string of quotation marks instead of your own thoughts.

9. After each quotation and each paraphrase, use a parenthetical source citation including author's last name and the page number of the source.

10. Remember to fully explain and introduce source material so that it blends in with your text. This is particularly important for quotations, which stand out like sore thumbs if you neglect to gracefully incorporate them into text.

11. Finish the research paper with a conclusion in which you wrap up your ideas, restate the thesis, and consider calling your reader to action, if appropriate.

12. Include a Works Cited page that adheres to the documentation style you are using.

Peer Evaluation Guide for Research Papers

1. What topic is researched?
2. Does the student have an interesting introduction?
3. Does the introduction end with a thesis statement?
4. What is the student's criteria for analysis stated in the thesis?
5. Does each body paragraph begin with a topic sentence?
6. Is a transition used to begin the topic sentence?
7. Is a transition used at the beginning of each body paragraph?
8. Has the writer used parenthetical source citations?
9. Does the writer use paraphrases?
10. Does the writer use quotes in quotation marks?
11. Has the student limited the length of quotations to not more than 25 words?
12. Has the student incorporated quotes and paraphrases into their own text?
13. Are quotation marks used around quotations?
14. Does the student place the author's name and the page number of the source in parentheses following the quotation or paraphrase?
15. Is the conclusion appropriate, based on the analysis in the body?
16. Does the writer avoid grammar, punctuation, and spelling errors?
17. Does the writer use mature and varied vocabulary and sentence constructions?
18. Did the writer choose an appropriate topic, one which is neither overdone or inappropriate?

On-line Outlaws

Student

The first thing *Time* Senior editor Phillip Elmer-DeWitt noticed was awry was that
he had somehow been registered for over one hundred different E-mail sources in
less than one day's time. Yet, almost as soon as he had unsubscribed himself from
every last one of them, he discovered that he had been enrolled in over 1,500 more.
Elmer-DeWitt states that his "file of unread E-mail had swelled to 16 megabytes,
and was growing by the minute" (77). With the help of his on-line service provider,
Phillip Elmer-Dewitt was able to reduce the flow of messages from a gargantuan
two hundred forty per hour to almost fifty per hour. What caused this phenomenon? Elmer-Dewitt was unfortunately the target of an E-mail bomb, an attempt by
an anonymous person to flood another computer's system with garbage mail
(Elmer-DeWitt 77). Even though events like this cause no real damage they are
annoying and are considered serious crimes. In fact, many new crimes have been
introduced to the world because of the rapid growth and expansion of the computer industry. The creation and release of destructive viruses, tampering with cellular phone networks, and a sundry of other crimes cause much chaos in the
computer world.

One illustration of a computer crime is the creation and release of destructive
computer viruses. Some viruses are destructive and lethal to the computer's system
and others are used only as bothersome pranks. One recent example of a destructive virus is the well-publicized Michelangelo virus. It was designated the Michelangelo virus because it becomes operational only on March 6, the birthday of the
famous artist, Michelangelo. This virus posed a threat to computer users because
it had the ability to actually destroy data on computer disks which could cause
computers world-wide to collapse.

Fortunately, the Michelangelo virus wasn't allowed to cause much damage
largely because of the extensive publicity and widespread detection efforts (Jenish
49). Where did the program originate? Most evidence seems to point towards a pro-
grammer in the Netherlands or Sweden. The virus became widely circulated when

"an unidentified Taiwanese software company unwittingly began distributing infected programs" (Jernish 49). Even though Michelangelo had infected many computers world-wide, it, however, did not have the distinction of being the most widespread virus. This honor belongs to the Stoned virus, which when the computer is booted up will clear the screen and produce "one of several variations of the message 'Your PC now is stoned'" (Jenish 49). A second virus becomes operational at 5 o'clock on predetermined days and plays the tune "Yankee Doodle" through the computer's PC speaker (Jenish 49). These viruses are contracted by sharing computer disks or running infected programs acquired online. To prevent the viruses, the computer must have a virus detection program (Booth 12e). This program can be arranged to automatically scan any incoming data before it is executed. In this manner, a computer can remain virus free (Booth 52).

A second type of computer crime involves cellular phone networks. Two methods of cheating this system are in known existence today. The first method, cloning, requires altering the computer chip inside the phone to match that of a legitimate cellular phone. Many times, the legitimate customer doesn't know what is happening until the bill arrives. Such is the case when "one U S West Cellular customer in Albuquerque recently received a hefty phone bill. Total: $20,000" (Flanagan and McMenamin, "Why Cybercrooks" 189). Fortunately, the cellular customer is not held responsible for such a bill, but it costs cellular phone companies approximately $300 million a year in illegitimate services. The second method, tumbling, makes use of the fact that cellular carriers allow customers to call outside of the home area. When the phone is used away from its home base, the verification process takes so long that the connection is completed before it is verified. If the call is found to be invalid, that office will not allow any more calls by the verification number. That doesn't matter to the phone, for it changes numbers every time a call is placed, therefore bypassing the confirmation check. Although the gamble of using chipped-up phones may be high, it is worth the risk, especially for immigrants and drug dealers who make frequent international calls (Flanagan and McMenamin, "Why Cybercrooks" 189).

Many amazing computer related crimes have been accomplished in the past. In addition, there are several kinds of computer hackers which commit these crimes. Computer stunt hackers are small time offenders who are merely out for an intellectual joyride while trashing someone else's computer system. For example, take the 1988 case of Robert Morris, who launched an attack on the world-wide Internet. He developed and unleashed a "worm" program which "jammed an estimated 6,000 computers tied into Internet, including those of several universities, NASA, and the Air Force, before it was stopped" (Flanagan and McMenamin, "The Playground Bullies" 187). Even though the aftermath cost at least $15 million to clean up, Robert Morris only received a sentence of three year's probation, community service of 400 hours, and a $109,000 penalty. The penalty was not as stiff as it could have been, for Morris's defense argued "that the worm did not actually delete or modify any files"; it only duplicated itself ceaselessly on every computer system ("Noted and Notorious" 152). Secondly, there are the hardcore hackers. These programmers are only out for their own gain. They cheat and scam their way into bank accounts, telephone companies, and government agencies, tricking people into giving away passwords, credit card numbers, and other personal information.

For example, researchers have discovered a new kind of computer fraud on the Internet. In this scheme, the computer hacker creates a webpage that is similar to a legitimate page on the web, such as microsoft.com. Instead of microsoft.com, the page is saved as microsOft.com, a close match. Once a victim has stumbled upon this site, the hacker can monitor any activity. If the user attempts to purchase something using a credit card or completes an application on-line, the hacker instantly takes a victim (Young A25). "A lot of this technology is being put out there without thinking of the consequences of what can be done to the Web users" says Eugene H. Spafford, a computer science professor at Purdue University (Young A25). Many times the computer user doesn't know what has happened until it is too late.

Finally, from the virus creators to the stunt hackers to the hardcore hackers, the world of computer miscreants is growing every year. Law enforcement considers computer crimes to be more of a threat than ever. As we face the 21st century, the frequency of these crimes increases, while the fines and prison terms lengthen. We only hope our law enforcement can remain one step ahead of tomorrow's cyber-criminal.

Works Cited

Booth, Stephen A. "Doom Virus." *Popular Mechanics* June 1995: 51-54+.

Elmer-DeWitt, Phillip. "I've Been Spammed!" *Time* 8 March 1996: 77.

Flanagan, William G. and Brigid McMenamin. "The Playground Bullies Are Learning How to Type." *Forbes* Dec. 1992: 184–189.

——"Why Cybercrooks Love Cellular." *Forbes* Dec. 1992: 189.

Jenish, D'Arcy. "A 'Terrorist' Virus." *Byte* Sept. 1995: 48+.

"Noted and Notorious Hacker Feats." *Byte* Sept. 1995: 151–162.

Young, Jeffrey R. and David L. Wilson. "Researchers Warn of the Ease With Which Fake Web Pages Can Fool Internet Users." *Chronicle of Higher Education* 10 Jan. 1997: A25.

Software Piracy

Student

"Global losses caused by software piracy totaled $13.2 billion in 1995, an amount that exceeded the combined revenues of the 10 largest PC software companies" (Anthes 24). Today, computer software, ranging from video games and educational programs to word processors and database managers, continue to be illegally copied. Crime occupies every facet of life, but computer crimes, like software piracy, are unique because of the wide ranged age groups, gender, races, life-styles and geographical locations. Anyone is capable of software piracy: "surveys indicate that the demographics of the people browsing the Web has shifted to more closely reflect those observed in the general population" ("Who's Using" 46). With the vastness of the Internet, software piracy continues to escalate despite the prevention tactics and the threat of punishment.

The Internet, also known as the World Wide Web, the Information Superhighway, cyberspace, and others, has gained enormous popularity, which has provided a rising ocean, full of ships, for the software pirate. "The fast-growing 'network of networks,' with some 30 million users around the globe" is only the beginning ("Piracy on the" 9). This increasing demand for service has spawned commercial and private network servers, expanding accessibility to the work place, to educational institutions, and even to your own home. With this growth and ease of accessibility, "software piracy, the illegal copying of computer software, . . . has become a widespread problem in university, government and business environments" (Sims, Cheng, Teegen 839). All types of information including pictures, sounds, videos, games, mail, shopping, newspapers, magazines, pornography, and pirated software are transferred on a daily basis through cyberspace. Subsequently, the web has become a hacker's playground, a virtually clueless crime scene in virtual space. For example, a continuous movement of illegal activity would be laborious to track in any environment. "Monitoring everchanging Web pages for content is difficult" (Deck 6). Hackers, software pirates, use the Internet to acquire, distribute, and display their conquered victims, copyrighted software. Mostly due to the size and population of the World Wide Web, software piracy is incredibly difficult to trace.

Equally important, anti-piracy (the prevention tactics of copying software illegally) is continually revised and revisited by industry, and supported by the government. "Software producers have tried just about everything to protect themselves from losses due to unauthorized copying" (Sims, Cheng, Teegen 839). Recently, one such method, "'cryptolope,' . . . cryptographic envelope," is software designed to house encrypted information allowing a prospective customer to sample a small portion by viewports displayed on the video screen (Ross 137). After purchasing the information, a key is obtained from "on-line or from a disk" to gain access (Ross 137). Other tactics include disk copy prevention techniques, which consist of using non-standard disk formats, creating burn marks and holes in the disk made with lasers, and unique coding (Sims, Cheng, Teegen 839). Since breaking the copyright law is a federal offense, the government is forced to take action, as well as expected to become involved. "Software piracy directly affects over 1,000 U.S. companies engaged in computer programming and software development" (Sims, Cheng, Teegen 839), which significantly affects profits of individual companies as well as tax revenue to the United States government.

The government is a major player in the litigation of anti-piracy concerns; "publishers of software, . . . said the bill, which is before the Senate, must protect them from electronic piracy" (Anthes 28). These bills were proposed to include the information superhighway in the legality of copyrights that are currently used for tangible media (Anthes 28). Despite the many bills passed and anti-piracy organizations formed, some consumers are unaware that they have committed software piracy.

Furthermore, the threat and severity of punishment for software piracy does not seem to deter the crime. Lawsuits are common throughout the software industry whenever there's a case of copyright infringement. "The Software Publishers Association (SPA) filed lawsuits. . . that charge two Internet service providers and a World Wide Web-hosting service with software piracy" (Deck 6). These suits accused three Internet providers of consenting to their customers intrusion of copyright laws by allowing users to post pirated software, to publish illegal identification numbers, and to display software hacking tools or to allow customers to upkeep addresses to "file transfer protocol sites" which contain unauthorized software (Deck 6). Until there's an understanding and an agreement of who is responsible for enforcing the copyright laws, many companies will continue to suffer a profit loss. Sometimes, the threat of a lawsuit is replaced by a fine.

For example, "'they want to fine us $5,000 per computer. If we pay, they won't sue'. . . said the . . . chief executive" (Garber 214). During a "surprise audit" by inspectors, 19 computers at the main company office had illegal copies of software (Garber 214). For this new company, $95,000 in fines was steep, since profits were at least 18 months in the future (Garber 214). Besides lawsuits and fines, the act of property seizure is another form of punishment against software pirates. For instance, "FBI officials seized computer hardware and documents as part of an . . . investigation, code-named 'Cyber Strike'" (Wong 24). Although this provides hard evidence against the criminal and will most likely lead to prosecution, the government can not knock on every door in the United States, or the world for that matter.

In conclusion, the Internet presents major problems with the issue of software piracy, due to ease of accessibility and lack of security. Meanwhile, the future, creative prevention methods introduced by the software industry, along with progressive government support look promising, but there are no guarantees of resolution. Although punishment is severe and well publicized, the number of offenders continues to increase. Finally, while ignorance of the law is no excuse, the true criminals are not always punished, because they are rarely caught, but you know where they have been by the tagged code-names left behind in pirated software.

Works Cited

Anthes, Gary. "Software pirates' booty topped $13B, study finds."
    Computerworld 6 Jan. 1997: 24.

——. "Cyber copyright issue sparks fierce debate." *Computerworld* 20 May 1996: 28.

Deck, Stewart. "Internet providers sued for software piracy." *Computerworld* 14 Oct. 1994: 6.

Garber, Joseph. "Piracy." *Forbes* 22 Apr. 1996: 214.

"Piracy on the Electronic Seas." *World Press Review*. Apr. 1995: 9.

Ross, Philip. "Cops versus robbers in cyberspace." *Forbes* 9 Sep. 1996: 134–39.

Sims, Ronald R., Hsing K. Cheng and Hildy Teegen. "Toward a Profile of Student Software Piraters." *Journal of Business Ethics* 15 (1996): 839–49.

"Who's Using the World Wide Web?" *The Futurist*. Jan./Feb. 1996: 46.

Wong, Wylie. "FBI targets BBS operators, seizes hardware in software piracy sting." *Computerworld* 3 Feb. 1997: 24.

The Homeless Epidemic

Student

Outline

Thesis statement: Learning about who are the homeless, what causes homelessness, and how being homeless affects children and adults may help society realize the urgency of the problem and how they can help to create solutions.

I. Who are the homeless?
   A. Educated people
   B. Working people
   C. Families with children

II. Why are people homeless?
   A. Increase in poverty
   B. Decrease in low-rent housing

III. Effects of homelessness
   A. On adults
   B. On children
   1. Emotional
   2. Health
   3. Developmental
   4. Social

IV. Homelessness is an epidemic of great proportion
   A. Little recent data
   B. People only care about the homeless two days a year

"Can you spare some change?" Chances are, most people have heard this from a dirty, ragged panhandler as they pass him on the street. Most people ignore him and walk on by. They seem embarrassed to be approached by such a horrendous individual and think he is just looking for an outlet to buy his next bottle of booze. What if these same people were approached on the street by an innocent, needy, eight year-old child asking for money? Chances are the child is not looking to buy drugs or alcohol but to buy his or her next meal. Even though children begging on the streets are not as commonly seen, the fact is that they account for 25% of the homeless population in the United States (NCH "Homeless" 1). Today's homeless are not just those with addiction disorders or mental illness. Learning about who are the homeless, what causes homelessness, and how being homeless affects children and adults may help society realize the urgency of the problem and how they can help to create solutions.

"The old stereotypes do not apply any more to today's homeless. It's not just a wino on the corner who doesn't care" (Gorder 22). Homelessness is not only a problem for the lazy jobless, weary mentally ill, or worn out veterans but, also, for scholarly college graduates, hardworking people with full-time jobs, and impoverished families with children. "The homeless are better educated . . . than ever before. Half are high school graduates. One in five has attended college. One in twenty has a college degree" (Gorder 19). Many are working full time, low paying jobs that are not sufficient enough to put a roof over their family member's heads. The cost of a car, housing, daycare, food, and healthcare is more than their meager minimum wage paycheck can sometimes handle. They are forced onto the streets, even though they are working 40 hours a week. A "survey of 30 American cities found that 22% of the urban homeless population were employed" (NCH "Who" 3). Nearly everyone thinks that something as terrible as losing their home will never happen to them, but as Betti Knott, director of the St. Vincent de Paul Society, noted "'Most people in America are only two paychecks away from the street'" (Gorder 19). The most unfortunate statistic is the growing number of homeless families with children. "In its 1998 survey . . . , the U.S. Conference of Mayors found that families comprised 38% of the homeless population" (NCH "Who" 2). Many of these families fight for space in shelters in attempts to keep their young children off the streets. Unfortunately, the shelters get full and have to turn families away, forcing them onto the streets where they have to find refuge in the trunks of old cars, in abandoned buildings, or in parks (Grisham 2).

Many things cause homelessness. Among the reasons, poverty and a decrease of obtainable low-rent accommodations are the two largest. "In 1997, 13.3% of the U.S. population, or 35.6 million people, lived in poverty" (NCH "Why" 1). These underprivileged people and families are on the edge of being homeless. All it would take to throw them out on to the streets, for example, would be a family member getting ill from cancer or in a car accident. The time off from work not receiving a paycheck would have catastrophic results. They would then have to choose between housing and other basic needs. Since housing is the majority of the expense, it would more than likely have to be the portion cut out (NCH "Why" 1). Over the years, poverty has been on the rise. One reason that poverty is increasing is the decline in wages. Although minimum wage has increased over the years, its value in 1997 was

18.1% less than that of minimum wage in 1979 (NCH "Why" 1). This decrease in value makes it very difficult for a family to afford housing. "In fact, . . . a minimum-wage worker would have to work 87 hours each week to afford a two-bedroom apartment at 30% of his . . . income" (NCH "Why" 2). Furthermore, a survey from 1999 found that a minimum-wage worker would have to earn twice the federal minimum wage of $5.15 an hour to afford that same apartment (McCoy 2). Another reason people end up on the streets is because of the decrease in affordable housing. It is not uncommon to drive through any downtown in the United States and see old abandoned buildings that have been boarded up. What once were places for low-income workers and their families to live are now just eyesores. Many of these buildings are torn down or converted into condominiums that are unaffordable for minimum wage America. A study found that from 1996 to 1998 the number of units renting for less than $300 declined from 6.8 to 5.5 million, a 19 percent decrease (NCH "Why" 4). As the number of low-rent units decreases, the number of people in need of low-income housing continues to increase, and unfortunately, so does the rent. "During 1997 and 1998, average rents nationally rose 3.2 percent while the consumer price index increased just 1.65 percent" (McCoy 1). It is a simple case of supply and demand. There are far more people demanding low-rent units than there are units. This causes people to either crowd in with relatives, find room at shelters, or live on the streets.

The effects of homelessness on adults and children are widespread and devastating. One example of this is the breaking up of families, when parents and their children are separated from each other. This happens because either the parents leave the children with friends or relatives to save them from living on the streets, or the children are taken away from the parents and put into foster care. The National Coalition for the Homeless states that in the New York City shelters for single adults as much as 60% of the residents had children that were not with them (NCH "Homeless" 4). With that in mind, it is not surprising that there are higher rates of depression among the homeless and that one-third of homeless mothers have attempted suicide at least once (NCH "Homeless" 4). There are many more effects on the adult homeless community, but the hardest hit are the children. Homeless children have many emotional, health, developmental, and social problems. Children of the streets are more depressed, angry, and anxious than are other children (NCH "Homeless" 3). They have low self-esteem and are uncertain about life (Goodnight 91). Homeless children are extremely deprived and do not grow up with the same opportunities before them as do other, more fortunate, children. A recent study found that 61% of the homeless children in New York City had not received proper immunizations (NCH "Homeless" 3). Therefore, the children are susceptible to such things as tuberculosis and whooping cough, diseases that run rampant through shelters (Kraljic 79). That same study also showed that middle ear infections among homeless children are 50% greater than the national average (NCH "Homeless" 3). These ear infections, if untreated, can cause hearing loss, which, in turn, can lead to serious learning difficulties (Kraljic 79). Poor health is one reason that homeless children are developmentally delayed. A Harvard study revealed that nearly one-half of homeless preschoolers studies showed at least one developmental lag on the Denver Developmental Screening Test, and one-third had two or more lags (Kraljic 25). Developmental delays are not the only hurdles that homeless children have to face when going to school. Enrolling without proof of residency is not acceptable in many school districts. A lack of school supplies, clothing, and transportation to and from school, also, make attending difficult (NCH "Homeless" 4). If these homeless children are lucky enough to go to school, they often are ridiculed and treated poorly by teachers and other students (Goodnight 55). The treatment these children receive at school is one example to prove that most of America does not understand or have compassion for the homeless.

Homelessness is an epidemic of great proportion. No one is immune to it, and it is not a problem that is going to disappear if ignored. In my research, many of my sources are very dated. Some are as far reaching as 1988. I found it very difficult to come up with recent data on the subject of homelessness. I find this very disheartening, because I am certain that the homeless problem has not vanished. Yet, not much press is given to this terrible problem that plagues the United States. In her book, Cheryl Gorder says that most of us only think about the homeless two days a year, Thanksgiving and Christmas. During these holidays, we donate food for families and toys for children (Gorder 22).

Subsequently, they are on their own the rest of year. Unfortunately, their problems do not appear and disappear with the holidays much like our charity. These homeless people face their destitution day-in and day-out. Only when everyone understands how terrible and widespread this matter of homelessness really is will we, as a country, be able to come up with long-term solutions to solve this dilemma.

Works Cited

Goodnight, G. Thomas, ed. *Homelessness: A Social Dilemma*. Chicago: National Textbook Company, 1991.

Gorder, Cheryl. *HOMELESS! Without Addresses in America*. Tempe: Blue Bird Publishing, 1988.

Grisham, John. "Somewhere for Everyone." *Newsweek.com* 9 Feb. 2000; 1-3 <http://newswek.com/nw-srv/issue/06_98a/nw_980209_014_1.htm> 19 May 2000.

Kraljic, Matthew A., ed. *The Homeless Problem*. New York: The H. W. Wilson Company, 1992.

McCoy, Frank. "In an age of plenty, a search for shelter." *U.S. News Online* 10 Apr. 2000: 1-3 <http://www.usnews.com/usnews/issue/000410/housing.htm> 19 May 2000.

National Coalition for the Homeless. "Homeless Families with Children." *Fact Sheet #7*. June 1999: 1-6 <http://nch.ari.net/families.html> 19 May 2000.

National Coalition for the Homeless. "Who is Homeless?" *Fact Sheet #3*. Feb. 1999: 1-5 <http://nch.ari.netIwho.html> 19 May 2000.

National Coalition for the Homeless. "Why Are People Homeless?" *Fact Sheet #1*. June 1999: 1-9 <http://nch.ari.net/causes.html> 19 May 2000.

Student Rating Form

To the Student: Your ratings of the reading selections will help us to plan future editions of *The Red Bridge Reader*.

Selection	Interesting	Not Interesting	Too Difficult	Readable	Too Easy	Didn't Read
Description						
A Guard's First Night on the Job						
Take This Fish and Look at It						
Graduation						
Summer Rituals						
The New American Man						
A Fable for Tomorrow						
What Do Women Want?						
An Athlete's Locker Room						
My Grandma						
An Urban Legend						
Learning Experience						
Narration						
Mind Your Tongue, Young Man						
A Total Eclipse						
Passport to Knowledge						
The Perfect Picture						
My Experience with Hunting						
An Eventful Flight						
Example						
Civil Rites						
What the Nose Knows						
Idiosyncrasies, Anyone?						
Were Dinosaurs Dumb?						
Naming Names: The Eponym Craze						
Bike Wear						
How to Save Fuel and Money						
How to Be a Successful Basketball Player						
Process Analysis						
A Hairy Experience						
Foundation Waterproofing						
How to Open a CD Box						
How to Poison the Earth						
How to Say Nothing in Five Hundred Words						
How to Write with Style						
Let's Get Vertical!						
How Not to Kill Yourself Water-skiing						
How to Mix a Song Using Professional Deejay Equipment						

Selection	Interesting	Not Interesting	Too Difficult	Readable	Too Easy	Didn't Read
Division / Classification						
The Big Five Fears of Our Time						
The Plot Against People						
What Are Friends For?						
Predictable Crises of Adulthood						
DeVry Students and Financial Aid						
Spare Time at DeVry						
Comparison / Contrast						
Neat People vs. Sloppy People						
Grant and Lee: A Study in Contrasts						
Second Thoughts on the Information Highway						
Get a Life?						
Gender Gap in Cyberspace						
Kansas vs. Hawaii						
A Comparison Between Business and the Life of the Non-Traditional Student						
My Two Sons						
Cause / Effect						
Children and Violence in America						
Fall of the Legends						
My Wood						
Why We Crave Horror Movies						
Fear of Dearth						
My Decision to Attend DeVry						
This Is Not a Tall Person's World						
Why I Believe Everyone Should Do Military Service						
What Makes a Good Internet Page?						
Definition						
Barrier Signals						
The Holocaust						
Pornoviolence						
The Bureaucrat						
The Sweet Smell of Success Isn't All That Sweet						
Television Addiction						
The Right Stuff						
What Is a Lamer?						
Failure						
Success						

Selection	Interesting	Not Interesting	Too Difficult	Readable	Too Easy	Didn't Read
Argument and Persuasion						
Get a Knife, Get a Dog, but Get Rid of Guns						
Putting in a Good Word for Guilt						
I Have a Dream						
Gettysburg Address						
Drug Testing Violates Workers' Rights						
In Praise of the F Word						
Welcome to Cyberbia						
Live Free and Starve						
America's "Garbage Crisis": A Toxic Myth						
A Modest Proposal						
The Psychology of the Future						
Wearing Motorcycle Helmets . . . or Not						
Requiring Senior Citizens to Retake the Drivers Test						
Homeless, Not Jobless						
The Research Paper						
On-line Outlaws						
Software Piracy						
The Homeless Epidemic